A Woman in Custody

Audrey Peckham is married with two daughters.
She now lives in Manchester.

Audrey Peckham

A Woman in Custody

Fontana Paperbacks

First published in 1985 by Fontana Paperbacks,
8 Grafton Street, London W1X 3LA

Copyright © Audrey Peckham 1985

Set in Linotron Plantin
Made and printed in Great Britain by
William Collins Sons & Co. Ltd, Glasgow

Contents

Acknowledgements

My thanks are due to Rod Morgan of the University of Bath, whose help, advice and encouragement I greatly valued.

Also to my daughters, my solicitor, and Mike and Beryl Vernon, who all read the manuscript at various stages of completion. Their comments, while not necessarily resulting in textual alterations, were essential for the clarification of my purpose.

'The Prison Department is responsible for holding those whom the courts commit to its custody in conditions which are not only secure, but do not affront civilized society. This is not always the case today.'

(Para 2.15, Her Majesty's Chief Inspector of Prisons, Annual Report 1982)

1 The Arrest

Whatever emotions I had to struggle with during my twenty-four hours in the police cells, regret was not one of them. I had been prepared for this, now it had happened, and I had to get on and make the best of it. The cell was rather like a cage at the zoo, with its bars spaced at intervals, which I recognized from many a film, the bare concrete floor, the rubber-covered mattress on a couple of boards. At least there was a toilet in the cell, and had I realized then that this was a luxury which would be unknown at the remand centre, where I was to spend the subsequent five and a half months, I would have appreciated it more. Instead, I worried as to whether anyone could see me each time I retired behind the barely adequate screening. It was cold, too; cold after the hot sun outside, and cold because I was in a state of shock. I asked for blankets, and the wardress was generous and gave me enough to warm me. She also brought me a cup of strong, hot tea.

I had been arrested at about one thirty on a glorious day in May 1982. That arrest was at once the culmination and the commencement; it truly marked a turning point of enormous proportions in my life. But, paradoxically, it was merely another step along a road I had begun walking years before, and which has not ended yet.

I was forty-four years old in 1982, and in the eyes of the world I had everything: a marvellous family, a successful career, a lovely home in the Gloucestershire countryside, money, holidays abroad, a car of my own – the list could continue. By profession I was a teacher, and a good one. I had risen rapidly to become deputy headmistress of a large coeducational comprehensive school. With a little more ambition, I could by this time have been headmistress of a school myself. Not exactly the kind of person one expects to find incarcerated in a police cell, but in a police cell I most certainly was.

Looking back on it now, it seems to me that it should have been obvious to those close to me that I was ill, and becoming more so. Dimly, it had been obvious to me, but there did not seem to be much I could do about it. This was an emotional rather than a physical illness and just as all my life I have believed that physical illness should be as far as possible ignored, I equally believed at that time that the emotional illness should be ignored, until, like tonsilitis for example, it went away. The trouble was that it was not going away, but rather getting worse.

I could not see that there was anything to be done about it except stick it out, and, as a matter of pride, conceal from those I worked with that there was anything wrong at all. I must have succeeded well in this, for everyone was utterly amazed by my arrest, and had no idea that I had been suffering from anything other than the usual strains of a very demanding job. And I had been able to go on working, right up to the day of my arrest. It had somehow been possible for me to live and operate on two totally different levels, neither of which interfered with the other. The underlying nightmare of my emotional life was not affected by the outward calm and efficiency with which I performed my official duties. Neither was that outward self apparently affected by the turmoil within. I was two people at once, not in the popular conception of the schizophrenic, having two personalities, but in some way able to experience two different sets of feelings at one and the same time, which is as difficult to envisage as the physical possibility of being able to experience both extreme cold and extreme heat at once.

All the time, the raging pain was there. It had never stopped. It had never ceased to be in my awareness. It had underlain everything I had done, everything I had been, day after day after day. Yet, at the same time, I had been able to get up in the morning, go to work, and work well the long day through. Often I had wished that I could have broken, have failed to cope, but I never did. Part of me had very much longed for someone to override my determination to carry on as usual, and enforce a rest, a change, a cure. But I realized that there was probably no such thing as a cure.

I had been ill, then. For several years, it seems to me now. The cause? I honestly do not know. I can see some factors which certainly contributed to a greater or lesser extent. A hysterectomy, which upset me more than I let anyone know; the death of my parents, one after the other; my children leaving home; the mid-life crisis of identity and purpose. Yet it must have been something more, as these things are faced by most people, and they do not end up in prison.

Whatever it was I was running from, I chose a path which could only lead to disaster. I chose the utterly banal and trite 'solution' of having a love affair with another man. Predictably, the affair went hopelessly wrong. It was that boring old triangle, with me as the unwanted angle. In the state I was in, this was more than I could take. The relationship had ended in August 1981, and for the next six months I went downhill with increasing rapidity. It still remains a matter of pride to me that nobody realized.

I had asked for help, though. In the June before the affair ended, I went first to the Samaritans, and then, on their advice, to my doctor. He was kind and sympathetic, and after seeing me several times he agreed to my request for psychiatric help, and sent me to a consultant. Both the doctor and the consultant prescribed drugs which cost me a small fortune at the chemist, but I could not take them. They simply sent me to sleep and made my days worse because I had to fight not only the pain but also the soporific effect of the drug all day. So I only took them at weekends, and those weekends had become for me as unreal as the time one spends in a physical illness with a very high temperature. Between sleeping and waking I existed in a deadened, drugged, unreal world. I was reading (very slowly!) Mervyn Peake's *Titus Groan* at the time, and the fantasy world of Gormenghast became for me the same as my own world of precarious sanity, where nothing could be trusted any more, nothing added up any more, and strange people went about the world on strange errands, with none of it making any sense or obeying any logical rules.

After a life spent largely hiding my feelings and getting on with the job, it was too hard for me to explain how I felt at this time to the psychiatrist. I knew it was silly: there was precious little point in asking for help and then being unable to say what was necessary to make the psychiatrist understand, but I could not. I was not surprised when he decided that I was just wasting his time, and turned me over to his psychiatric social worker for monthly sessions, but I did feel vaguely let down. I felt he ought to have been able to see a little further into the millstone than that. However, it probably did not make that much difference. There was no magic cure, and if I had been taken into the local psychiatric hospital they could only have patched me up and sent me out again with the real problem unresolved.

I remember how I felt during that six-month period of steady deterioration. After all, I had been through it before, and I knew how the healing process worked. You just had to hang on, and after you had got up and gone to bed enough times, slowly other things began to matter more and the pain began slowly, slowly to recede. I knew myself, and knew that this process could take several years, but it would happen, if I could just hold on. What I had not realized is that perhaps our emotions are a bit like our physical body in their reactions to damage. If you keep doing yourself serious physical damage, eventually the wound will not heal, because there is no living flesh, only scar tissue from which new or repaired organs cannot grow. This time, the wound did not begin to close over, rather it festered and bit ever deeper. I got steadily worse instead of slowly better.

So I continued for eight months. Then, in April 1982, I made another turn of this giddy spiral into insanity. It began to seem to me that I was being presented with a challenge, which it would be weakness to ignore. I twisted things until I saw them as they were not. I felt that I was being required by some higher power to make some kind of supreme effort, supreme gamble, which, if successful, would result in my being able to take hold of my life and force it to go the way I needed it to go. I felt that I was being asked to put into one scale of a balance all I was, all I had, and all I could ever be, and weigh it against the one fact of the possibility of the broken affair being renewed. Only if I were to risk absolutely everything would I have the remotest chance of success.

I translated this into a demand that I should do something positive to remove the other woman from the scene so that I could get the man back. I felt also that I had been shown the way I was to set about it: I knew, for he had told me so, that she was frightened of the violence she encountered in London, and wanted to move out. It began to seem to me that all I had to do was to engineer a little violence and she would go. I was certain of this, with the certainty of the totally irrational. I convinced myself that it was so. The only problem was to engineer the violence. Where was my reason? Where was my morality? Where was my common sense? Not in my head, that's for sure. What I thought I was doing I cannot say, except to repeat that it had become to me a challenge which I could either accept nobly, or refuse cowardly. Black was white to me in those days of early May.

Why I decided to go to a private detective I have no idea. I am not a reader of detective stories, neither do I watch that kind of film or television programme. The plan came to me, that was all. I would go to a private detective and, telling him the absolute minimum of the background, get him to put me in touch with a criminal who would . . . What? I had no idea then, I have no idea now. Perhaps I would have done better at my trial if I had been able to say what I had in mind, but I am not a violent person and my mind would not consider what exactly I envisaged this 'frightening' to be. 'Mugging', I suppose, but then I still have not a very clear idea of what 'mugging' actually involves. My daughter has been mugged, but not physically injured in any way – merely frightened so that she left her flat for a new one.

The detective I spoke to jumped to the immediate conclusion that I meant murder. I knew he had done, but I was so besotted by my determination to tell him as little as possible that I allowed him to continue to think it. That was a serious mistake, because naturally he went straight to the police and told them that he had been approached by a woman who wanted to 'take out a contract'. At the time, I would not have understood what the jargon meant. The whole business was beginning to get totally out of hand and assuming proportions of drama which simply had no bearing on the facts of the case.

However, the police had a week to prepare their elaborate stake out. Oh, I know the jargon now. You learn a different language in prison. I had a week during which I was rushed off my feet, and I do not remember giving much thought to the meeting which the detective had arranged for me. I know that I felt no excitement, no elation, no fear. It would all happen, or more likely it would not. I had my lines to speak, laid down for me; my required movements to make. The development of the plot was not my responsibility.

I knew what I was doing was wrong. I knew it was against the law. I thought that there was a fair chance that it would go wrong and that I would end up either in prison or in some kind of mix up with criminals. I almost expected to be blackmailed: I was in a very vulnerable position. I did not have to reconcile my behaviour with my status as a high-ranking teacher: the 'teacher' me had nothing to do with the 'other' me. One of them was a charlatan, but to this day I have no idea which. Both, probably.

When I left the house to go to the meeting I said goodbye to the cats and to the house, but that was all. I made no attempt to tidy up the litter of half-unpacked things from my parents' house; I left the work I had been doing on the table; I left the windows open. None of it seemed to matter very much. It was as if everything was already a long way behind me. It had no more significance than if I had stepped off the set on a stage to resume a real life, a real existence, leaving all the props behind me. I might or might not return, that day or in the future. It didn't seem to matter much.

The day continued to fulfil its promise. I drove down to Bristol with the car window down, the May sun hot. One small part of me was in a panic, but mostly my feeling was simply of having embarked upon a course of action to which I was now committed, come what may. I do not remember ever considering that it would be perfectly possible not to go through with this after all. It seemed that, whatever happened, I had no choice any more. The outcome was with God, and I had no reason to believe that God was very likely to be on my side. I had, actually, very limited hope for the entire enterprise. Somewhere deep inside myself I knew perfectly well that I had been doomed and damned a long time ago. I regarded God as a positive evil: how could He be anything other when He allowed to happen the things which do daily happen? He had got it in for me anyway, and there was no doubt about that. I was simply going wearily through the motions of a game which was lost before it had been begun. There was no elation, and very little hope.

I parked my car in the multistorey, and made my way down the hill to the Wimpy bar which was the place of assignation. I was early, so went into a nearby newsagent to buy a *Radio Times*. Assuming I was neither arrested by the police nor kidnapped by criminals, both of which were beginning to seem more likely, I needed to know what was on television the following week. I wandered back to the Wimpy, and took up my stand outside. I was very nervous now, my heart racing and my mouth dry. Yet still it never crossed my mind for a single instant that I could save myself by simply going home.

In fact, it was already too late, as the police had me in the sights of binoculars from the detective's window, and they had several squad cars strategically positioned in the area. Had I gone, I would have been followed and no doubt taken in for questioning. I was glad that there was a bus stop outside the Wimpy, so that it could look as if I were waiting for a bus and not a person. I hated, always, to be conspicuous.

It was now just before one o'clock. There were other people hanging around. No one approached me. A bus came, and several people got on. The well-built, good-looking young man beside me did not. It was well past one now. I thought, hell, he's not coming. Now what do I do? I moved from foot to foot a bit, restlessly, to show that I was getting fed up with waiting, just in case anyone was watching me. Nothing happened. I moved away a little, strolling to the corner. I had almost decided that enough was enough; I would give up. But the well-built, good-looking young man had also moved, following me the few steps to the corner. So I strolled back. So did the young man.

I thought one of three things. 'Either I'm about to be picked up, which would be a bit embarrassing at this particular moment; or he's a policeman; or he's the man I'm waiting for.' I wasn't left wondering for long, for the young man (having received the signal to go in for the kill) suddenly and decisively folded the newspaper he had been pretending to read, and said, not looking at me:

'Are you waiting for anyone?'

'Yes,' I replied. 'Are you?'

And it was as easy as that. Later, my family refused to believe that I had had any idea that he might be a policeman; that I would have been stupid enough to go on with it if that thought had crossed my mind. I was never able to make them understand that for me it was like being on a roller coaster when it moves off: you're on and you can't get off, and you don't really want to, even if you have more than a suspicion that you are not really going to enjoy the consequences of having bought a ticket for that particular ride. Had I been in my right mind, I would not have been in that situation in the first place. Being in the state I was in, I was not only in the situation, but helplessly committed to following it through, wherever it led, whatever the price.

Nor, later on, when it was all over, did I feel differently about things. I was often asked if I would do it again if the clock should be put back, and the honest answer was 'Yes'. To smash my life up seemed to be a reasonable price to pay God, given what a bastard He was, for the hope of something as fundamental to me as that broken relationship. It was worth it, and never at the darkest time of the months that followed did it cease to be worth it. Today, more than two years after these events, I can still understand why I felt as I did then, I can still accept the logic of the situation. But today, being somewhat more secure in my head than I was then, or for many months thereafter, I know that now I would never allow such a thing to begin to happen.

But it was a glorious May afternoon, with the life of Bristol normal around us. Groups of people were sitting out on the grass during their lunch hour, enjoying what was really the first decent day of what one hoped would be the summer to come. At the young man's suggestion, we crossed the road and joined the sunseekers on the grass. It was really hot; I had my jersey off, but the young man kept his leather coat on, which I noticed without thinking about it too deeply. As the half-hour conversation progressed and the young man began to sweat with the heat, I wondered more actively why he did not take off his jacket.

The answer to that of course was that very dramatically he was carrying a cassette recorder and microphone, and also a radio 'mike' which was relaying our conversation to yet another recorder in a police car parked nearby. I must have cost the ratepayer something that day. What utter nonsense! What resources of police technology and manpower to catch one middle-aged schoolteacher having a breakdown! But, so it was. The conversation was taped, and there can be no argument about what was said. The only disagreement possible was about the exact meaning. Words like 'kill', 'murder', 'destroy' were not used. How could they have been, since no such thought was in my mind? Yet, I did use phrases which were capable of being construed differently, as I have done above when I spoke of 'removing the other woman from the scene'. That does not have to mean murder, does not mean murder when I use it, but I can quite see how the police, who had been told by the private detective that I meant murder, could eagerly construe it as such. So because of my muddle as to what I did want, and the infelicity of my expressions, I dug myself a beautiful trap to fall into, and then fell into it, while all round the grassy square plain-clothes policemen were stationed for the kill. (Now there's an interesting use of a word . . .)

After half an hour, the well-built, good-looking man felt he had enough, or the tape was running out, or something, and he suddenly sat up straight and announced that he was a policeman, and that he was arresting me for 'threats to murder'. I could hardly pretend to be surprised; I saw only too clearly what had happened and how. I did not object to being arrested – looking back now I wonder if perhaps the whole thing was my way out of a situation I could no longer handle. What I did object to, and this comes over very clearly on the tape, was the dramatic way in which they made the arrest. Enormous policemen appeared from every direction and grabbed hold of me, police cars started howling and screeching to a halt, and I felt as though I was in a very second-rate film indeed. I was not resisting and I protested about being dragged about. One of the policemen understood the reason for my distress and assured me kindly that I would not be put into a marked police car, though it must have been obvious to everyone in Bristol what was happening.

I was put into the car with a plain-clothes WPC and several burly men. Who on earth did they think they had caught? I wondered then and I wonder now. At the station I was put behind some kind of barrier in a room at the end of a number of long corridors. It seemed to me that all the policemen in Bristol crowded into that room to have a look at me, as if I were Crippen or the Yorkshire Ripper. But, in no way was I dangerous to anyone except the other woman, and that was over now. I was merely, it seemed to me, a middle-aged woman, feeling my age, about to be charged with an offence I had not committed, and totally unworthy of the drama and histrionics that the police had displayed with that elaborate stake out. I felt very angry about it, and hoped sincerely that the police felt as foolish as they jolly well ought to have done – after all that painstaking preparation, to have only caught a little teacher having a breakdown.

They took my name and address, took away all my possessions, and sent me down to the cells with the WPC. Her job was to supervise the strip search. Had I known then just how many times in the future I would have to strip in front of another woman, I think my heart would have failed me. The policewoman was young, and very kind to me. 'If you want to tell me anything at any time,' she said, 'just ask to see me and I'll come straight down.' I'll bet you will, I thought to myself. I could not see the police as in any way my enemies, but I was very disinclined to say anything to anybody at that stage. I do not remember feeling frightened, or worried, or apprehensive. I was caught in a machine which would roll on according to its own laws, carrying me with it. That was all.

So there I sat in the cells on that May afternoon, wrapped in blankets. Not really thinking, just sitting. Not yet in any way upset. Waiting like an animal for what was to happen to me next. The locked door did not bother me unduly. I was not tormented by regret, or fear. I never wished I hadn't 'done it'. For the minute, I was entirely placid and passive. Later on it was going to hit me that what had happened to me would have enormous repercussions on my family, on my colleagues, on the school, and when that understanding penetrated my thickened brain, then I would feel pain and shame and worry. But not now. Not yet. Now it was really rather peaceful to sit there, without a shred of responsibility for my own future. Other people would decide what was going to happen to me.

But, of course, if they really were going to charge me with 'incitement to murder', then I was in serious trouble, and I needed help. From time to time during that long afternoon, one or another of the police on the case came to see me. They tried various approaches from the 'I only want to be your friend and help you' to the severe 'You're in dead trouble, girl, and your attitude isn't making things any easier'. Once there was even an element of bribery: 'Come on, tell me all that happened, and I'll see that you have a quick trial at the magistrates' court. If you don't it will mean going to the crown court, jury, witnesses, everything.'

Such psychology! To all these approaches I answered only, 'I want a solicitor'. I was not moved by the friendly approach, nor frightened by the rougher one, and certainly not fooled by the attempt at bribery. I knew perfectly well that the kind of charge I faced would have to be tried in a crown court. But the police had me to themselves for several hours, trying to get some kind of confession out of me, without any attempt to provide legal representation, and I do not think this is right.

At last they gave up and a sergeant appeared and asked if I had a solicitor who they could contact. I had not, my dealings with solicitors having been restricted to conveyancing only. He offered to bring the list or to tell me three names from which I could pick one. I could not be bothered with the list, they were all names to me, so the sergeant recited three names and I chose the only one I remembered. In this unsatisfactory and haphazard way I got myself a solicitor. I was entirely fortunate that the solicitor I chose was in fact first class, and had an excellent reputation. The sergeant need not have included his name among those he offered me, but I am grateful that he did so. David Ticehurst proved a good friend to me, and did much more for me than he was bound to do. He was always efficient and always firmly sympathetic, and this approach is exactly what someone in my position needed then.

The sergeant said that he would contact the solicitor, but that it might be some time before he could come to see me. He asked if there was anything else I needed, and I asked to see a doctor. I explained that I was on medication, and the sergeant clearly thought it was Valium. I added the information that the pills I took were for depression, and that I had been seeing a psychiatrist. I thought it would do no harm for him to know that. The sergeant promised to ask the police doctor to see me, and then added, 'You know, you were lucky you got stopped. One day you'll be very glad we stopped you. You don't want a thing like that on your conscience.'

I remained silent, staring at him. A few minutes' conversation, and he thought I would be fool enough to relax and talk. I felt far too shocked and stupid to be able to talk to the police: they would dig traps for me, and I would be fuddled enough to fall into them. The only safe thing was to say nothing at all to them, then they could not trap me. I said 'I want a solicitor' again, and he shrugged, said, 'Have it your own way', and left me.

I continued to sit wrapped up in my blankets. I stared at the graffiti written and scratched on the wooden partition between the bed and the toilet, and wondered dully how they had managed to get a biro, and whatever implement had been used to scratch away the shabby paint, into the cell. I myself had nothing. Everything had been taken away from me upstairs except my book and my glasses, which, with extraordinary presence of mind under the circumstances, I had saved from being put into that plastic bag now containing my watch, my comb, and even my wedding ring, which they had insisted I should take off. My clothes had been returned to me after the strip search, but my sandals and socks had not, and were on a table at the end of the cell block. It worried me to be separated from my property, and my feet were very cold. With great daring, I called the wardress, and asked for my socks. She explained that I was not allowed to have them, and offered me another cup of tea. She was a kindly person.

The only trouble was that when the wardress brought the tea, I had to unwind my blankets and go to the bars to take it, which meant that my feet got cold again; in addition I did not like walking about barefoot on the concrete floor of the cell. It didn't look too clean to me, and I had visions of people being sick and the floor not being cleaned properly. The wardress was kind, and told me not to worry too much. She began to ask me about my family, but, rather to my relief, was interrupted by the woman in the cell opposite mine (from whom I shrank away, not wanting her to see me), asking for a light. I got back on to the bed, to be as far away as possible. There was nothing to do but think.

I could not face the reality of what had happened to me for the moment. It was something I had known could happen. I was not surprised, and I was not afraid. On the other hand, I was destroyed. I was in prison, or at least in police cells, and I had committed a serious crime with my eyes open; and I was a middle-aged, highly respectable and respected schoolteacher, who only yesterday had been mouthing platitudes to the sixth form about how they should live their lives. I felt very sorry that it had been necessary to do such violence to my other self, or rather my other image, my mask, my disguise. Like a sleeping 'mole', I had lived for so long in the role that I had at times almost forgotten that it was my cover, and thought it was myself. But it wasn't myself, and it was because I had been true to myself at last that I was where I was.

Without my watch, I had no idea how much time was passing, but it seemed several hours before the sergeant returned, and with him my solicitor. The cell was unlocked, and David came in and sat on the bed beside me. The mere fact of his presence was suddenly immensely reassuring. I had thought of solicitors as many things in the past, but never as them being members of a caring profession. Yet, so it seemed to me then, and seems to me now. This man was my friend in an entirely hostile and unfamiliar situation: this man would help me. I was no longer alone; there was someone who knew the rules of this nightmare game; who would see me through, and to whom the police could not deny access to me. I felt overwhelming relief, and with the relaxation of the guard I had till then maintained came the tears.

David no doubt had seen it all before. I maintained my innocence of the charge, but he had no doubt heard all that before as well, and reserved his judgement. With quiet efficiency he diverted my mind from the possible charge to the more immediate practical problems I faced: my husband, my children, my cats. And the tears came again as I remembered. How could I have forgotten? My elder daughter had recently qualified as a state registered nurse, a just reward for her hard work and tenacity of purpose. The next day was the day of her presentation, and I had been going to London for the event, and afterwards to take her and her boyfriend, now her fiancé, out for a meal. How could I miss so important a function because I was in prison!

There was also the effect that all this would have on my daughter's relationship with her boyfriend, which I knew was very important to her. How would he react? How would his family react? Would my disgrace break up the relationship? This fear was to haunt me more than any other in the weeks ahead, until he himself came to visit me in the remand centre and reassured me that what had happened to me would not affect his relationship with my daughter in any way.

It was agreed that David should try to contact my husband, and get him to tell my daughter that I would not be able to attend the presentation, but without telling her why. Looking back now, I wish I had tried to get bail, but even then I was seeing it as inevitable that I should be held – inevitable and desirable. The world would have to get along without me. The cats, left with no one to look after them, also worried me, though my husband would be back home the following evening and could feed them.

When David left, I felt much better. It was not long before the police doctor came to see me and gave me a quick examination. He left an Ativan tablet with the wardress to be given me later on, and I was relieved, for I knew the knock-out effect Ativan has on me and that I would sleep.

Later, David returned to say that he had been unable to contact my husband, but would do so first thing in the morning. He had contacted my headmaster, but the thought of school and what I had done to the people there was so awful that I could not bear it. David advised me to try to sleep, and asked if I was strong enough to say nothing whatsoever to the police, no matter what they asked me. I thought I was. It must have been fairly late by now, as tea was brought while David was still there. He left me to it, and I managed to eat a little. Then I asked if I could have my Ativan, and when it was brought I took it eagerly, put myself to bed, and slept, exhausted, till the morning.

The following day was one of great confusion. The wardress who brought me breakfast told me that I could have a bath if I wished. I said yes please, but later wished I hadn't when I saw the filthy bath. I washed standing up in a trickle of water, but at least I had washed, though there was only a sliver of soap and a tiny towel to dry on.

Soon after, my solicitor appeared again, and said that he had finally contacted my husband, stressing that he should get in touch with my daughter. David also said that he had heard the tape, and that he thought it unlikely I would get bail when I was charged and brought before the magistrates. I was utterly numb and not really able to experience this situation. It was like reading a book or seeing a film, it seemed to have nothing at all to do with me.

At some time later I was taken with my solicitor across the corridor to another room where the police interviewed me. It was very short, and merely established that I was who I was, that my money was my money, that other articles in my possession were mine, none of which I wished to dispute. I was returned to my cell. Later still, I was walked along several corridors to have my fingerprints taken, and that did shake me. It was a very upsetting experience.

Lunchtime came and went, I ate what I could. I was formally charged by a policeman in my cell, with my solicitor present. On his advice I said nothing at all, though it was hard to remain silent when charged with such an offence, of which I was innocent.

I remember all this, but then my mind began to close down, and I have no consistent memory of the rest of that day's events. What we cannot bear to remember we mercifully forget, and I see the next few days in glimpses rather than as a coherent narrative. I was not yet in the state of complete collapse which I was to reach, but I was well on the way. I can see myself in the dock at the magistrates' court, but I have not the faintest recollection of how I came to be there, and no memory at all of what was said. All I can remember is wishing I were not wearing jeans, as it did not seem to be suitable attire for an appearance in court. I do not remember being led into the dock, and I do not remember being led out. I have no idea whether I was crying, as I did on subsequent appearances, or not. It would be a lot more interesting for me as well as for my readers if I were able to record that I thought such and such, felt so and so, but I have absolutely no remembrance of what I thought or what I felt. To all intents and purposes I was dead.

I have one more glimpse of myself standing with a policewoman at the top of some steps, blinking at the bright sunlight. I knew I had to go down the steps and get into the car waiting at the bottom. The policewoman had her hand on my arm, and I remember asking her not to hold me, as it seemed to me that we were in public, and I felt shame. I remember nothing else. I assume that the car was the one which took me to Pucklechurch Remand Centre, but I have no recollection whatsoever of actually getting into the car or of being driven to the remand centre.

I wonder where I was in that fortnight leading up to my complete devastation as a human being? Not in my head, that is for sure, for

I have a cataloguing brain which wants to know exact detail, and files it away. When my daughters were born, the first thing I wanted to know was the exact time. I wonder what time it was when I entered Pucklechurch for the first time? Sometime in the afternoon or evening of 14 May 1982. For me, that isn't really good enough, but it is all I can do.

2   Early Days at Pucklechurch

I cannot remember very much at all about the first days at Pucklechurch. I think that I was in a state of deep shock for some considerable time: many weeks at least. I cannot remember coming into the place through the great gate that first time. I cannot remember how I got into the building, or what my first impressions may have been. I remember odd fragments of my first experience of the reception procedure. Like being put into the tiny cubicle I later came to know as the 'horse box' – for that is what it resembled, this tiny rectangular box measuring about two foot six by three foot with a piece of wood across one end to act as a seat. It would have been impossible to lie down in the box; one pace and you were at the end of it and had to turn round. I have no idea how long I was in there. I remember being asked to take a bath and wash my hair, and that I was glad of the one and resented the other as my hair was clean. I remember having a medical inspection, but not much about it except that my sex was checked, in case I suppose I was a man seeking the unlimited opportunities afforded by a women's prison.

I remember distress when I sat at the table opposite an officer and all my things were catalogued and many of them put away as unnecessary: my handbag and comb were taken, but I was allowed to keep my watch, my wedding ring and my glasses, though the case for the glasses was also taken away. The process could not have lasted long as I had only the clothes I had arrived in, my handbag and its contents. I do not remember being taken to the wing and locked in. I wish I could remember what it felt like to be in a remand centre cell for the first time, but I can't. I have no idea what time it was except that it must have been some time in the late afternoon or evening. I expect I was given food, but I have no recollection of it. I do not know what I did in the cell, but I think I probably got straight into the bed, which was clean and warm.

That day was a Friday, so the next day introduced me to Pucklechurch Saturday, which was the day of rest. No cleaning was done on that day, and a church service was held in the chapel in the morning for those who wanted to go. I was not allowed to go that first week, as I had to see the doctor, which was customary for new admissions. I remember that first thing in the morning the sister had come in and found blood on my pillow, of which she was suspicious. I thought it had probably come from my gums, which do sometimes bleed at night. But she didn't seem to believe me, and informed me that anyway I would be seeing the doctor later, which I found reassuring; though I did not like my first experience of automatically being disbelieved. Later, I was to get used to this happening, but I could never accept it.

I remember watching the others all go off to church, and being reassured that they did not seem too bad. Corinne and Caroline in particular, who were to become my first friends in Pucklechurch, looked completely normal and spoke to me kindly. I don't remember the doctor, but I know that the examination was cursory and included a blood test. (Later on I was informed that I had not got VD which took me slightly aback as I had never considered it a possibility.) A few days later I also had a gynae examination, and it was reassuring to know that all was well there.

Having had a hysterectomy I was never subject to the indignities which other women had to suffer at the time of their periods. We were not allowed to keep sanitary towels in our cells, so every time you needed one it had to be asked for. Tampons were handed out sparingly, if at all. I can imagine what it must have been like to be locked up all night with a heavy period and no access to a clean towel; to have to use the pot and have nowhere to wash your hands. And if, by any chance, you had managed to get an extra towel in the cell and could change, you then had to live in the cell with the soiled towel and its smell until you were next unlocked. On the other wings many cells were shared. It must have been a brutalizing experience. I know that one woman who was on remand at Holloway tried to avoid menstruating by taking her contraceptive pills, and these were taken away from her. The doctor apparently told her that used sanitary towels in the cells did not constitute a health hazard.

So they might not have done, but the incident shows the callous attitude of some doctors in the penal system to their patients. Unless you are actually dying, it is difficult to get appropriate medical care. Some doctors give their time grudgingly it seems, and although the inmates may request to see the doctor on any working day, the quality of care is below that given outside.

Because there had just been an outcry against the use of drugs to quieten inmates, I found both at Pucklechurch and at Styal that the pendulum had swung right in the opposite direction, and that getting drugs out of the doctors was a major problem. At Styal in particular, after the judge at my trial had decreed that I should have psychiatric help, I had to fight really hard to keep my twice daily doses of Tryptyzol, which is a very mild drug indeed.

Drugs were used, though. For a long while we had a diagnosed schizophrenic at Pucklechurch, who could become really dangerous. I saw with my own eyes how she was given her drugs: when she was too violent for the nurses to enter her cell, and she threw the drugs away if they were given through the hatch in the cell door, the nurses used to keep her short of liquid until thirst got the better of her: then she was given orange juice with some drug in it. 'Carrie's Cocktail' one sister used to call it. But the nurses were the first to say that Carrie should be in a psychiatric hospital where she could have been cared for properly. The sister in charge told me this herself before Carrie was finally sent to hospital at her trial.

Wherever possible they administered medicine in liquid rather than pill form, as it is a lot harder to retain the liquid in the mouth for long. Many of the sisters really did watch like hawks to ensure that the medicine was taken by the right person at the right time. Nobody was allowed to have any kind of drug in their possession: not a mild headache relief such as many women carry regularly outside, not contraceptive pills nor pills to reduce period pains. I am not a pill-taker myself, so not having them available did not bother me, but some people found it very hard to be deprived of their standbys. Many women had been on Valium or something similar outside, and this was almost always discontinued.

Several of the young ones coming in to Pucklechurch were drug addicts, some on heroin or cocaine. Entering Pucklechurch meant, of course, the end of their supply, and one of the extra tensions of the place was people being forcibly taken off drugs. This naturally caused them to become very upset and unpredictable. They were put at once on a steadily reducing course of Methadone, and were supposed to be cured in the space of just over a week. Heavy drug-users found the Methadone an entirely unsatisfactory substitute, and it must have been very difficult for them. One girl was in a really bad way, not only with withdrawal symptoms but also hepatitis caused by her drug abuse. She was kept in quarantine in her cell for weeks and weeks, and I cannot imagine what it must have been like for her: to be seriously ill, to be forcibly taken off her drug, and to be kept in what amounted to solitary confinement as well.

On that first Saturday I was not sorry to miss church to see the doctor, but after the event I decided that I would have been better off going to church. The chapel was a separate building in the centre of the compound. If you wanted to go to church you answered in the affirmative when the nurse came round and shouted 'Church?' through the door. Nearly everyone went, because the alternative was being locked up. We gathered at the bottom of the stairs, and when they were ready the escorting nurses unlocked the door, and we walked down the administration corridor, through the visits room, and out of the building. We turned left for the chapel – to the right was the main gate and freedom. There was no question of making a bolt for it, as a line of officers guarded our way across the open space and safely into the chapel building. This little walk was in itself a high adventure, particularly after being on remand there for several months.

The chapel was a pleasant building, clean and new, and unlike prison, except that the doors were locked behind us, and many officers stood round the walls. We hospital girls always had a nurse or nurses accompanying us in case we had a fit. We were not allowed to sit where we liked, only in rows according to what wing we were on. Hospital girls always sat at the front on the left in the first two pews. It was possible to communicate with girls on the other wings, which was another reason why going to church was popular. The chapel was interdenominational, and the three chaplains took it in turns to take the service. But whether it was the Anglican, Catholic or Nonconformist chaplain in charge, the service always took the same form: a lot of hymn singing, a short talk, and a few prayers at the end.

I was always surprised by the hymn singing. Having come from schools where the popular feeling was that people did not want to sing hymns, and school assemblies were becoming more and more secular in tone, it was surprising to see these tough girls – who only a year or two before must have been the fifth-year terrors – choosing and singing the old and well-loved hymns with pleasure and gusto. (Singing hymns is acceptable in prison apparently, but not in a school assembly.) Sometimes the chaplain would choose the hymn, but usually he asked what was wanted and the girls called the numbers of the favourite hymns. We were accompanied at the piano by a very elderly man known as George, who gave up his Saturday mornings to play for the services. He was quite a good pianist considering his age, but would sometimes feel it necessary, especially when he thought the chaplain had not been sufficiently religious in his talk, to stand up between hymns and tell us how Jesus had come to be his personal saviour, which caused me, at least, acute embarrassment.

It was a very emotional atmosphere in the chapel, what with the excitement of a break in routine and being with other wings. The hymns were frequently too much for many people; some had to be escorted out, many just stood there helplessly crying. Yet week after week the girls would choose hymns like 'The Lord is my Shepherd', 'Dear Lord and Father of Mankind', 'Abide with me', which are emotional enough at the best of times. Every week we sang 'Lord of the Dance', which the Anglican chaplain used to refer to as the Pucklechurch National Anthem. Children's hymns such as 'All Things Bright and Beautiful' were often chosen. I recognized this as an attempt – which the girls were not ashamed of then and in that particular place – to recreate the atmosphere of Sunday school, or perhaps infant school, when things were safe, before they had become disillusioned and their lives had begun to go so terribly wrong. It was always taken tremendously seriously, this singing of the hymns of childhood, by a collection of embittered, tough and hopeless human beings.

I was not ashamed to cry with the rest of them. I shared their feelings. There were a few older women there who had obviously been churchgoers, who chose hymns which meant to me what 'All Things Bright and Beautiful' meant to the others. Little else recreates a former existence more than the music of that time. I had been a churchgoer, I knew the old Anglican hymns by heart, and it was an emotional experience to sing them again in such a place. In fact, the nurses used to keep a special eye on me because they knew I was going to be upset, but I never lost control. I came nearest to it when the Anglican chaplain decided we ought to widen our repertoire with that lovely new hymn 'Lord Jesus Christ, You have come to us, You are one with us, Mary's Son'. I had first heard that hymn sung at the confirmation services of my daughters.

So why, some may ask, go to the chapel in the knowledge that the music was going to provide an upsetting experience? Why not steer well clear of it, and keep one's equilibrium? Well, in real life, I do. I cannot, even now, easily tolerate music of any kind for the memories and regrets it makes me face. I avoid it. I have to. But then, church was the highlight of the week, and who knows, maybe those tears were therapeutic. Once learned, 'Mary's Son' became part of the Pucklechurch Saturday morning, and never once could I sing more than the first few lines before the tears hit me. I knew the words by heart, but I used to sing with my head in the book, though I don't know why I bothered as everyone knew I was crying, and nobody minded. Corinne used to cry, and even my brave Gillian, whose determination not to show emotion was the strongest I have known, used to have damp eyes at the end of some services.

That first Saturday, when the others came back from church and the doctor had finished with me, I was introduced to what was known as 'wing association'. I came to hate this more than any other part of Pucklechurch life, as time went more slowly then than at any other time. 'Wing association' simply meant that we were left unlocked, and could be out of our cells, but were not allowed off the wing to the normal association room. Later on, we were locked up more often when we got back from church, but at first we were usually unlocked, made to go up to the top corridor, and there was absolutely nothing to do but mooch about. Those first few weeks I was there there were not many people in Pucklechurch, so it was possible to sit in the chairs at the end of the corridor and chat. That was fine for a few weeks, but eventually you got to know exactly what everyone else was going to say anyway, and it became very boring. I am not a social being at the best of times, and spending hours and hours with nothing to do but chat about old crimes got me down.

On that first Saturday afternoon I had my first visit from my family. I have the feeling that I remember it quite well, but from time to time my family tells me something I said to them of which I have no recollection. It was of course a very difficult visit, as it was the first time I had seen them since my arrest. They were all three there, and all three looked shattered. I know that I was trying to be as calm and normal as possible, so as not to upset them. I told them that the place was not too bad, and indeed it did not seem too bad to me. I had lost control of myself to the extent that I was really quite glad to be safe in Pucklechurch and away from the torments and worries of the outside. I really did not mind being there, and I tried to get this over to my family. But, of course, they took the view that any sane person would take, which was that if I really did not mind it, there must be something wrong with me, and they were just as worried. In fact, I was well on the way to the complete breakdown which was to overtake me a few weeks later, but I did not know that. I thought I was quite sane.

Inevitably, tears were shed and they promised to do all they could to help me, though there was of course nothing they could do. I had the presence of mind to ask for some clothes to be sent in, and some books, and my knitting. Then the short visit was over. Why, I wonder, are prisoners on remand not allowed to have as long a visit with their family as they want? Families often travel a long way for these visits, and to restrict them to a quarter of an hour seems most unreasonable. My younger daughter had to travel all the way from Manchester. It is a bit like the bad old days in hospitals when visiting was so strictly limited. Given that a prisoner on remand is innocent until proven guilty, why are these visits restricted? This is another example of the way in which remand centres treat people worse than prisons, for the visits at Styal, although restricted in number, were for two hours, which really made sense of the visit. What can you say in a quarter of an hour or, with the chief's permission, an extended visit of half an hour?

At the end of the visit, my husband and my elder daughter went out, though reluctantly, and emotionally. My younger daughter, my baby, in spite of her twenty years, burst into terrible racking sobs, the reason for which I knew well, and we clung to each other. The officers on duty, in pity, allowed her to stay an extra ten minutes until she was more composed; allowed us to hold each other, until I had calmed her, and told her over and over again that it was not her fault, and that I was all right. It must have been the hardest thing she had done, to pull herself together and go out to rejoin her father, and leave me there. I shall remain grateful to those officers for their compassion for ever, but I protest against a system which makes this sort of situation necessary. I was not a convicted criminal: why could my daughter not stay with me?

And thus began the pattern of all my visits in Pucklechurch. All were painful experiences, which I could well have done without. It was impossible to talk to my poor husband, though there were things which I should have said. Every Saturday he made the journey to see me, and every Saturday we conversed as strangers, as I found it impossible to do anything else. I grew to dread Saturdays, simply because it meant that I would have to go through the torture of the quarter-hour visit. I found it easier, but not much, to talk to my children, though I did not see them very often. The journey from Manchester was long and expensive for my younger daughter on a student's grant, and my elder daughter was abroad much of the time, at my insistence. I saw no reason why her plans should be disrupted because of me, especially as there was absolutely nothing that anyone could do.

On a normal Saturday we came back from exercise in the afternoons, and we were allowed to sit and watch the little black-and-white portable TV which the hospital wing had for its own use: hospital girls were not allowed to mix with the other wings in the evenings when they watched TV in the association room. As there was never anything but sport on a Saturday, this was a bit of a non-event for me. As the summer went on, we frequently spent Saturday afternoons locked up, so it came to be that even watching sport was preferable to being locked up.

Among the things of which I have no recollection are that first weekend, but I must have been introduced to the unfailing Pucklechurch Sunday morning routine of cleaning the whole wing: both corridors, and every room, including the offices, the staffroom, Sister's room, the kitchen and the staff loo. When I heard there was a kitchen, I wondered if it would be possible to make coffee in it, but I soon learned that the kitchen was for the exclusive use of the staff, that it was kept locked, and was only cleaned by the women with a nurse standing on guard to see that nothing was touched except the floor. They cleaned the surfaces themselves. At first I used to enjoy the work; it got us out of our cells, gave us something worthwhile and useful to do, and provided a bit of much-needed physical activity. But after cleaning the same floors every week, and sometimes during the week as well, for five months, it began to pall a little. By the end I hated it and, like the others, spent as much time as I could skiving. We were not allowed to clean any other way than the hard way: with scrubbing brushes and floor cloths, down on our knees. I could not see the reason for this: there was an obvious reason for the need to keep the place clean, but to be made to do it in such a way smacked of punishment, and why should we, unconvicted prisoners under the presumption of innocence, be punished? There was not even a vacuum cleaner for the office carpets. They had to be swept by hand with a hard brush, down on our knees again. Why?

That first Sunday there was an unusual break in routine for me. There were no visits on a Sunday, but my husband had left a bag for me at the gate full of things I had asked for. Although it was not strictly according to regulations, the bag was sent up to reception for me, and I was told to go down there while my things were checked in. This was my introduction to the concept that a woman's property was not her own in the remand centre. Everything my husband had sent in was written down on my property card, and then the officer decided what I could and could not have in my cell. I suppose it was reasonable to limit us to only three sets of clothing, but it was not at all reasonable, nor was it in accordance with the rules, for the officer to go through the books which my daughter had sent in for me and decide that I could not have certain titles. I was forbidden Iris Murdoch's *The Accidental Man*, and told that it was because it was pornographic. In actual fact, it is about the least explicit of her works, but I can only suppose that there was a ban on certain authors.

I think now that if I had made a fuss I could have obtained access to my books, but at the time I was too ill to care, and accepted whatever happened with dumb acquiescence. At no time was I told what my rights were: there was a booklet in my cell but, couched in legal jargon, it defeated my powers of comprehension in the state I was in at the time, and I imagine could only be understood by one per cent of the average remand centre population anyway.

Back to my cell I went with about half of what had been sent in for me. The rest was kept in my holdall in the property store in reception. I hated being separated from it, but what could I do? My knitting had been sent in, but I was not allowed to have it in my cell; it had to be kept in Sister's office, and I had to ask permission if I wanted it. Sometimes it was allowed, sometimes it wasn't. I was a suicide risk, I found out later, and knitting was therefore highly dangerous. They used to assess my mood before allowing me my knitting. I knew nothing about all that at the time.

As to the permitted three sets of clothes, my God how tired we got of our clothes after weeks and weeks of them. Most of us tried to keep one set for visits, which narrowed it down to two. While appearing on remand every week, it was essential to have a 'best set' kept only for court appearances and visits. My 'best set' consisted of a green skirt and cardigan and a blouse of which I used to be very fond. I also kept one pair of sandals for court. This left me one pair of grey cords, one pair of jeans, one blouse and two jerseys for daily wear. I lived in these for five months. It was theoretically possible to get permission from the chief officer to have one set of clothing exchanged for another, but in practice few of us did. It was not worth the hassle. It was trouble enough getting my coat and shoes sent in when the summer was over, and a new set of clothes for my trial.

As far as my books were concerned, I had been told that it was not necessary for me to have books sent in as there were books on the shelves for us to borrow. It was certainly true that there were two shelves of books on the wing, but what books they were! And what a state they were in! There was a library, but that consisted of two tall cupboards of books by the association room, which were kept permanently locked up. I only saw the cupboards open a few weeks before my trial, when an officer was checking the books. I asked if I could borrow some, and was told that they were for the convicted prisoners, not the girls on remand.

I read every one of the books on the two bookshelves, plus a few more, since one day we were allowed to exchange our books for those in the bookcases on the other wings. The problem was that almost every book had been mutilated in some way. Often the last few pages had been torn out, sometimes the first pages, sometimes both. All the books had been written in, and the graffiti was unbelievable. Even in the Bible there was writing and drawing of a most unsuitable kind. There were pathetic messages in some, written by one despairing person and cast loose to be read by those following her. Later, I copied some of these into my exercise book.

Today is Thursday 9/10/80 and tomorrow i am going to Court 10/10/80 at Swansea Mag. i am going to get Borstal most prob but what the hell theres not much happeneing outside only my bloke Colin but then theres this trouble with his mother she hasnt got long left and i dont fancy being there when she dies but i hope she lives for many a year yet. Well good luck to who ever reads this i hope you have better luck than myself.

I wondered if a psychiatrist would be interested in the way the pronoun 'I' was written 'i' throughout.

I also wrote this in my exercise book:

When they have books, they do not read them, but they either write in them, or take the longest word on each page and see how many words they can get from it, or cross out every letter 'a' or 'e' wherever it appears. Someone of great perseverance had gone through every single page of *My Cousin Rachel* deleting every single 'e'. Or another variation is to delete the 'a's on the first page, the 'b's on the second, and so on through the book and the alphabet. The writing is sometimes ordinary graffiti, sometimes tales in the form of a letter to a loved one, sometimes in the form of verse, of which the best example I have seen is:

Oh how happy they must be, Carol and Steve
The new man and wife
They are starting a new life.
That could have been you and I a week or so ago.
What happened to that, where did it go?
Down the kneck of a bottle, that's where it went
And me into hell which is where I must of chose to go
Did I choose? Did I have a choice? Or was it on
Listning to that other voice that makes me mad and insane
To do things I shall never do again.
Now no future just a past
I know life without you will not long last.
I thank you for the love I thought I would never find again
It meant so much I could never explain
Sorry is not a big enough word for what I have done
There is no way to undo what I have done. Who to? And where
    do I go from here?
You will no longer want me near
Who have loved me and held me dear
You are my life as you know
So without you there isn't far to go
Never together, never near, is the greatest thing I fear.
Always that battle I will have nightmares about
If only it was a nightmare and I could awake.
Never one sip would again pass my lips
As just one sip I can tell you so well
Doesn't lead to delight, it leads to hell.

I have reproduced this in full because it seems to me to be the true voice of Pucklechurch. I have no idea who wrote it, or when, but I can imagine a girl, tough, uncaring, resentful of attempts to help her, watching her life go uncontrollably wrong without being able to do anything about it. Then, one day, locked up alone in her cell, she found words to tell the story of her misery, and wrote it in the book for others to see. I imagine it was written in white heat, just as it came, the words putting themselves on to the page.

Exercise book again:

I wonder very much at this writing in the books. Some of it is bitter, angry, full of swear words, cursing the police, the prison, other girls, their boyfriends, everything. Or it is pathetic, sorrowful, grieving for the mistake they made, longing to see the boy or the children again. While it is usually evilly misspelt and inarticulate, it seizes the attention by its obvious sincerity. It is, though they do not know it, creative writing of a high value. If only they could have learned in English lessons to get it out of their systems in words! Much, though, is articulate, and I have seen one example (and I think I know who wrote it) which was perfect in grammar and spelling, written in complicated constructions, but totally insane.

I have never understood the desire which so many people obviously have to write their names up everywhere. Often the writing in the books is in the form of a letter to a man, names and nicknames given, but never surnames. I feel no desire whatever to leave my name or that of anyone I care for written anywhere in here, or anywhere else either.

On Sunday afternoons we needed the books, or something to do, because after the great clean-up in the morning, we regularly spent Sunday afternoons locked up. This was because the officers had a meeting at that time, though I did not find this out until much later. It was never explained to us why we were locked up: ours not to reason why – ours just to get in our cells and remain quiet for the whole afternoon.

For the first two or three Sundays I did not know what to do with myself. I spent most of the time asleep, for which I paid by not sleeping at night. Later, I learned to organize myself, and saved my letters to write on Sunday afternoons. This I did for the whole five months. It could take a long time to write a letter if you spun it out a bit. I devised other ways of passing the time, but I remember those first never-ending Sundays with dread. This really was how I had visualized prison. On my first Sunday I had no way of knowing that this was not to be the pattern of every day: nobody said to me, 'You will only be locked up on a Sunday afternoon. Tomorrow will be quite different.' It was a long time; we came in from exercise, if we had exercise, at about 1.30 p.m. and were then locked up until 6.00 when we might or might not be unlocked for the evening. We had only a brief exodus from our cells to fetch our tea from the trolley at 3.45. If we had no exercise we were locked up from midday till six o'clock on Sundays, and six solid hours of one's own company with nothing to do is difficult to bear. Difficult to bear, especially when the last thing you want to do is think.

Mentally, in those first days, I was very precariously balanced indeed. Perhaps I was not really balanced at all. I had a short interview with the psychiatrist, and was given hope, and also drugs, including sleeping pills at night and an antidepressant. I think I must have been more ill than I realized, because when Friday came, and with it my appearance at the magistrates' court, I did not have to go. The psychiatrist had the power to provide a note saying that I was too ill to attend. Unfortunately, that was the last time I was excused court attendance, but week after week I used to hope that I would be. But then the regular psychiatrist went away on a month's leave, and his replacement was the coldest, hardest man I have ever met. I am by no means sure now that the regular man would have excused me more than once, but at that time I was convinced that the new man did not understand my problem.

I repeatedly asked to see him, and at last I was forced to ask him in front of everyone else if I could see him. He asked why, and I had to say that it was because he had the power to allow me to miss going to court. He gave me the coldest, most contemptuous look I have ever had in my life, and said, 'Ah, but I believe in letting the law take its course'. Another one who had condemned me before my trial. On the basis of what?

There were those in Pucklechurch for whom the weekly remand appearance was not the ordeal it was for me. There were those who positively looked forward to it: it meant a break in routine, a voyage outside the gates and the chance to see their family. Although I only saw my husband once at court, the police sometimes allowed family to visit the prisoner in the cells at court, and many took advantage of this.

For me, however, it was different, and I cannot find the words to describe the feeling of horror which the weekly court appearance created in me. I was all right the rest of the time, but when Thursday came and I knew it was court the next day, I began to get strung up, and by the time I arrived safely back in Pucklechurch after court at lunchtime on Friday, I was prostrate. I have known some bad times in my life, but nothing to equal those Friday appearances.

What was known as the 'wind up' began at some stage on the Thursday, when an officer would appear in class or association or wherever we were, and call me out. I went with her to my cell, and then all my belongings, everything down to a biro, were collected and crammed together in plastic bags, usually white plastic bags, but sometimes they proclaimed themselves as Sainsbury's or Tesco's. The clothes, underclothes and sandals which I wished to wear to court were kept separate, but taken away, often bundled over the officer's arm in a manner which undid the careful ironing which had gone into them. Some officers were sensitive to the prisoner's feelings about her belongings, some were not, and appeared to regard it all as so much clutter. I would be left with nothing but my nightclothes, my washing things, the clothes I had on, and my book from the shelf. Later, I got canny, and passed a lot of things over to my friends to keep for me, but this was strictly forbidden, and although I knew, and the officers knew, that I would be coming back, they had to pretend that I might get bail.

So the Thursday evening and night would be spent in a bare cell. I always slept badly before court, and I know I was not the only one. The Friday morning found me trying, and really I did try, to control my steadily mounting panic. Some sisters insisted that I washed my hair on the night before the court appearance, in spite of my pleas that to do so made me look like a guy the next day, and so it did. I have problem hair, which needs to be pinned down after it has been washed, and of course we were not allowed to have hair curlers or hair grips to do this with. So, frequently on the Friday morning my hair was standing out in all directions, which did nothing for my self-esteem. I later learned to wet the front bit and simply wrap the rest in a towel, and none of the sisters ever took the trouble to discover that my whole head had not been washed. But those Friday mornings were spent in the knowledge that I looked just about as awful as it was possible for me to look.

We did not have breakfast on the wing, but early in the morning an officer, sometimes two, would come to collect me and take me down the administration corridor, and into reception. I would be in my nightclothes and carrying a bundle of my other clothes and washing things, my book from the shelf having been put back as I left the wing. Only once was I allowed to wash on the wing before being taken to reception. I abandoned my bundle of clothes on the big table in reception. I was told to go behind a curtain and take off my nightclothes. Not that the curtain afforded much privacy, as the officer stood behind me and watched. I stood there naked, and then had to turn around with my arms above my head so that the officer could inspect every external inch of my body. Then I had to lift my feet one after the other so that they could be checked for anything taped to the soles. I was then allowed to put on a kind of dressing gown.

This is the infamous strip search, to which everyone in English remand centres is subjected. Many of those who have to undergo it are entirely innocent of any crime. The police cannot be right 100 per cent of the time; inevitably they make mistakes and innocent people are remanded in custody. It is an appalling thought that an innocent person can be taken off the streets or from their house, and subjected to the ordeals of the remand centre, the most traumatic of which is probably the strip search. I never could understand why such a search was considered necessary. Anyone who wanted to get something into or out of the remand centre would secrete it in the obvious places, and I know for a fact that this was done. This made a mockery of the strip search, and I think it should be discontinued at once as being totally unacceptable in a free society.

To be fair, however, I do not think that the officers enjoyed this part of their job either. To be confronted with all those disgusting, saggy, scarred female bodies first thing in the morning must have been a terrible experience, but they did it because they had to do it. With someone like me the search was often omitted, because I was sometimes allowed to go to court directly from the hospital wing, or on my return from court I was frequently allowed to go back to the wing without going through reception because I was in such a state.

Having gone through that process, I was given my court clothes, which had been searched the previous day, and put through into a little room at the back of reception where I was supposed to wash and dress. The trouble was that another ten or twelve women might also be trying to wash and dress there. There was one very small washbasin in the toilet, which was invariably filthy, and how could one wash properly when other people were waiting to use the toilet? Also, it was unusual to be allowed to keep your washing things, so how we were supposed to wash I never did work out. Many times I appeared in court unwashed, until I learned that there was in fact a basin in another room which, if I was lucky and had to wait in the anteroom before my strip search, I could use. If I was taken straight through, then that was that. No wash.

There were not enough chairs in the little room, and only one tiny handmirror, made not of glass but of metal. I found the other girls frightening, I hated mixing with the girls from the wings, as they were so loud and tough, and I was always terrified that one day I would see someone I had taught. I could imagine what I would have to go through then. Fortunately, that never did happen, but it was possible. We then had to wait in that overcrowded room – for up to two hours in my case, as I was only going to Bristol and did not therefore leave until 9.30. Breakfast was brought to us on a tray, but sometimes there was not enough to go round, and if you were not prepared to push, you did not get any. More than once, however, one of the young ones would sense my fear, and see to it that I was given my share. Not that I ever felt like eating much, but I did need the tea.

While we were waiting, the officers in reception checked our property against our property cards, packing our things in their plastic bags. They did as much of this the day before as they could, but the clothes we had been wearing the day before still had to be checked, and there were always some queries. Sometimes they could not find an item of property, and came into our room to ask the person concerned what had happened to her red pants, for example. Almost always the fact was that the woman had thrown the property away, which we were not supposed to do without permission. (Please Chief, my red pants are worn out. Can I throw them away?) I must say that the property procedure was very efficient – I was always expecting them to lose something, but they never did. Even so, what a performance to go through every week. Was it really necessary?

The girls were dealt with in the order in which they were going to court. Some had long distances to go, and left at 7.30 in order to be there by 10.00. A few girls, who had to go right into Cornwall, had to leave even earlier. Fair enough, but why then was I, who did not have to leave until 9.30, made to sit in that room for two hours with absolutely nothing to do? One by one the girls left, and the room cleared slowly. Often it happened that I was the only one left, with three-quarters of an hour or so to wait by myself. I was never sure whether it was worse to have other people with me smoking and shouting, or to be alone with nothing to do but think.

At last the door would be unlocked, and the officer who was to escort me would come in with my property cards to sign. We had no idea, of course, whether the property was all there or not, but we had to sign to say that it was. Then I was allowed out of that awful room, worse than a cell to me, and into the reception anteroom to wait until an escort and taxi were sorted out for me. I always had a nurse with me; it was usual, but not inevitable, for a nurse to accompany a woman from the hospital wing. The officers always took the plastic bags loaded with my property, and we would leave the building using the door outside which the taxi had drawn up. A senior officer was always standing by the open door. 'Who are you and where are you going?' she intoned. I used to wonder sometimes. The expected reply was 'Audrey Peckham, Bristol Magistrates'', to tally with the paper she had in her hand. One officer went out before me and got into the back seat and I was supposed to follow. The second officer and the driver dumped my plastic bags in the boot. The same officer got in on the other side of me, the nurse in the front, and we were off. Sometimes if there was more than one, we went in a minibus, which I liked better as we were not all so crowded together. I wonder how much it costs the government to provide all this transport to take prisoners backwards and forwards from court?

I was never pleased when the double gates shut behind us and we were outside. I was frightened. Pucklechurch had become my refuge from the terrors of the outside world, and I hated to leave it. I didn't feel safe. I just wanted to stay inside for ever in a state of suspended animation. Invariably, as the gates closed and I was outside having to face the shame and hostility of the world, I began to lose control. The journey to Bristol took about twenty minutes, but by the end of it I was almost always crying hopelessly. I am not proud of this; I do not understand it. I am not normally given to crying, and I did not believe that it could be possible for anyone to cry continuously for the length of time I did on those court days. If I could have controlled myself I would have done so. I hardly ever cried inside Pucklechurch – it was coming out which did for me.

The car would drive right into the underground car park beneath the magistrates' courts. I and my plastic bags would get out, go further underground down a flight of stairs and along some corridors. The officers and nurse would hand me over to the police wardress, who would sign for me and my plastic bags as if there wasn't much difference between us. Then they went, leaving me in the care of the police.

On every occasion but one, I was placed in a cell next to the room where the wardress sat, so that she could keep an eye on me. It was always the same wardress, who saw my distress and told me that I would have to toughen up or I would not stand the things that would happen to me. She was kind to me, and I often wonder if she is still there, down so deep underground, where, as she said, in winter she never saw daylight at all. What a terrible job! I never saw many other women when I was there, but she said that some days it got very hectic.

My solicitor would usually come down to see me before court, but once or twice I would go to see him, up some stairs to a long narrow room filled with little cubicles in which solicitors sat, like a row of battery hens, interviewing their clients. I am left with the vague impression that most of the clients were young and male, but I was not in a state to be very aware of my surroundings. Poor David was very sweet to me always, though he must have often wanted to wring my neck, as he could never get any sense out of me on court days. I just sat and cried. He used to have to come out to Pucklechurch if he wanted to talk to a sane woman. I was always glad to see him, I trusted him absolutely, and he always made me feel better, even if I still could not stop crying.

He would always try to arrange things so that I went into court as soon as possible, and only once did I have to wait any length of time. Soon after 10.30 the policewoman escort and a male colleague would come for me, and I would be escorted upstairs in a lift, and sat down on a bench outside the court to wait. By this time my senses had become blocked, and I could hardly see or hear anything. I sat there like a caged animal, until the policewoman got hold of my arm and led me into the court. She went into the dock first, I followed, and a male policeman brought up the rear. If my life depended upon it I could not describe the courtroom or the magistrates. I never saw them. I kept my head down and tried to cry quietly, not noisily. It was all I could do.

The procedure was always the same. I was asked who I was, managed to agree that I was Audrey Joan Peckham, and was allowed to sit down. That was better, I could hide my face completely in my hands. Things were said, but the only thing I remember is that every week I was remanded in custody again 'because of the nature and seriousness of the offence, the likelihood of further offences, and your psychiatric condition'. Only once, after an appeal through my solicitor, did I get them to say 'the nature and seriousness of the *alleged* offence'. As to my psychiatric condition, upon what evidence they based that remark I do not know: I never heard any. And if they thought that I was a psychiatric case, why was I not allowed to go to a psychiatric hospital where I could have had treatment, instead of being held on remand where I had to heal myself as best I could?

One of the things which my solicitor had done when I was first arrested was to get the psychiatrist who had been treating me before my arrest to agree that if I were given bail, he would make a bed available for me in his hospital, or arrange for me to be treated in the local Bristol hospital if the court preferred that. Presumably in either place I could have been locked up so that I did not escape. Yet I was never given bail. At the time I did not care, but looking back on it now, I think it was disgraceful that I was remanded in custody for such a long period. I was not well, I needed help. Help was offered to me, but the magistrates would not grant bail, so I went without any help at all. If I was a suicide risk, as I was considered to be at Pucklechurch for I don't know how long, then surely I could have been better looked after in a hospital. As for the likelihood of further offences, by which they meant the possibility that I would have had another attempt at 'murder', that was impossible for me to do. A minute's thought would have made them realize the success of my 'scheme' depended upon secrecy.

It had to be. Less than a year later I was to be set free. What about the possibility of further offences then? If indeed I did have murder on my mind I could have committed it at any time during the past year. Oh, it was such rubbish. It would have been better for me to go to a psychiatric hospital, it would have been better for half the people I met at Pucklechurch to be in a hospital. There was a place for me in hospital, but I was not allowed to take it.

But this is all as I see it now. At the time, I did not care where they sent me, so long as I got out of that courtroom. I did not want to go home, I knew that. I did not think I could cope on my own any more. I knew I could not go back to my job. If I were in the same position now, I would try hard to get bail, and I would do my utmost to make the community see me as innocent until proved guilty. I would go to school, and say, look, I am innocent of that charge, and I am also innocent of anything until I have been found guilty. Why should I resign? Why should I behave and be treated as if I were already condemned? But at the time I was not myself. The horror of it all had overwhelmed me, and I could not think straight. It is even possible that my attitude was taken as a tacit admission of guilt, rather than of shame.

The worst experience in my whole life was having to stand in the dock, having to hear that charge read out, and be unable to declare my innocence of it. The court was not concerned with whether I was or was not guilty. That would be tried by a higher court. Their interest was only in what was to be done with me for the next week. I can understand why the idea grew up that prisoners should be produced before the magistrates every week: to give them a chance to ask for bail if circumstances have changed, to give them a chance, even if only a theoretical one, to complain about their treatment, to let the magistrates reassure themselves that the prisoner had not been 'done away with', but was alive and well. Yet the weekly remand only lasts until the prisoner is committed for trial at the crown court. After that, he stays in the remand centre for months and months, and nobody cares whether he is alive and well or not.

In my own case, I first appeared before the magistrates on 14 May 1982. On the 21st, as I have already explained, I did not attend court, as I was not considered to be well enough. But every Friday thereafter I had to go through my ordeal, until the day I was committed for trial at the crown court. That made seven Fridays, seven ordeals. I was committed on 9 July. I then had to wait in Pucklechurch for another twelve and a half weeks until my trial. It seemed to me that if I could be held for twelve and a half weeks without anyone seeing me after committal, then I could quite as well have been held for the weeks before the committal, and remanded again in my absence, to avoid going through that weekly farce. What it must cost the taxpayer! That period of weekly remand seemed never-ending to me, but my solicitor assured me that in fact it was all dealt with very quickly – nine weeks in all – and I was committed long before I might have been.

And why, I ask now, is there such a long delay anyway? Why did it take nine weeks for me to be committed, for the DPP to decide that there was a case for me to answer? Why did it then take a further twelve and a half weeks before the case could be heard? I know of people who have spent more than a year on remand in custody waiting for their case to be heard. One of the things most wrong with the remand system is this awful delay. Week after week after week. It is inhumane in the extreme.

Mercifully, my Friday appearances in the dock lasted for only four or five minutes at the most. Then I was taken back to the cell to await return transport to Pucklechurch. Again, I was treated with kindness and humanity in that wherever possible I was sent back to Pucklechurch by car as soon as one was available. But there were occasions when I would have to wait all morning and well into the afternoon before I could be sent back. Those long hours in the cells with only a few magazines to read were some of the worst of my captivity. If I was kept over lunchtime I was given a cup of tea, a pie and a few biscuits, but I didn't feel like eating much anyway.

On two occasions I had to be sent back to Pucklechurch in a Black Maria. It was utterly degrading, but both times the police warders apologized for this. Inside it is divided into little cubicles with just enough room to sit down on the ledge seat provided. There is a little window. The door to the cubicle is locked behind you. It made me feel claustrophobic: what I wonder would happen to someone who was really unable to tolerate being locked into such a tiny space? But I preferred the Black Maria in one respect – at least no one could see me. I hated driving through the streets of Bristol in a marked police car, as I felt everyone would know that I was under arrest.

It might be thought that after the court appearance I would recover a bit; but I found that being shut in the police cells and driven back to Pucklechurch was as bad as anything except the actual court appearance itself. I still could not stop crying, and was unable to read the magazines provided because of my swollen eyes. With nothing to do but sit and think, it all came to the forefront of my mind so that I could not escape it. I could only survey a life in ruins, though by that I do not mean what most people would mean. It was my own private ruin I was considering, not the public disgrace; though that only added to my misery. I couldn't help but go over and over it in my head, over and over. I suffered on those Fridays.

I was always returned to Pucklechurch, usually at about lunchtime, in a state more or less of collapse. The longer I had to wait the worse I was. I was often allowed to go direct to the hospital wing without going through reception. Oh, the mercy of this. On one of these occasions, I was supported along the corridor by an officer and another person. Only at the end of the corridor did I realize that the other person was the chief herself. She said nothing, but had taken the trouble to come out of her office and help me. I shall never forget that.

There were occasions when I did have to go through the reception procedure. Into the anteroom, to be signed for again. My money was tipped out and counted in front of me and my police escort. I neither knew nor cared how much money I had. Then I was put into the horse box for a long or short time, depending on when the officer running reception could get round to me. Nobody ought to be locked up in a little cubicle like that for any time at all, and certainly not for the lengths of time I have spent there – sometimes half an hour, an hour, or more than an hour. Once or twice I was given my lunch in there, and once I was taken out rapidly and returned to the hospital wing with no more ceremony because I began screaming. I wasn't trying it on. I really couldn't help it.

Normally, however, it was out of the horse box into reception, where my belongings were checked again against my property card and I signed for them again. As I could hardly write, my signature on those cards is pretty unrecognizable. This was followed by a compulsory bath and hairwash, 'because we don't know what you have picked up in those police cells'. Out of the bath, strip searched again, and my own clothes to get into. The rest of my things were bundled up in a pillowcase, and then back to the wing at last. Sometimes we had to go back to the wing in our nightclothes.

On the wing I would always be locked up for a while. I put my few things away, and then fell on the bed, in a state of total exhaustion, to sleep. Depending which sister was on duty, I would be locked up until teatime, or allowed out to join the others in the association room.

The first time I went through this reception procedure after a court appearance, on Friday, 28 May, I could not believe it. I hoped familiarity would lead to a lessening of the horror, but it never did. If anything it got worse. But there was worse yet in store for me.

It was, I remember, Wednesday, 2 June, the week after my first experience of the remand procedure. I was called out of class to see the psychiatrist. This was the temporary man, the hard, cold, unsympathetic man, not the regular psychiatrist who was on leave. Nonetheless, I went in hope. He barely glanced at me as I came in, and said something like, 'Well, you shouldn't have done that, should you?' I replied, 'I didn't do it. Can I tell you about it?' He actually said, 'If you must', and looked at his watch. I could say nothing after that, and he began to flip through my file. He allowed it to rest open at the front cover. He was reading the first page, but I was reading the press cutting which someone had stuck to the inside of the cover. 'Deputy Head in Murder Plot' it said in letters half an inch high.

And that is when I broke down completely, lost all sense of reason and finally had the breakdown towards which I had been moving for months past. I had not been thinking straight. I had not realized the implications of what I was doing. I had not realized that the press would be involved, that the school would be involved. Until that moment, it had been to me my own private nightmare. Suddenly I had to face the fact that it was not private any longer, that I was now at the mercy of the whole world.

They took me away and locked me up. They let me out after dinner, and as Wednesday was the day the chaplain came round, I asked to see him. He gave me about two hours of his time, and seemed to be trying to help me. But he went and told the sisters that he thought I was seriously suicidal. They did nothing with me until the evening, but I suppose they were watching me. After supper, I was sitting on my bed, and one of the sisters came to talk to me. She had already made up her mind what she was going to do. She had merely come to tell me that I was going into 'strips'.

At a call from her, other nurses came in, and all my furniture and all my things were bundled into the corridor outside the cell. I was left with only a mattress and my plastic mug. I was told to take all my clothes off, and given a strip gown to put on. This is a tunic-like garment made out of specially strengthened material, so that it could not be torn up and used to strangle yourself. Two strip blankets were given to me, which were of similar material, but quilted like an eiderdown. For two days and two nights that is all I had in my cell. The strip gown was fawn and the blankets were navy blue. I was left alone with my misery. Fortunately for me, I do not now remember much about it at all.

Sometimes I slept on the mattress on the floor, sometimes I did not. Food was given to me on the usual plastic plate, but it was all cut up for me, and I only had a spoon to eat it with. I was not allowed my glasses, but I wasn't in a fit state to read anyway. I remember there was one time when there was a nurse outside the cell, continuously watching me through the peephole. I couldn't see her, but I could hear the jangling of her keys. That first night and day I went under and came up several times. A nurse came in to me once and spoke kind words. I don't really know what was happening to me, and I have no words to describe the way I felt. Thankfully, the memory of it soon faded.

Yet not even that was sufficient justification for missing court on the Friday. This was one of the occasions when I went straight from the wing and not through reception. They pushed me into my clothes and then pushed me into a car to take me to court. My solicitor was not there: he had two weeks' leave. A partner was there, but I could not tell him what had happened to me at Pucklechurch. Strangely, even after that, I did not want bail. I never told my family anything about it. I was returned to Pucklechurch in such a state that I could not breathe properly. I suppose now that I was only displaying all the usual signs of hysteria, but I thought I was dying, and I may say I hoped I was. Why, oh why, could I not have been in a proper hospital at that time, instead of the 'hospital' wing of a remand centre, which was in no way a hospital?

Another sister was in charge on the Friday evening, and she let me 'have my bed back', as we put it, which meant that the furniture was moved back into my cell, and I was considered to be normal again. The next day I could have gone to church with the others, but I was so annoyed with the chaplain, who I quite unfairly blamed for my being put into strips, that I did not go. Nor did I ever forgive him as long as I was at Pucklechurch.

This was the absolute rock bottom of my time on remand. It was the bottom both from the point of view of my physical state, because, having been put into strips there isn't much more in the way of physical degradation that can happen in the prison system of this country; but more importantly from the point of my psychological state. It seems that I had to go all the way to the bottom before I could come up again. What happened to me during those two days in June was the inevitable end of the road I had begun walking in November eighteen months previously. I have been pretty tough in my life, and I have taken a lot for forty years without breaking, but that was too much. I broke, and I lay on the floor in a strip cell in Pucklechurch in a state of total collapse.

So from then on there was no way to go except up. That is the comforting thing about being right at the bottom; things can't get worse, can't remain the same, so can only get better. And from the time I got my bed back on the Friday evening, I was on my way back into the real world from the hell in which I had been living for the past year. It was a long process. In my heart I know it is not completed yet, but one day it will be. Not that I could ever be the same person I was before the events of those years 1980 to 1983; but I shall be a person again.

I began to improve. I began to take an interest in my appearance again, although it was not much good being too fussy, as we were not allowed hairpins or razors. Theoretically, we were allowed to use a razor under supervision, but the effort involved to get a razor made available was so enormous that most of us settled for hairy legs. I began to take more of an interest in the routine of the place and the other people in with me. On 14 June, I was considered to be sufficiently well to be moved to a room on the upstairs corridor, which was a real 'promotion': the upstairs rooms were for people who could more or less be trusted, while the downstairs rooms were for those upon whom the sisters wanted to keep an eye.

And so began the period of time, from 14 June to my trial on 6 October, when I became absorbed into the Pucklechurch routine and learned from that long experience what life is like in a remand centre in the England of the 1980s.

During my whole time at Pucklechurch I was on the hospital wing. I felt desperately in need of some kind of therapy. But I realized, after two brief sessions with the prison psychiatrist (a friendly and fatherly man), that therapy of any kind was not part of the prison system. Our interviews were strictly diagnostic – to see whether I was a suicide risk. Once it had been ascertained that I probably wasn't, they ceased. My longing to talk about my case, my breakdown, my feelings, could not be met by the prison psychiatric system. I wished – as other critics of the prison system have suggested – that my own caring GP and psychiatric social worker could have continued to see me.

3 Pucklechurch Morning

A little later, in July, I was to write in my exercise book of these early days:

> When you settle into any institution you must first learn what you need to know for survival: how you get food and water, where the toilets are, who you can trust, who is kind and who is not. Then you can set about learning the system. Then you learn to manipulate the system to produce conditions of greater comfort.

And again:

> When you first come in there is a babble of meaningless noise echoing through the uncarpeted, uncurtained corridors. Slowly you sort it out; slowly, as the routine of the prison becomes understood, the noises cease to be meaningless. Feet thundering down the corridor and the jangle of keys might mean that I am going to be unlocked, or it might mean the duty officer checking the fire door; or simply one of the nurses coming to the loo. A door may be unlocked, but unless there is also the sound of the lock fixed back, nobody is coming out.
>
> As familiarity grows one can tell which of the sisters is coming: walks are as distinctive as voices. The tramp of heavy feet after trouble means strips for someone. Two pairs of official footsteps and a low monotonous voice means someone is having a report read to them. A shout of 'Medicine, Sister' means that the girls from the wings have been brought over after breakfast or lunch for their medicine. At 8.00 p.m., the trolley of drugs crashes its way over to the wings for night medicine. An abrupt loud ring is the riot bell, often followed by considerable drama.

Thus confusion and meaningless noise becomes ordered and classified into understanding the sounds which make up a typical Pucklechurch day.

The following extract from my notebook shows that I still had the feeling that I was safe and moderately happy in Pucklechurch:

There are good things about being in here. The fact that nobody can expect me to do anything about anything. I just rest in this very sheltered place, away from the stresses outside. There are some good people in here, and in the forcing house of our common trouble one gets to know people quickly. I have made some good, if temporary, friendships. The magic appearance of food four times a day which I have not had to think about, shop for, cook, or clear away. The almost constant hot water, which means a bath a night which I don't have to pay for. Spoiling myself with canteen Mars bars. Also, at times things can be really funny; I have laughed in here more than I have for years. And the occasional break in routine such as the goings on on August Bank Holiday comes with a meaning out of proportion to what it is.

Typing this out now, a year after my release, I am capable of seeing that this attitude must have been a manifestation of my sickness. Nobody in their right mind would have been content in Pucklechurch: I was not in my right mind. That is how I felt at first, and I have included the extract to demonstrate it. Slowly, slowly, my attitude changed, as I began to pull myself together again, but I cannot honestly say that I ever really hated Pucklechurch life as I would have done had I been normal.

The Pucklechurch day began at 6.30 a.m. with the ringing of an electric bell to wake us up. At first I leapt out of bed, thinking that something must be going to happen and I had better be ready for it, but in fact we had another hour and a half of being locked up, so I soon learned to ignore the bell. I used to stay in bed dozing until 7.00 when I would put my little radio on and listen to the news. Between 6.30 and 7.00 we would be checked twice, once by the night officer going off duty, and once by the sister coming on, presumably to make sure that we were still all alive and on the premises. At some point the officer on patrol would thunder down the corridor and check the fire door. Does it open? Is it locked? It always was. If we were awake, the night officer and the sister would exchange a few words with us.

In my first days at Pucklechurch I was almost always asleep, oblivion being the preferred state of being. Later, through the summer, I tended to wake up earlier and earlier, as the life of enforced inactivity began to get me down physically. Later still, I could hardly sleep at all because of my forthcoming trial, and I was always awake and often out of bed by the time Sister came round.

I used to try to stay in bed as long as possible, listening to the 'Today' programme on Radio 4. Often, though, an item would bore me and I would have to get up because I could no longer bear to be in bed, but as there was nothing to get up for, it was a bit pointless. Sometimes I lasted up to the sports news, but that would always drive me to get up. I would potter round my cell, tidying an already tidy locker, and strip my bed and fold the blankets neatly. It all filled in time.

As I could not get to the toilet until I had been unlocked, and as it was a matter of honour with me not to use the ghastly plastic pot provided, I used to wait with increasing impatience and discomfort for the sound of keys and doors being unlocked at the other end of the corridor, which meant that soon I would be 'out'. For me, that meant straight into the toilet, while my less continent sisters had to undergo the trail down the corridor to the sluice, plastic pot in hand – and sometimes plastic pot overflowingly in hand, too.

Unlocking was at 7.45 in the morning, or was supposed to be, but often, in fact, we were unlocked later than that. Breakfast was supposed to be at 8.00, so we often had less than ten minutes to wash. Had there been sufficient basins, this might just have been possible, but there were only four basins on the wing, and these might have to be shared by up to fifteen or sixteen women. When they first came in, people would try to wash properly and then dress, but if you did that, it tied up a basin for the entire ten minutes available, and was not therefore fair to the others. So we fell into the habit of dressing in our rooms before unlocking, so that as soon as the door was opened we could make a rush for the basins, and either get there first, or be early in the queue. The old stagers were always the ones who washed first.

Of course, there was no privacy at these basins, no curtains which could be drawn. The modest would struggle with inadequate-sized towels to hide their nakedness; the less modest, or more natural, would simply strip off and wash, regardless of who saw what. Those who suffered most were probably the genuine lesbians. I came to understand that for them the implications of nakedness among other women was the same as it would have been for me among men. One lesbian girl tried to evade the overwhelming sexual implications of all these naked and semi-naked female bodies by washing in the bathroom. The door did not lock, but at least it ensured a reasonable amount of privacy. One sister saw to it that this young girl was made to wash at the basins with the rest of us. Her protests earned her punishment, and the resulting trauma upset the delicate balance of her emotions for the rest of the day.

I cannot complain that we were made to be dirty, because in fact most of us had the chance of a bath every night – one of the advantages of being on the hospital wing. Those in the main part of the centre had fewer baths. Yet, having been locked in for at least twelve hours with only a plastic pot and no facilities whatsoever for washing our hands, we yearned for the chance of hot, soapy water in the morning. Somewhat to my surprise, the water was usually hot, but, knowing that there are four or five other women to use the basin after you before eight o'clock, all you can manage is a quick rinse, when what you yearn for is a long soak!

I am fortunately blessed with a strong bladder, and it was a source of pride to me that in fact I never used my plastic pot during the night, except on the occasion when chicken curry had been one of the two dishes served for lunch. All the women who had eaten the curry woke in the night with food poisoning, and I was one of them. I had better leave it to the imagination as to what it is like to be locked up with food poisoning, a plastic pot and no washing facilities. For our doors, once locked at night, could not be unlocked by the night staff except in cases of life-threatening emergency. To be fair to the officers, on this particular night some of them were recalled to duty so that the worst-affected food poisoning cases could be unlocked to

59

empty their pots and wash their hands, but there were so many women affected that some of us, including me, did not get unlocked until the next morning.

Our unlocking always depended on the number of officers on duty. It was strictly against the rules to unlock prisoners unless the ratio of officer to prisoners was maintained. This ratio differed with the number of category A (dangerous) prisoners the centre held. There were occasions when we were not unlocked in the morning because sufficient officers had not come on duty. We might be unlocked singly, or in twos, to go down and get our breakfast from the trolley. If sufficient officers did not come on duty, or if after breakfast the number of officers required to escort people to court had reduced the ratio of women to officer left behind, then we were simply locked up again for the morning or the whole day. One very bad period occurred in the summer when I suppose many officers were taking leave. We were locked up almost continuously from one Thursday to the following Tuesday. I have reserves within myself to deal with long periods alone, but by the end of that spell, I could feel alterations in my attitude taking place. How do people cope with really extended spells of solitary confinement without becoming hopelessly disorientated?

For those of us who were having medication, the time allowed for washing in the morning was further reduced by the fact that early medicines were given out before breakfast. Sometimes, we had barely been unlocked before the shout would go up from the sister on duty: 'Medicine!' We were then supposed to leave whatever we were doing, and queue up at the hatch to receive our morning pills and liquids. It rather depended which sister was doing the medicines as to the latitude she would allow. Some were furious if everyone did not appear the second the shout went up; others were more reasonable. It was, however, one of the major frustrations of remand centre life to have to stand in a queue for medicine before I had washed, because the call had come (as it frequently did) while I was still in the toilet – a morning ritual which after a long night could not be hurried!

We waited for our breakfast at the foot of the stairs by Sister's office. We always waited for everything there, unless we were sent to wait upstairs. The reason for this was simply that at the foot of the stairs there was a widening of the corridor, with space for half a dozen chairs (the school, stacking, wooden variety). Fewer than half the women usually held in the hospital wing could sit on the chairs. The rest stood around. I usually made no attempt to sit on a chair because the cigarette smoke from the others at close quarters annoyed me, especially first thing in the morning. I used to stand on the other side of the corridor, propped against the radiator. No matter how you braced your feet there, if you were leaning on the radiator they would slowly slide from under you. We all discovered that game; and I must have spent hours of my time inside, propped against that radiator, watching my feet slowly sliding. It was quite mesmeric, and infinitely better than thinking. Besides, the radiator was outside the glass partition of Sister's office, and a pair of sharp eyes and ears could discover all manner of things, if they were lucky. The espionage came later though, at first I just stood.

How powerful the force of habit. What 'glass' partition? Of course it was not, it was plastic, as were the cell windows and all the other transparent partitions – except for the one along the upstairs bathroom. That was genuine glass, and like many others I made a note of the fact for possible future reference. Glass was a very forbidden thing, but there was an amazing lot of it which was hoarded away for the time when death seemed preferable to life, or violence against fellow inmate or prison officer was contemplated. Slivers of glass from broken windows were plentiful in the little garden quadrangle where we took our exercise. It became a game to see how many you could pick up and bring back inside, and although some of the staff had eyes like eagles, many did not.

Eventually from behind the locked door at the end of the corridor would come the cry 'Sister!' This meant that the trolley bearing our breakfasts was there. One of the staff would go and unlock the door and the 'trusty' from the kitchen would wheel the trolley in. Not so trusty, either, many of them, and frequent notes would change hands at this time. I only saw anyone caught at it twice. I was often surprised at what did go on right under the noses of the staff; and this sort of thing of course heightened the boarding-school atmosphere.

When the trolley was in, we queued up, or didn't, according to our nature. In spite of the charge I was facing, I am not a violent person, but I did once, and totally seriously, threaten a woman that, if she pushed in front of me again, I would thump her. I would have done, too, only fortunately she never did it again, or if she did, she caught my eye and retreated to the back of the queue. It wasn't her fault, poor thing. She was desperate with anxiety, and could not bear to wait for anything. She was not at all well, and I should have been more tolerant. But I was not at all well then either, and my sense of proportion had totally gone, as this incident shows. Also, I would have hit her and I would have found pleasure in it. After a while in Pucklechurch, the desire to hit someone very hard indeed becomes more like a serious temptation than a vague feeling. How the people who are violent by nature must feel I do not like to imagine. Thankfully, they mostly took it out on their cells, but on occasions the feeling of barely suppressed violence in the air was almost tangible, as is the increase of pressure before a thunderstorm.

The food was certainly not worth quarrelling about. At first I ate it because I did not care, and then it became a habit. Then I got used to it, and only when I was moved to Styal did I realize just how loathsome the Pucklechurch food had been. Breakfast was always a three-course affair, but what courses! There was almost always porridge, except on Sundays when we could expect cornflakes. Nothing else ever appeared. There was of course no milk, and sugar was limited to one plastic eggcupful twice a day. Oh, those red plastic eggcups, half full of sugar! The second course might be a sausage, quite alone on its plate, or a tiny bit of streaky bacon ('rasher' would give entirely the wrong impression!), usually alone like the sausage, but sometimes accompanied by a dollop of what I am sure was reconstituted dried egg left over from the war. There might be a tinned tomato, or a boiled egg on Sundays. There was no choice, one or the other of these delicacies appeared each morning, and you either ate it or you went without. The meal was concluded by two pieces of toast and a pat of margarine. On Sundays they usually – but not always – provided marmalade. This repast was accompanied by a mug of tea, and I will say one thing for Pucklechurch: the tea was always hot and strong, and as I do not have sugar in my tea it was enjoyable. Those who preferred their tea sweet suffered very much from the sugar rationing to which we were subjected.

All this food had to be carried from the trolley to our rooms, and we were then locked in to eat it. In a short while, one of the staff would come round to collect the dishes, but we were not let out. We were supposed to have stripped our beds and neatly folded the blankets before breakfast, and now was the time to make the bed again. Then it was a case of waiting, for we never knew for certain what would happen next. Just before I left Pucklechurch, a morning exercise period was created at 9.00, but during the majority of my stay there was no exercise in the mornings.

In theory, we were supposed to be let out daily at 9.00 in order to clean our cells, but although this usually happened, it by no means happened every day. It all depended on the ratio of officers to prisoners, as I have explained above. If there were not enough officers, then we simply stayed locked up all morning or all day, though in this case we were usually allowed out singly or in twos for only ten minutes to clean our cells. On a normal morning, we all trooped downstairs to our stairwell, for the cleaning things were kept in the cupboard under the stairs. We each possessed ourselves of a broom, dustpan and brush, bucket, cloth and scrubbing brush. If you were lucky, there was a bit of soap in the bucket. We filled the buckets with water from the downstairs bath, and queued at the kitchen door to be given disinfectant in the water. I always asked for rubber gloves, not to keep my hands beautiful (I do not normally use gloves for housework), but because my nails were splitting and I was trying to protect them from water.

The corridors and cells in Pucklechurch were floored with thermoplastic tiles, which gave a cool effect, and not an unpleasant one. But they had to be washed, or rather scrubbed every day, and mops were not provided. Kneelers were provided, however, so it was down on our knees to clean like old-fashioned charwomen. Exactly how much cleaning went on depended on what mood everybody was in and which staff were on duty. Some people would get away with barely flicking the broom round the room. Others would scrub the cell out thoroughly every day. At first, I used to clean fairly thoroughly, mainly because I found the manual work soothing. It was at least something to do which was necessary. Towards the end, though, I became as adept as anyone else at pretending to do the room properly for the most part. The utter pointlessness of all this cleaning got me down. I was not so dirty that my room had to be scrubbed every day.

Not that one could really complain about this part of the Pucklechurch regime. It was clearly important that the place was kept clean, and it was fair enough to expect us to make our own beds and clean our own rooms. The place was not a hotel. The rest of the wing, corridors, stairs, offices, staffroom, kitchen and treatment room, was cleaned by a wing cleaner, who was usually a convicted prisoner from B2, the wing where those prisoners who had been convicted and were serving their sentences at Pucklechurch were housed. However, it often happened that for one reason or another there was no wing cleaner, and then we would have to do all the cleaning ourselves. Again, at first I welcomed the ordered activity, and got myself a reputation as a good cleaner, but by the end I hated it.

Due to the large number of inadequate people usually housed on the hospital wing, the burden of all the cleaning fell on those of us who were more balanced. It was also very noticeable that the young ones did much less than we older ones, yet the young ones might be supposed to need the activity more than we did. The one thing about it which I hated in particular was that while cleaning any of the offices, the staffroom or the kitchen, there always had to be a nurse standing watching to see that you did not get up to anything of any kind. I could see the reason for this, but that did not stop me feeling great resentment at being watched over at my work, as though I were untrustworthy. I simply could never get used to the idea that just because I had been arrested, guilt or innocence apart, I was suddenly not to be trusted in any way at all. That was very hard for me, and I could not accept it. It is another of the ironies of the system, that at Styal, as a convicted prisoner, I was trusted in so many ways, but as an innocent prisoner at Pucklechurch I was not trusted an inch.

One of the good things about all this cleaning under supervision was that it did provide the chance to chat to the nurse standing watching. They were usually thoroughly bored, indeed I can't imagine many things more boring than just standing watching other people work day after day. There were many nurses, and many women, and it was usual for almost everyone to find some member of staff with whom they felt at ease, and to whom they could talk. Many of the staff were exceptionally kind to me, and with three or four of them I was able to talk in quite some depth. I suppose that discussing fears and hopes with a sympathetic figure in authority, while taking out my frustration on the kitchen floor with my scrubbing brush, was a kind of therapy.

This period of my life also left me with a much less fastidious attitude to other people. There had been times at home when I had balked at cleaning the lavatory after members of my own family. Now I had to clean lavatories and baths after all and sundry, and they were sometimes left in an unbelievable mess too. At first, I no longer cared about anything, and for weeks I cleaned up behind other people in a kind of dream, not really knowing what I was doing, or realizing how horrible it was. As I began to feel a bit more together, I found that I was still capable of doing jobs that at one time would have revolted me beyond measure. I worked in my rubber gloves, and I cleaned urine, faeces and menstrual blood from the lavatory floors, and pubic hair and grease from the baths. At one time I would not have believed that I could do such things.

On an ordinary day, when the cleaning had been finished we returned to our stairwell to wait for 'class'. I began to sit on the stairs early on: there were not enough chairs to go round, and it saved a hassle, as well as keeping me away from the cigarette smoke. The stairs, of course, were uncarpeted, made of that stone-effect material used in schools and public buildings of all kinds. The walls were plastered and then sprayed with that sort of paint which stands out from the surface in little blobs and streaks. This was practical: it showed the ravages of dirt and damage much less than an ordinary, flat, emulsioned wall would have done. Some of the walls were sprayed with yellow paint, some with blue; and the effect was quite pleasing. The same material was used for the walls of the cells.

At about half past nine, 'Teacher' would arrive. It really was a bit like a kindergarten. We would move to the door at the end of the corridor through which our meals appeared, and when the staff had sorted themselves out, we would 'go through to class'. The door would be unlocked, and we would file solemnly through two more locked doors, and into the association room. This was a large and not unattractive room, with long tables and stacking chairs. Teacher would unlock the cupboards and the morning's work would begin. The theory was that what we did in class was work, and it was there that we earned the money which we would spend in the canteen on Fridays. The 'work' however was so varied as to be able to provide something for everyone, and was of an almost exclusively practical nature.

The options included making soft toys, or dresses if you were ambitious. There was knitting, painting, copying from books to make a 'project', and later on in my time there I embarked on rug-making, while a friend of mine took up macramé. When I first went into the association room, I was with the two people who were to be my friends during the first part of my time at Pucklechurch. I sat at the table at which they sat, and ever after it was to be 'my' table.

Caroline was a little younger than me, in Pucklechurch for arson. She had attempted suicide at one time, and her neck was disfigured with the scars of the razor she had used. After a long wait, she was sent to a psychiatric hospital at her trial, where she should have been all the time. The remand centre did her no good whatsoever. She was not a criminal, came from a good background, and had done what she did out of desperation with the way her life was going. Her problems were with her relationships and her inability to make sense of her life, not with the law.

Corinne, also younger than me, was from Birmingham. She was very quiet, with a sweet smile, a little woman who looked as if she could not harm a fly. She had been in since January, and she always said it was for shoplifting. She had to wait seven months for her trial, and then she too was sent to a psychiatric hospital. She never told me what she had really done. One day after Corinne had left, Caroline tried to tell me what she had really done, but I stopped her because by then I had worked it out for myself.

During the course of idle conversation, Corinne and I had been talking one day about the trials of pregnancy and childbirth. She spoke as one who knew, yet her official story was that she had no children. How much pain I must have caused that poor woman, going on and on about my marvellous children. Corinne also had problems with her mother, and with her husband who had left her. I could well see how she had fallen into a state of depression, with children to bring up alone, trying to keep her job, and at the same time having to maintain the ridiculous standards of perfection in housework that her mother insisted upon, where everything had to be done thoroughly every day. That impossibly hard winter of 1982 must have been the last straw for her. I do not know what happened or why, and I am not interested in nosing out the details of someone else's agony, but Corinne's children disappeared, and she would never wear tights.

As I began to realize what must have happened, I found it impossible to condemn her. She was obviously always afraid that if people found out what she had done, they would hate her for it. Indeed, for a woman to kill her own children is a terrible thing, and a short while before, I would no doubt have condemned her, saying that there was no excuse whatever for her action. But I knew Corinne before I knew what she had done, knew her sweetness and her diffidence, and the look of suffering in her eyes that nothing will ever remove. I could only think how she must have been driven and tormented, and how unlucky she was that she failed to kill herself, but woke to a world made worse by her attempt to solve its problems for herself and for her children in the only final way.

So the three of us, Caroline, Corinne and I, became fast friends, although not one of us told the truth about what we had done. Corinne told Caroline the truth the night before she was moved to Risley Remand Centre before her trial in Birmingham. I never told anyone, but I needn't have worried because Caroline told me the night before she went for her trial that she had always known what I was charged with, as she heard it on the local news the day I was remanded in custody. No doubt she had also told Corinne. But they did not judge me, accepting me as one like themselves, and indeed we were three of a kind in that not one of us was a criminal. We should all have been in psychiatric hospitals rather than in the remand centre, and we had all been driven to do terrible things by the pressure of intolerable lives and the breakdown of relationships.

Sometimes I wonder how much that terrible winter of 1982 had to do with it. Of course, I am not suggesting that just because one is snowed up for a week one must rush out and murder somebody, but the fact of being shut up with our thoughts for so long was an added difficulty when life was already only marginally tolerable. Who knows?

Corinne was lucky in one way. A man who had known her before, who must have known all the awful details, and who nonetheless visited her regularly in Pucklechurch, said that he wanted to marry her. As well as facing the trial, Corinne was beginning divorce proceedings to free herself from her husband, so that if and when she was released she could marry Bernard. He came to see her every week, and she came alive at the time of his visits. They wrote long letters to each other, but Corinne said: 'He never so much as holds my hand, because he says I am still a married woman'. I used to wonder whether Bernard was as genuine as he seemed, and what would happen to Corinne if he let her down after all. She used to say that she was not dependent on him, but the only time I saw her upset was when the expected letter from him did not arrive on a Tuesday (they always wrote to each other on Sundays, after the Saturday visit), and she convinced herself that he had had a car accident on the motorway. I hope with all my heart that they are married and together now, for I cannot imagine what Corinne would do, how she would face the world, by herself. This man has taken on a serious responsibility in making her trust him at the time of her greatest vulnerability. I saw him once or twice, when her visit coincided with mine, and I must say he looked very sincere and very kind. But don't they all.

So we sat at the same table in class and talked. Caroline did most of the talking, and almost always about herself and her problems. Corinne was always knitting, nothing in particular, just a long piece of knitting that may have started out to be a scarf, but was now just her knitting. There was no purpose to it, and she would sit there smiling gently and listening to Caroline, while her foot moved up and down, up and down – the inexorable sign of the stress she was forever under. She rarely stopped knitting.

I was not able, then as ever, to do anything as pointless as Corinne's knitting. I have always knitted, but I used to regard it strictly as a spare-time activity, something to be done while watching television or talking to the family. I had been knitting a pullover for my daughter when I was arrested, and my husband had brought it in with my clothes on the first Sunday, so that to the best of my recollection

I had it in class from the beginning. I was very pleased that I was allowed to continue with this pullover, and although I proceeded very slowly, and made a fearful mess of some of it, I was able to spend my mornings in a pleasant and therapeutic way. I finished the red pullover for my daughter, and went on to make a brown one, a gold one, and then a navy blue one. They were all the same pattern, a cable stitch which I knew well. I did not feel up to coping with a new pattern, so I just went on knitting pullovers in the same pattern. There was a break in the middle when I got restive and changed my activity to rug-making, which I had always wanted to learn, but had never had the time for. I also knitted a child's coat in white. I finished everything I started, and ended up with only a few days immediately before my trial when I had nothing really to do in class, but by then the time was dragging badly, and I could not settle to anything at all anyway.

We stayed in class until half past eleven. The nurses and the teacher sat at the top table and gossiped. The teacher was not really there to teach, though she would help anyone who wanted to learn. The whole thing was not much more than a holding operation, and as most people were not there for as long as Caroline, Corinne and myself, it was not really worth their while to get involved in anything. Some people were bored by class, but for me it was the best part of the day, when I could get on with something constructive, and mix with other people.

The two issues in class time over which the staff and the women came into conflict most were sitting down and cigarettes. We were supposed to stay sitting down all the time. They hated us to be up and walking about. Yet people under stress find it easier to be walking; but we were not allowed to do it. If anyone got up, it was 'Sit down', at once. At first I did not mind, but soon I found it very aggravating always having to be sitting down. Women found the same excuses to be up as children do in school – a visit to the lavatory, just asking somebody something, just getting a pencil. I suppose that there was probably a good reason for it, I suppose that trouble was more likely to break out if people were wandering about than if they were all sitting down peacefully. But after five months of perpetually sitting down, I had had more than enough of it, though I must admit it did do wonders for my varicose veins!

But no amount of sitting down could solve the problems of those who smoked. There was always, as a constant background to everything, the need of the smoker for her cigarette. As prisoners on remand, they were all entitled to have as many cigarettes as they liked brought in, but of course this led to immediate problems when some people had regular visits, with frequent and plentiful gifts of cigarettes, whilst others had few visits and perhaps no cigarettes. The more inadequate the person, the less she was able to ration herself so that her smokes would last from visit to visit. The staff used to attempt to ration them for these women, which only led to more trouble as the person knew that she had cigarettes which the staff were keeping from her. Tobacco was stolen, people would pick up dog ends from ashtrays and, horribly, even go through rubbish bins and the incinerator looking for tobacco. It seemed that there was always someone on the wing whose entire life revolved around her next cigarette. Undoubtedly, all the serious trouble I saw in Pucklechurch was caused by tobacco, or rather the lack of it.

People would attempt to exchange sweets and toiletries for tobacco, which was of course strictly not allowed. One woman I knew when I first went there, who was absolutely obsessed with tobacco, made the lives of smokers intolerable by always asking and asking for cigarettes. When she had been shouted at enough times to stop her asking, she would just stand there as close as she could get to whoever was smoking. This woman, Mildred, was quite tall and really thin. She was not able to cope with anything, and was hopeless at cleaning or making anything in class. She was usually quite quiet, but would then, for no reason, suddenly start on a long, involved story which was utterly meaningless, and sometimes developed into a conversation with herself. Wild bursts of laughter would accompany this behaviour, which might take place in class or in the privacy of her cell.

Poor Mildred was so odd that she was difficult to befriend, not that anyone really tried. It was impossible to have a rational conversation with her. We never found out what she was in for, as her stories varied so wildly, and had very little connection with reality. Yet when she spoke, she was very articulate, and used complicated language. She must have had an education before her life fell to pieces. According to her, she had been well off and lived in a nice house. It may well have been true. One of my most enduring memories of Pucklechurch is Mildred: tall, thin, obsessed, walking as she did, quickly along the corridor with tiny steps which made her look as if she was run by clockwork, holding her yellow plastic mug at chest level as if it was some sort of weapon against the world.

I could not stand the woman, and that made me feel guilty because I knew she was much more ill than I was. It looked as though she was never going to get better either. She was the first person I ever saw rummaging through the rubbish bucket for dog ends, and I despised her hopeless obsession with tobacco. She was always scrounging, yet when she had tobacco of her own, she would never pay back her debts. She used to sit in class and cry because she had not got a cigarette, and it seemed to me intolerable that anyone could let themselves go so far for an addiction. I wonder now if my hatred of her behaviour was not in part a reflection of my discomfort at how far my own particular addiction had led me. Who knows?

Mildred was also unclean. It was an unpleasant experience to use a lavatory after her. The lavatory door did not of course lock, and had spaces at the top and bottom. We often used to see Mildred's feet through the space at the bottom of the door facing the toilet bowl as if she were a man. Hardly surprising that she made such a mess. She was also entirely revolting when she had her period, dripping blood everywhere, and making a sickening mess of her bed. She would often be seen walking along the corridor clutching a soiled sanitary towel, on her way to the incinerator, and no amount of shouting at her could get her to wrap up the offending object. Sometimes she would drop a used towel into her pot, and then walk along the corridor spilling a mixture of blood and urine after her, which someone else had to clean up. How can a woman get into such a state?

As a result of all this, she smelled disgusting, and also had a habit of standing as close as she could and scratching her crotch. We complained many times to the nursing staff, but they assured us that there was nothing physically wrong with her, that her scratching was a nervous symptom. So it may have been, but it was decidedly off-putting. Dirty as she was in so many ways, Mildred had an obsession about her hair, which was a lovely coloured brown and naturally curly. With her startling blue eyes and her lovely hair, she must have been very attractive once. She washed her hair at any odd moment of the day, regardless of what she was supposed to be doing. As soon as it was cleaning time, you could be sure that Mildred would be washing her hair.

It was Mildred who was involved in two of the worst scenes of violence I saw at Pucklechurch. On one occasion, she was sitting next to one of the young girls in the chairs at the end of the corridor where we used to sit when we were not allowed downstairs. I have no doubt that the young girl was getting at Mildred. That was normal, and Mildred laid herself open to being got at in so many ways. But this time she had had enough, and with a strength amazing in one usually so negative and silent, she picked Colleen off her chair, flung her on the floor, and began banging her head up and down on the tiles of the corridor floor. It took three of the heftier members of the nursing staff to get Mildred off Colleen.

Of course, Mildred was not going to get away with that, and a new kind of tension filled the atmosphere as we all wondered when and how Colleen would get her own back. The staff did their best to keep them apart, which meant that poor old Mildred spent more time than usual locked up, but they could not watch us for ever, and after Colleen had given a solemn undertaking not to hurt Mildred, their vigilance slackened. A time came when we were upstairs alone, and Mildred went into the washrooms to wash her hair yet again. Colleen leapt like a panther from her chair, and Mildred got a bloody nose. Colleen got a week of loss of association, which meant being locked up most of the time, but she said it was worth it.

Mildred also got into trouble when she stole a whole half ounce of tobacco from Josie. Josie cornered Mildred later on in the washroom and thumped her there. That occasion caused me considerable concern, because I saw what was going to happen, and said 'Josie's going to get Mildred'. Another woman went off screaming down the stairs to the staff, and Josie was caught coming out of the washroom. She thought I was responsible for this, and threatened to get me next. Josie was not the sort of youngster you got into a fight with. She was Welsh, and very powerfully built, and was in fact in Pucklechurch for murder, having killed with her bare fists a man who had been molesting her. She was only eighteen years old, and her background was one of family tragedy, with the death of her mother, aged twenty-eight, when Josie was only seven, and subsequent rejection by her father. There was a grandfather in the background, but he seemed to care no more for Josie than anyone else did. She had led the usual wild childhood, in constant trouble at school, frequently under suspension, drinking too much, experimenting with drugs, getting into minor trouble with the police, and now faced not only a murder charge but drugs charges as well. She had drugs in Pucklechurch with her, in spite of the strip search, and after this episode with Mildred, as a result of which Josie was sent to the silent strips for a while and lost her room upstairs, she was desperately worried that the drug would be found. I happened to be in her room, talking to its new occupant, when Josie rushed in, retrieved her little packet from its ingenious hiding place, and rushed out again, saying 'You never saw nothing' as she went.

There was not as much violence at Pucklechurch as I had expected. It came as a terrible shock to many of the older women from good backgrounds that the young ones were so ready to fight. I suppose my job had prepared me to a certain extent for many of the things among the younger ones which the women of my generation found shocking – the foul language and the fighting among them. I was shocked by it also, and really wished they would not do it, but at least I knew it happened. A spell on dinner duty in the average secondary school soon inures you to the fact that the younger generation uses words without thinking which at their age I did not even know existed, and the sight of two girls squaring up to one another is not as rare as it ought to be. On one occasion a group of us older ones began to take to task a particularly foul-mouthed youngster, pointing out to her that she used the same couple of words in every breath, which was extremely boring for anyone listening to her, and also that when anything really bad happened, she had no swear words in reserve, having already used the worst words in the language as a matter of routine speech.

So I was not surprised when Josie went for Mildred. In her book, as in Colleen's also, it was inevitable that physical violence should follow any kind of 'liberty' taken; and from Josie's point of view, stealing tobacco in prison was about as low as anyone could sink. Josie was a goodhearted girl, and had given Mildred more than one of her precious roll-ups, although I always advised against giving her anything, as the more you gave, the more she ground you down with begging. In many ways, Josie was a decent kid, and more than one or two of us older ones longed to rescue her from the situation she was in, which to me at least appeared to be a result of lack of love and little else. She was younger than my own two daughters, and I longed to be able to help.

Josie's worst problem was her ungovernable temper which led her into all her scrapes. She had killed the man who was molesting her in a temper. She got worked up easily, and once started could not be reasoned with. So it was that when she hit Mildred, the staff rushed upstairs, the riot bell was pressed, and officers appeared from all over the centre. When the riot bell rang, all officers (except one on each wing who had the job of locking the other women in) dropped what they were doing and ran, for it meant serious trouble. We were locked in, but could hear Josie clearly, beside herself and, who knows, perhaps encouraged by the general air of drama, defying the officers and refusing to go to her room.

I imagine that the staff had decided that Josie was not to be trifled with, for they simply took hold of her and hurled her into her room, which was almost opposite mine. Josie would not calm down, and proceeded to destroy her cell, with much screaming and crashing. The officers took counsel outside, and then went in after her. They always worked out who was going to do what: one would go for the right leg, one the left, two more for each arm, and there was always someone whose job it was to grab the chair, which was the most obvious weapon in the cell. They reckoned to overpower by sheer force of numbers, and of course they were always successful. But it was a dangerous job, and not one that I would have liked at all. Officers did get hit, kicked, and scratched on these occasions.

So, soon after she came in to Pucklechurch, Josie was dragged off, screaming all the way, to the silent strips. This was a cell, passed with fear by most of us as we went out to exercise in the yard, where there was nothing but a concrete floor and a concrete plank on which a mattress could be put if the woman inside was not likely to destroy it. There was no window, and a permanent smell of urine about it, though whether this was because no pot was provided or because the pot was usually smashed up, I do not know. I would imagine it was the latter. There was no bell, and when someone was in this cell the officers maintained a regular visual check on the person inside. It was virtually impossible to harm yourself, as you were usually put into this cell naked, or at the most in a strip gown made of special material which cannot be torn. Short of banging your head on the concrete, there is nothing you can do in this cell but sit until you have calmed down.

This cell was called the 'silent' strips because it had no call bell. Every other cell in the prison had a bell, which was supposed to be used only in emergencies, but was often used to annoy the staff. The constant buzz of someone's bell usually hung over the place. These bells could be switched off in only two cells on the hospital wing: Room 5 and the padded cell. Elsewhere, they were not supposed to be switched off at all. These bells kept buzzing automatically, until the reset button outside the cell was pressed by a nurse answering the bell. But the nurses hated these bells, and we would often see a nurse standing outside a cell with her finger on the reset button, which meant that the woman inside was making everyone's life a misery by continually pressing the bell. When we were locked up there was usually someone buzzing for something, so answering was a full-time job. I often heard an exasperated nurse point out in no uncertain terms that the place was not a hotel, and that the bells were only supposed to be used in emergencies. People rang mostly wanting a light, or wanting to know when we were coming out.

The bells in the wing which could be switched off were only switched off very rarely, and it had to be done with due solemnity by the chief officer. Visual checks then had to be made regularly; of course every cell had a spy hole through which the woman inside could be observed at any time. Covering up this hole was a serious offence. I suppose it was essential that the staff could keep an eye on us, but it was very annoying never knowing when you were under observation either asleep, or using the pot, or getting dressed.

When Josie returned to us from the silent strips, she was put into a room on the ground floor, where she stayed for the rest of the time I was there. The rooms on the upstairs floor were for people who could be trusted not to have a 'funny five minutes', as one nurse used to put it. Most people began on the ground floor, and then were moved upstairs when they could be trusted. Any unoccupied rooms were kept locked, so that poor Josie had to wait until the room she had been in was occupied and unlocked again before she could retrieve her little packet. The rest of her belongings had been bundled up and moved out by the staff, and Josie must have been very worried about her illegal possession. As to how she got it past the strip search, as I have already said, all such things move in and out of prison in hiding places in the body which would need a medical examination to reveal.

When Josie first returned from the silent strips, I made it my first priority to make the woman who had shouted for the staff, which got Josie caught after hitting poor Mildred, own up to having done so. By the time all this happened, I had been in Pucklechurch long enough to know that it does not do to acquire a reputation as a sneak, or a grass, and I was absolutely certain that I would be next on Josie's list if she thought it had been me. The woman who had grassed had a withered arm, and I was pretty sure that Josie, who as I have said was a decent kid in her way, would not hit her. If she did hit her, that was too bad. I was not going to take the aggravation for something I had not done, and Josie's threats against me as she was led off to the silent strips had been most alarming. I was learning to take care of myself in this hostile environment, and while it was a near thing once or twice, I got through my eight months unscathed.

So, with these kind of undertones, class could often be a pretty tense place. It was a highly strung, volatile environment, and a very unstable one. Often someone went to pieces and started shouting at someone else, or refused to sit down, or simply went to pieces quietly in a corner. And there was always Mildred, quietly sobbing to herself because she hadn't got a cigarette. It must have been a difficult job for the staff, who never knew what was going to happen next, and had the responsibility of dealing with whatever violent or dangerous situation arose. They used to put the 'Jimmy Young Show' on in the hope that it would have a soothing effect, but the youngsters would have preferred Radio 1 and there was always too much noise to hear the bits which would have interested me. Still, it was better than the awful despairing silence which sometimes fell over us otherwise, and was usually the precursor of some outburst or another. I used to wonder if Jimmy Young knew that his 'prog' was used as therapy in a remand centre.

Just before 11.30 we would begin to clear up. Most people left their work behind, locked in the cupboards by the teacher, but quite early on I was told by a sympathetic nurse that I could take my knitting back on to the wing to do in my room. I think she realized it was therapeutic. So I began quite a craze for taking things back on to the wing, and soon more people were taking things than leaving them behind. Of course, we were not actually allowed to have the knitting in our rooms freely available, it had to be kept in the office or the staffroom, and asked for when we were locked up. Even spare balls of wool were taken away, presumably because they were dangerous. For a long time I was allowed to carry my own knitting along the corridor and back on to the wing, but then there was a tightening up, and it suddenly became too dangerous for anyone other than a nurse to do the carrying.

The cigarettes situation was made worse in September, when the policy was changed from allowing cigarettes at more or less any time to sticking rigidly to the rules and allowing them only at set times: first thing in the morning, at 10.00, lunchtime, 3.00, and so on. This meant that instead of only Mildred getting worked up because she did not have a cigarette, everyone got worked up. Class became one long whine for cigarettes, and I got so sick of it. I suppose this was introduced partly to get over the difficulty of some women having plenty of cigarettes while others had none.

Josie was one of those who never got a visit, never got cigarettes brought in, so had to make do with a little tobacco which her wages of about one pound a week would buy. It did not seem to me to be sensible to lay down that because some people did not have as many cigarettes as they wanted, nobody should. Yet I do see that there is a serious unfairness in the system, where some people on remand get things, like books, clothes, sweets and fruit as well as cigarettes brought in while others get nothing or very little. Those of us who were visited regularly used to share our goodies with those who were not, but Josie used to get very worked up about accepting things when there was no way she could repay. And it was Josie one Friday, learning it was my birthday, who went to the canteen and spent some of her precious money on a Mars bar for me.

When we had all filed back through the three locked doors on to the wing, it was a case of hanging about and waiting for lunch at 12.00. We were not usually allowed to wait in our stairwell at this time, as there tended to be a queue of women from the other wings waiting to see the doctor at that time. We were not supposed to mix with the other wings, who regarded us as dangerous lunatics for the most part, but again this situation provided an opportunity for notes and messages to be passed, which they were. We were sent upstairs to await lunch on the top corridor. There were windows at the end of the corridor, and three surprisingly comfortable chairs. The first three women up the stairs had the comfy chairs, while the rest of us stood around, or brought wooden chairs from our rooms to sit on.

I used to spend this time walking up and down the corridor, for I felt very deprived of exercise. It was quite a long corridor, and I must have patrolled its length a hundred thousand times. Corinne used to be quite happy just sitting, but Caroline and I would walk up and down, up and down. When Caroline left, I walked by myself until my next crony, Gillian, was admitted. At the opposite end of the corridor was another window which overlooked an industrial estate, and we used to walk up the corridor, watch the lorries, and the men working, walk back, and so on. The lorries belonged to a distribution firm, and we had it all worked out as to how to get into one of them and hide until it started off. I used to wonder whether, if anyone did get out, the authorities would disrupt the routine of the industrial estate, because that was the obvious way to get clear.

I don't think the staff liked us walking up and down that corridor. To them, movement seemed to be a sign of disturbance. Well, of course we were disturbed, but more than that for me was the need for exercise. And the longer I was shut up, the more I needed to prowl, and the quicker I went up and down the corridor. I wish now that I had counted how many turns it was possible to make in half an hour, but I never did. This perambulation would be interrupted at around 12.00 by the shout of 'Medicine!' from below, and I and anyone else on a midday dose went downstairs to queue at the hatch.

By this time lunch had usually arrived, sometimes arriving before the medicine. It came on the same trolley as breakfast, and we queued in the same way. Lunch was a revolting meal. The meat, whatever it was supposed to be, was inedible, tough and more often than not 90 per cent fat or gristle or both. The exceptions to this were the pies and the chicken curry which were quite nice. I could never understand why they did not give up using meat and try soya instead, as the school meals service does. It would not be meat, but at least it would be edible. The meat came with two great scoops of unappetizing potato, and a vegetable, usually cabbage, which had been boiled to extinction, and frequently contained caterpillars, slugs and snails, also boiled, poor things, to extinction. I am fussy about my food, and I cannot now imagine how I ate Pucklechurch provisions. It shows what a state I must have been in, and certainly the longer I was there the less I ate. The puddings in contrast were usually good. I never ate the semolina (shades of the war!) but the 'stodge' and the rice pudding were good. Towards the end I used to eat seconds of the puddings whenever I could get them, which wasn't always because I was in competition with Josie and the other young ones, who seemed to be perpetually hungry. I never felt hungry, but I used to eat the puddings because I liked them.

Balancing our plates on our dessert bowls, and clutching our mugs of tea in the other hand, we went back to our rooms and, as for breakfast, were locked in to eat. It was surprising how important a place food held in our lives. Mealtimes broke up the day, marked the passage of time, and were a kind of focal point, something to look forward to. It sounds pathetic, but that's how it was: visits, letters and meals were all we had to look forward to, and for those women like Josie, who had neither visits nor more than the occasional letter, all that was left was food. The preoccupation of prisoners with their food is a well-observed symptom, and although I certainly experienced it as much as anybody else, I still don't really understand how meal-times came to be of such importance. No doubt it was really all psychological – substitution or something of the kind. Yet as soon as one meal was over we would be wondering about the next. Corinne, who had been there a long time, had got the rotation worked out and remembered, and was always able to tell us what the next meal would consist of. She was very rarely wrong.

I still sometimes look at the clock at just gone midday, and think: there they are, all sitting in their cells at their little tables, eating that dreadful cabbage!

4 Pucklechurch Afternoon

The nurses came quickly to clear away the lunch plates, as they wanted to be off duty at 12.30. Sometimes they were delayed by a panic: a fork had been lost and had to be found. The cutlery was counted carefully before and after every meal, to make sure no one could possess themselves of a dangerous weapon. Not that the Pucklechurch cutlery was that dangerous: like the plates and mugs, it was all plastic. But if a fork was missing or even a spoon, everyone stayed locked up until it was found. I should think something went missing a couple of times a week at least. If it happened at lunchtime it always put the staff in a foul mood, because it meant they were late to go off duty. One or two people from time to time used to hide things deliberately, just to see the nurses in a flap; and would then 'discover' them when they had extracted enough enjoyment from the situation. I took to drawing the collecting nurses' attention to the fact that I was handing in one knife, one fork and one spoon, so that they would know that wherever the missing object was, it wasn't in my cell.

In many ways, the time between having our plates collected at about 12.15, and being unlocked again officially at 1.45, but more usually just before 2.00, was the hardest of the day. There was a great temptation to go to sleep during this time, and indeed some of the staff referred to it as our rest time. For the first weeks I used to go to sleep, but I learned that if I slept in the afternoon, I didn't sleep at night. Also, I personally always feel terrible for the rest of the day if I do sleep in the afternoon. It was hard not to, though, as there was nothing to do but read or sit and think, and sleep seemed vastly preferable to either of these activities. Later on I devised a way of passing the time, which kept me awake, even if sometimes with difficulty.

After my plates had been collected, I would read whatever was my current book for the fifteen minutes or so till 12.30. I was first almost entirely incapable of reading at all, and this as much as anything else was the measure of my illness. It struck me as being very ironic that I, who had spent my entire life with so many books I wanted to read and no time to do it in, now had all the time in the world, and simply could not read. When I say I could not read, I mean that my concentration and my memory had entirely gone. I have always read very quickly, and had an almost photographic memory for what I read. I can see the page in my head, and simply read the words off as if I were really reading it from the actual page. Very useful at exam time!

But now, I opened the book where the marker was, and stared at the page, trying to remember what on earth the story was all about. Often, I would have to go back to a bit I did remember and read on again from there, and it was as if I were reading it for the first time: I would have no memory at all of what was happening. I was reading only things which were light and easy: paperbacks my family sent in for me, but I might as well have been attempting a weighty tome for all the ease with which I read. My family kept me well supplied with paperbacks, and I hadn't the heart to tell them that I simply was not able to read them. Slowly, slowly, my concentration came back, but it was not until I had been released from prison for several months that I really began to read properly again.

I would sit there trying to concentrate, trying to make sense of the words, and often I would give up before my set time of 12.30. For the first time in my life I understood those children to whom reading is not a pleasure but a penance, and who would rather do anything than read. At 12.30 I began the next bit of my lunch-hour duties: my daily bit of the Bible. I had decided that I might as well re-read the parts of the Bible I had loved as a child and never found time for since. So from 12.30 to 12.50, I read first a bit from the Old Testament then from the New Testament. I began the Old Testament with Isaiah, and read my way solidly through the minor prophets, whom I had once studied for A level. In the New Testament I began with the Acts, and read through the Epistles. I kept away from the Gospels, as I didn't think Jesus had much to say to me, nor me to Him. I was reading the Bible for its literature, not its religious content. There were many modern versions on the shelf, but there were also two copies of the Authorized Version, and I was rather shocked to find that even these had not escaped the general vandalizing of books that went on, with pages torn out or defaced with graffiti.

In order to avoid falling asleep completely, I used to read the Bible aloud, and hope that no member of staff would creep up and catch me at it. It helped to read aloud, but I still could not often remember which Psalm I had last read, or whereabouts I was in Galatians. I used to read the last verse several times, hoping to impress it on my memory, but often the next day I would have no idea where I had got to. At one time, I tried to learn a few verses every day, to try to stir my memory into action, but this was such a total failure that I gave up. I tried to time it so that I could read a bit of the New Testament and a bit of the Old Testament every day, and end in a sensible place.

At 12.50, duty done, I gladly closed the Bible, and got my little wireless out, for the weather forecast and 'The World at One' on Radio 4, though, again, if you had asked me at the end of the bulletin what had been broadcast, I would have been hard put to tell you. It was the summer of the Falklands War, but I am left with the distinct impression that I know very little about what was happening. It was only after I came out that it really penetrated that some of our ships had been sunk. I heard it all, but like the reading, the information just did not get through into my brain. I was not able to attend to the affairs of the outside world. My own situation precluded it. Not that I spent much time thinking about my own situation, but what had happened to me seemed to have put a barrier between myself and everything else. I tried to pay attention to my children, but I did not really want to know; rather, I was not really able to know about anything else.

While I listened to the radio, more for comfort than for information, I did my exercises. These had nothing to do with losing weight. I was putting on weight, but only slowly and it did not worry me at all. Having been two stone underweight for most of my recent life, I could afford to put a bit on. It was the eternal sitting down that did it, I am sure. No, my exercises were to wake me up. A bit of energetic bending and stretching in the middle of the day got rid of the sleepiness induced by a stodgy meal and too much sitting about.

The only thing that did worry me was the tops of my legs, where the muscles created by years of hard walking were turning to fat or, as I now understand it, were fading away with disuse and being replaced by fat. That only became noticeable at the end of my time in Pucklechurch, and there wasn't much I could do about it in Styal. I had to let them go, and hope to build them up again when I was released.

Apart from waking me up, the exercise I took secretly in my cell was designed to help with another problem, but it never did. I am sure that the basis of it was psychological, but almost everyone in Pucklechurch suffered from constipation. Later, I was to discover that this is a common problem in remand centres. At Holloway, people used to take it in turns to stay in from exercise so that they could be alone in the cell to perform their natural functions. I didn't have that problem, as I was not in a shared cell, but like everyone else, I found it very difficult. I could not bring myself to use my pot, and there was little opportunity for an uninterrupted communion with nature when we were unlocked. I think the worst thing was that you never knew when you would be interrupted. Quite early on in my time at Pucklechurch, there had been a panic just as I got settled. The riot bell had gone, and I had been yelled at by a nurse to get out of the lavatory and into my cell. After that, I never felt secure, and of course the more constipated you are, the longer it takes. There was also no privacy at all, not only did the door not lock, but there were always people moving round the washroom.

All this had a very inhibiting effect on each one of us, and constipation was the order of the day for everyone. Some people worried about it very much indeed. I found it uncomfortable, and just one of those extra annoyances that people outside would not dream existed. For me, it lasted the whole of my time in Pucklechurch, and was only cured by a return to a more normal way of life at Styal. All the staff know that this is a problem suffered by remand prisoners, a result perhaps of the emotional and nervous tension they are under. Nobody seemed to care very much. It should have been possible for some other arrangements to have been made, so that there were chances for everybody to have five minutes in privacy at some point during the day, to use the toilet, and not merely to be told to use the pot in their cell.

With luck, my exercise, 'The World at One' and our midday lock up all ended within a few minutes of each other at 1.45. The staff came on duty at 12.30, and were supposed to unlock us for exercise at 1.45. As visits began at 1.30, some people were unlocked for a visit before the rest of us. If it was raining, we were usually not unlocked. But most days I would hear the unmistakable sounds of a nurse working her way up the corridor, unlocking the doors and fixing back the bolts on the locks so that the cell could not be relocked accidentally. The volume of noise in the corridor increased as one after the other the women were released from their 'rest'. Josie was usually remarkably silent for her, as she was usually only barely awake. In my first days in the place, I found it a nasty shock to be woken suddenly by the unlocking of my door.

We all drifted downstairs, and waited as usual in the stairwell. The smokers had cigarettes on their minds, but usually had to wait until we were outside. When everyone was collected together, a nurse unlocked the door, and we went out. There were two places where we could take our exercise. When I was first there, we used to have to go through the building, past the silent strips, and out into the little exercise yard. We were not allowed to mix with the other wings, and although we could see them in the big yard, a nurse would stand at the wire to prevent us from communicating. The little yard was very little, and I used to hate it. We just walked round and round in this tiny, asphalted space. It was worse than the ones you see in a film of the exercise yard at a prison, because it was so small.

Much to be preferred was exercise in the garden. The buildings at Pucklechurch formed two squares. Within one square, bounded by the block of B1 and B2 wings, the workroom, reception, and A wing, nothing had been done. The place was just asphalted over and left bare. But in the little quadrangle created by the admin. corridor, the hospital wing, the other side of A wing and the dining hall, a delightful little garden had been created. There was real grass in the centre, and beds all around, which were filled with colour. To begin with, there were wallflowers in their hundreds, later it was antirrhinums and marigolds, and later still, asters. Round the outside of these beds was a paved walk, and in the very centre of the grass was a flowering cherry tree. The nurses, I think, preferred our exercise to be taken in the garden, because they found it a more pleasant place to be. Certainly, I did. One problem was the pieces of glass in the flowerbeds, from previously broken windows. No one could have completely cleared them and there was a continual risk of a disturbed prisoner picking up the glass.

It always surprised me just how slowly people would walk round and round on exercise. Some of them barely moved at all. I always went at a good quick pace, which sometimes meant that I walked alone, as Caroline and Corinne never hurried, but they did not go as slowly as some people either. Later, when Gillian joined me, we used to go at a cracking pace, lapping all the others several times. As exercise, it was a fairly pointless period; the most it did for the majority was to get them out into the fresh air.

We were very rarely allowed to sit on the grass in the centre of the little garden, but only occasionally, when the weather was really hot, and some good nurses were on duty. But we often had to come back indoors on a beautiful day, and sit in the overheated association room. 'This is not a hotel', we were told when we complained. True; but neither was it a prison. Why should not people on remand be allowed to sit outside on a nice day? We were innocent in the eyes of the law; many of us really were innocent. Why should we be treated as if we had already been found guilty?

Fortunately, the summer of 1982 was not a good one. Most often the weather was cold and wet, and we were only too glad to get back inside. We very rarely had the full half hour's exercise which we were supposed to have, and I suppose that that is why towards the end of my stay at Pucklechurch the morning exercise period was introduced. There had been a big Home Office inspection of the place, and I suspect that one of the things they found was that we were not getting enough exercise.

So, back inside we went, sometimes to be locked up again, but on a normal day we went through to the association room to watch TV until 4.00. That was without doubt one of the most boring periods of the day for me. As usual, we were made to sit down all that time, and there was only the most awful rubbish on the telly at that time in the afternoon, and frequently nothing but sport. The only things I enjoyed watching were repeats of the 'Survival' series, and a travelogue on Canada, which I did find fascinating. The films might have been good, only almost always we missed either the beginning or the end. And programmes like 'Fantasy Island' still haunt my nightmares!

I solved the problem of the television early on, by getting permission to take my knitting over with me, so at least I could do something constructive. How I depended on that knitting! And how utterly bored I got with it at the end. Also, it was uncomfortably hot in the association room in the afternoons – it was a prefabricated building, and had the kind of airlessness which those buildings tend to have. Often the wool stuck to my fingers, and I had to give up knitting and just sit which I hated!

There were frequent interruptions during the course of our couple of hours' association. This was the time of day when letters might well be brought round. (Though you could not be sure: letters might come at any time up to 8.00 at night, and Corinne once had her Tuesday letter from her Bernard pushed under her door at 9.30 at night.) When I was first at Pucklechurch, letters did tend to come during the afternoon, but later, as the censoring officer changed, they came at teatime, and then not until the evenings. This used to drive Gillian mad, as she needed to get her letters regularly and on time, so that she could reply to them. Her husband was also on remand, and they wrote to each other every day.

What can I say about my friend Gillian? She was younger than me, in her thirties, and facing more than one serious charge. She had two children, aged nine and twelve – the worst age possible to face the trauma of having their parents arrested. Gillian came up to me the first morning she was in Pucklechurch, after unlocking, and said, 'You don't look as though you belong here either'. From that moment we were two of a kind. Gillian suffered more than I did, for I firmly believe that she was innocent of any crime whatever. She could not have kept up a lying act, day after day, for all the long months we were there together, with someone as close to her as I became, any more than I could have done with her.

Gillian was one of the bravest people I have known. She was determined to show no weakness, to ask no favours, and to hide her suffering. The one thing which always broke her was her children, whether she saw them on a visit or had a letter from them. Her own agony she could stand, only just, but not that of her children. Did the magistrates who remanded her in custody, I wonder, think of the effect on those innocent children, or on Gillian's brave mother, herself not a well woman, who had to accept responsibility for their care? What terrible crimes could Gillian possibly have been going to commit which led the legal system to shut her up in the remand centre for a whole year before trial, a year during which her children became less and less able to cope with the situation, and which turned Gillian from the happy, gentle person she was when she came in to an embittered and depressed woman? Until she could not even conduct an efficient correspondence!

I didn't mind so much when I got my letters so long as I got them, and all letters of course, in or out, had to be censored. At the time I took it for granted, but now I wonder why. We had to leave our letters out unsealed: they were sealed and stamped by the censoring officer. Incoming letters came to us opened, and with the stamp removed. This was in case there were drugs concealed under the stamp – another example of the remand centre being more like prison than prison, for at Styal incoming letters came with their stamps left on. Even the best system breaks down, and on one occasion I was highly delighted to get three, stamped, unopened and uncensored letters: they had been put in my property one Friday when I went to court, and when my property was checked back in, nobody seemed to notice that the letters had not been opened, and they were given to me with the rest of my things. I kept those envelopes for a long time, just as a reminder of the uselessness of the system.

We were allowed to write out one letter a week, and you could also buy as many letters as you wanted, within reason. Gillian used to order two every night, and go up the wall almost every day when they were not delivered. The inefficiency of the system was beyond belief, and totally unnecessary. We were not supposed to have more than three letters in our possession at any one time, because the letters had to be checked in case they were used for wrongful purposes, such as communicating with other prisoners, and I suppose it was not easy to check if everybody had too many letters. Yet this was a Pucklechurch rule. Gillian's husband was allowed as many letters as he wanted, and used to get them in batches of ten and twenty at a time. Really there was no reason why we should not have been allowed more letters at once, but that was the system: you could order two, or at most three, every night, and if you were lucky you got them the following day. It was unfortunate that the censoring officers we had when Gillian came in were not very efficient, and it used to upset her tremendously that it took such a hassle to get letters.

I suspect that the real reason for it all was that the vast majority of people were illiterate or nearly so, and one letter a week was as much as they could cope with. Someone like Gillian ordering a dozen letters a week was very much the exception. I have seen people dictating a letter to a nurse because they could not write, and having its answer read to them because they could not read. I, of course, am literate, and I suppose might be expected to write a lot of letters, but I did not want to write at all, except to my children. I wrote weekly to them, as I always do, and sometimes I would write another letter or two in reply to ones written to me.

I was not sure what to do about my friends. At first I was too ill to write to anybody but then, when I recovered a bit, there were several letters, and not all from the people I had expected to write. So I made a rule that I would not write to anyone unless they first wrote to me, which I hoped would avoid embarrassment for them. But every letter which I received, I would answer, however difficult it was to do so. And this I did. The only letters I wrote which were not replies were to my headmaster, which in the fullness of time elicited a frozen reply leaving me in no doubt that he had judged and condemned me before my trial; and, when I could cope with it, to my bank manager to make some kind of arrangement about my financial situation, for I had a lot of standing orders going out every month and nothing now going in. This was a situation which would have worried some people to death, and maybe should have worried me, but I fear I was not concerned with my financial situation, and only wrote after being nagged and nagged to do so by my husband. He had tried to sort out my finances himself and been told politely by the bank that my finances were no concern of his.

The only other letter I wrote to someone who had not written to me was to my fellow deputy at school. Teachers are always told not, ever, to collect money from children and keep it themselves. Yet this was exactly what I had done. I was not sure of the exact amount, but I knew that I had been holding quite a sizeable sum of the children's money, paid as deposit on the trips we were to make at the end of the summer term. This money really did worry me, and what I wanted to do was to find out how much I owed and write a cheque for it. So simple it would have been outside, but the saga I was involved in over such a simple matter was beyond belief.

First, I had to ask permission to have a cheque brought in from my chequebook. Then I could not get the amount I owed sorted out. My colleague apparently phoned the remand centre and told them, but the message was not passed on to me. Then an officer appeared with the cheque, and asked me to make it out and sign it, and they would fill in the amount. Naturally, I refused to do so. Finally, a senior officer came to me with the cheque and the information that I owed just over sixty pounds. In her presence I wrote the cheque, and it was solemnly enclosed in the letter I had previously written to accompany it. Of course, it was all my own fault; I should not have had the money in the first place. But the hassle I had to go through to repay it! They said they were only protecting my interests, but clearly the presence of a cheque in a remand centre was a very dangerous thing! Nor do I understand how asking me to sign a blank cheque was construed as protecting my interests.

One other incident occurred concerning letters, or in this case a postcard. My elder daughter had worked and saved for literally years to go on a trip round the world with the boy who was to become her fiancé. At my insistence, and against her will, she had in fact begun this trip while I was in Pucklechurch. It was to take two years in all, but the first part was to be a summer in Europe. I used to get many postcards from her, both for my sake and because she was going to use the postcards, as we did in our family, as a pictorial remembrance of the trip. These postcards usually arrived with the stamps still on, though sometimes a zealous censor would scratch the stamps off with a knife. This particular postcard was pushed under the door, as I was finishing a letter to my younger daughter.

To my horror, I saw that the postcard had been defaced by having the whole corner where the stamp had been torn off. I was absolutely furious about this, and as I was writing to my daughter, I told her what had happened, without thinking, and certainly without intending to get anyone into trouble. This must have been read by another censor, who passed it on to a senior officer, because shortly afterwards my door was unlocked at lunchtime, and a young officer said that she had come to apologize for tearing off the stamp. I was horrified when I realized that she must have had a telling off, since she was one of the really nice officers – a bit vague, but she had been kind to me – and I wished I had not got her into trouble. My postcards arrived intact from that time on!

All our letters were censored, including those from our solicitors, which strictly speaking they should not have been. Letters to our solicitors had to be put in unsealed, and when Gillian took to sealing hers, saying that under section 37 of the Prison Rules she was entitled to write an uncensored letter to her solicitor, the staff were not happy about it. We reckoned that they opened it anyway. Letters from solicitors were always opened on the grounds that until a letter was opened they did not know who it was from. I am left, however, with the impression that they were exceeding their duty in opening letters to and from our solicitors.

They were certainly exceeding their duty in taking photocopies of letters going out, and I was the one who discovered that this was happening. I saw on my file one day in the doctor's office an unmistakable photocopy of what was unmistakably my handwriting. I was even able to recognize which letter it was. They had also photocopied the name and address of the person to whom I had sent the letter, and there were other photocopies of other letters, presumably, which I could not read, but which were in my writing, as I saw while the doctor rifled through the papers on my file. I said nothing at the time, but I knew they should not be doing it, and I told my solicitor.

He wrote an indignant letter to the governor, with a copy to me, and a request that if I felt myself being victimized in any way as a result of bringing this to light, I was to let him know at once. I thought it was interesting that he should have said that. The attitude of the sister in charge, always cool, became positively frozen towards Gillian and myself, for she had also written to her solicitor telling him what was going on. Some days later, I was sent for, out of association, to see the deputy governor. He had the job, which he obviously did not like, of apologizing to me for what had happened, and I listened with surprise as he tried to excuse it by saying that they had taken photocopies so that my letters would not be delayed in order to be seen by the psychiatrist, and assuring me that it would not happen again. He then had to do the same with Josie's friend, Laura, who had also seen photocopies of her letters on her file. It was a wondrous victory, especially as the sister in charge was there to hear me being apologized to. It was a little like being up before the headmaster. The deputy governor sat in Sister's chair behind Sister's desk, Sister and the chief officer stood beside him because there was no room for them to sit as well, and I stood in front of the desk with my hands behind my back. I was very polite and called him 'Sir', and hid my glee.

After which, if there had been any doubt about it before, Gillian and I were marked down as troublemakers. Though I must say, nobody did try to take anything out on us, and apart from the fact that the sister in charge was obviously very annoyed with us, that was the end of the incident.

The woman I remember most vividly as being an illiterate, and regularly having to have her letters read and written for her, was called Elsie. She was older than the rest of us, in her fifties, and hers was a sad story. She looked utterly defeated, there is no other way to describe it. She was thin and bowed down, she walked with her head bent as if everything was too much for her. She said very little, and what she did say was always kind and forgiving. She was pathetically grateful for any kindness, any attention, and she roused in us all feelings of protection and anger that she should find herself in such a situation. She never complained about anything at all. Elsie had come from Launceston in Cornwall, and unlike the rest of us, who were on weekly remand, she had to make that long journey twice a week. She would arrive back in a state of collapse, crying, and needing to talk.

At first she said very little about herself, but under the influence of the universal kindness she received, she began to talk. (One of the girls who spent most time with Elsie was rough tough Josie, who moderated her language, and showed the loving side of her character in Elsie's company.) Elsie, it turned out, was no stranger to confinement. Indeed, she had spent thirteen years in Broadmoor, for a crime which she confessed to us only with shame and loathing. Like Corinne, she had murdered her daughter. I used to wish that Elsie had come in while Corinne was still there: they may have been able to help one another, but Corinne and Caroline had both left before Elsie arrived.

Elsie felt that because of what she had done, there could be no forgiveness, and she wanted the whole of the rest of her life to be a punishment. Restrictions and confinement she accepted gladly, as being what a monster like her deserved. She gave away everything she had, feeling that she was not good enough to own anything or be anything ever again. Because I used to talk to her, being the nearest to her in age, she tried to repay me by giving me presents of soap and shampoo, bought from the canteen. She could not believe that anyone could want to talk to her because they liked her. This put me in a difficult position, because the giving of such presents was strictly forbidden, and I could have been in serious trouble if we had been caught. Anyway, I did not want to take them from her. When I gave her things which had been brought in for me at visits, she promptly gave them all away again. You couldn't win with Elsie.

I was never convinced that we knew the full story of what Elsie had done this time, but by her own admission she used to drink a lot, and she said that she had got drunk and hit her husband over the head with a garden gnome. He had called the police, and because of her record she had been held in custody. Gillian and I loved Elsie, and were furiously angry to see a human being reduced to the depths of abasement that she was, but the thought of Elsie hitting her husband over the head with a garden gnome reduced us to helpless hysteria, never of course in front of Elsie. We could not help it. It was partly the garden gnome, and partly the thought that anyone as helpless and damaged as Elsie could ever find the courage to hit anybody with anything. If Elsie could hit back, there was hope for us all.

As her trial approached, Elsie became more and more precariously balanced. She used to knit in class, her head bent down almost to her knees. Then her knitting somehow got lost, and I tried to give her a constructive thing to do by getting her to knit a sleeve of the jersey I was doing at the time. Elsie's knitting was erratic at the best of times, and I had to pull it all undone after she had gone, but she said it helped her cope with being locked up if she could have a bit of knitting in her cell. She was not allowed the class knitting because at the time the teacher was refusing to allow her needles out of the association room, a couple of pairs of knitting needles having gone missing after being taken into the staffroom. We all knew that a nurse had borrowed them, and they did eventually turn up, but I did not see why a conflict between the teacher and the nursing staff should mean that Elsie had nothing to do. My needles were my own property, and I was allowed to take them back to the wing. The wool was also mine. Strictly speaking, the staff should not have allowed Elsie to borrow another inmates' property, but they did, and I am glad. She would never ask for it, though. I had to do all the asking every time.

Like Josie, Elsie was promoted to an upstairs room, and then demoted downstairs again because she had a 'funny five minutes'. In Elsie's case, this occurred in the middle of the night, and took the form of an hysterical outburst, combined with a little restrained violence in the form of battering her door with her pot. Nothing was actually damaged, except Elsie's reputation for meekness, but the staff moved her back downstairs where more of an eye could be kept on her. Elsie looked round for something to do to atone for her outburst, and quietly began not eating. She was already bone thin, but the effects began to show on her face. She looked really ill. Because we ate alone in our cells, nobody realized for a long time that Elsie was throwing her food out of the window, where it was pounced upon by the birds. She was only discovered when she was moved from a cell facing the outside of the block to one facing inwards over the garden, and there as we took our exercise were the remains of Elsie's lunch, day after day.

She then took to hiding her food in her pot, and emptying it down the lavatory when we were unlocked. Caught at that, she moved on to hiding it in her cell, and disposing secretly of little packets of old food whenever she thought she was not observed. Poor Elsie, she had not only the staff to contend with, but also us, for we were all very worried about her, she seemed determined to kill herself this time. At last a nurse sat with Elsie while she ate, and made sure that she did eat, and she was weighed every day. Poor Elsie hated to be made to eat all her awful food, for which I can't blame her, and eventually she promised that she would eat properly if she was no longer watched and made to eat everything. So she was allowed to eat alone again, but weighed regularly, with the threat that if she lost weight again she would be made to eat everything once more.

As her trial came closer, Elsie calmed down a little, and seemed to be more lively than she had ever been in a normal way. We feared that she might go to pieces, but she did not. At her trial, like Corinne and Caroline, she was sent to a hospital. Her three months on remand had done her no good whatsoever. We understood that her husband was prepared to take her back. At first he had not written at all, and he never came to see her, but as time went on she began to get letters from him, which she would pretend to read when they were delivered in front of the rest of us, and would then have to have them read to her later. She dictated the replies to a nurse. She was shy about her inability to read and write. Other people were quite open about it, and would dictate letters in class to another woman, quite often Josie, who was always bored in class, and welcomed something constructive to do.

Another interruption to our association time was 'Chief's Aps'. In prison it is usually the assistant governor who deals with the requests of prisoners, but at Pucklechurch that pleasure fell to the lot of the chief officer. If you had a request, query or complaint, you could 'book chief' in the evening, and you would be sent for at some time the next day, usually in the afternoon. This must have been quite a chore for the chief, because you had to ask permission for absolutely everything. Permission to have a cheque sent in, permission to have it sent out, permission to have an extended visit, permission to have a special letter to write to your solicitor. One girl asked permission to have her teddy bear (made in class) in her cell. Permission had to be asked to have the things made in class put in our property. (This is the prisoner's belongings which are not allowed in the cell, but have to be kept, usually in a cardboard box, in reception.) Permission to have wool sent in. Permission to have a completed article sent out. Permission to have a change of clothing, a coat, a stronger pair of shoes. Permission to correspond with a friend sent to prison. Permission to breathe, we sometimes felt. One girl had to ask permission to have her false teeth sent in. I had to ask permission to have my knitting in my cell, which was given, subject to Sister's agreement.

To be fair, permission was almost always given, and, by the chief who was there for most of my time, given graciously. A tall, imposing woman, with the quietness of assurance and authority about her, she was always pleasant, though there was a hint of steel in her eyes, and I would not have liked to get on the wrong side of her. When ushered into her presence by the officer on duty, we were supposed to stand to attention and recite our name and number, but she always forestalled this, with a quiet 'Hello, Audrey' to me, and no doubt she also greeted the others by name. At least she knew who we were, and I wondered if that was the reason she bothered with such trivia as she had to deal with during Chief's Aps. Her deputies were not so human. I think they rather enjoyed the standing to attention and the recitation of our names and numbers. Good for discipline, no doubt.

Standing, whether to attention or not, in front of the desk, the request was stated and the chief wrote it down in a massive book, and indicated that the request was granted in the book, though she never actually told me that any of my requests were granted. A smile meant assent, I learned. Presumably if they had not been, I would have been told. Once the chief had granted a request, it was 'law', and had to be carried out.

The chief's humanity was also apparent when I went into her office one day, and her dog, a little King Charles spaniel, was there. The dog came up to me, and I totally forgot where I was, who I was, and that I was supposed to be standing to attention, giving my name and number. I knelt down and petted the dog, as I had not seen an animal for so long, and I yearned for the touch of animal fur. How much I missed my cats was brought home to me by the little friendly dog. The officer on duty was having apoplexy behind me, but the chief said nothing by way of reproof. I said I was sorry, that I had quite forgotten my position, and made my request.

Now it occurs to me to wonder how I had got so institutionalized that I could have thought it 'wrong' to pet the dog. The atmosphere of discipline, the assumption that in some way we were lesser forms of life, who had given up our rights to be treated and to behave as ordinary people, had made us feel and behave as if we were indeed lessened, and subjected. This atmosphere had a powerful effect. But why? We were all under the presumption of innocence. Was such powerful discipline necessary? Why on earth should I not pet the dog? Why was the chief some kind of goddess figure? The only answer I can give is that the remand centre worked on the principle that whatever the law may say, if you had been arrested you were *ipso facto* guilty, and therefore to be treated as such. It is a point to ponder.

Other interruptions to association time came in the form of solicitors, social workers, the laundry, canteen, 'the Welfare', and the officer to collect clothes for court. I am sure that there was not a single day but someone, and often many people, were called out of association for one or other of these reasons; and of course, visiting time was between 1.30 and 3.30.

A new girl coming in once asked me what time we went to the laundry. She also wanted to know what time 'canteen' was, what time 'private spends' was. At Pucklechurch there was just no answer to questions like these. I could only say that canteen would be sometime on Friday, private spends sometime on Wednesday. Laundry might or might not happen at any time. I loathed the laundry, I really hated it. We were called in ones and twos, and, as I have said, at any time. The theory was that every girl got to the laundry once a week, with those going to court taking precedence over those who were not. I know for a fact that the theory did not always work in practice; there were several weeks, including one when I was still going to court, when I did not get to the laundry.

I seemed mostly to be called in the afternoon. It was hot, it was furiously noisy, it was crowded. There were convicted prisoners from B2 who worked in the laundry, and were there all the time. They operated the machines which washed the towels, the PE kit and the clothes from the men's side. Sheets were sent out to Leyhill Open Prison, where they had a proper laundry. We did our washing by hand, which suited me as I always wash by hand anyway. But the machines made an incredible noise, the girls shouted, and Radio 2 was turned up to full volume. After the clothes had been washed, they had to be spun dry, which I did not like, as I dry my washing on the line in the good old-fashioned way. Then they had to be put in the tumble

97

dryer, and we had to stand about waiting for them to dry. This was a marvellous opportunity for exchanging gossip with the girls from B2, with whom we were of course not supposed to mix. The laundry was the central clearing house of information as to who had come in, who had got off, and who had got what after their trial. Snippets of scandal from people's letters were exchanged: what was going on in Hull; where so and so's old man was; what Bill at Strangeways had said to the governor and, *sotto voce*, that Joe and Tim were back on the old racket again, and Karen was helping them. When you went to the laundry, you imparted some information, and you learned far more.

There was of course an officer in charge of the proceedings, and she was there all the time. But she could not be expected to hear and control the flow of information which passed from girl to girl. When we girls from the hospital wing were there we were usually accompanied by one of our nurses, and when someone potentially violent like Josie was there, both the nurse and the officer had to be on their toes. I was often sent in with Josie; I suppose because they knew they needn't bother about me, and could concentrate on her. If the officer left the laundry for any reason, we all had to go trooping round with her, as we were never, of course, allowed in the place by ourselves. I have seen girls sent out of the laundry for failure to behave properly, and it was certainly one of the real danger points of the remand centre. Any trouble there could have been very serious indeed.

I used to whip my clothes out of the tumble dryer as soon as I could, and iron them roughly dry, because I just wanted to get away from the awful noise. Then I would stand, holding my pile of clean clothes, and fix the officer with my eye until she phoned for a nurse to collect me, or took me back herself. The hospital wing was only just round the corner from the laundry, and I was usually the first to be delivered back. Sometimes, however, I had to wait a very long while, and that was the worst thing. I found that my head would start to spin, and I would come nearer to screaming than at any other time. The officers were supposed to check that all clothes leaving the laundry were dry, but most of them, thank goodness, didn't bother. I spread the clothes round my cell to dry off completely. Dry clothes were not the imperative: getting out of the laundry as fast as possible was.

We did not wash our 'smalls' in the laundry, but in the basins on the wing. We were not supposed to wash anything but underclothes on the wing, but I extended it to anything I could wash without ironing, as that cut down the time spent in the awful laundry. I used to hang things out of the window to dry, although we were not allowed to do so. This earned me several tellings off, especially when I was moved to a cell overlooking the admin. corridor, where the sight of my blouses blowing in the breeze seemed to greatly upset the senior officers. One of the rooms I had, when I was first moved upstairs, only overlooked the roof of the association room, and I used to hang everything out of that window, with nobody being any the wiser.

As I have said, the afternoon was also the most usual time for canteen and private spends. Canteen was the little shop selling sweets, toiletries, tobacco, biros, where we spent the money we had 'earned' in class each week. This was decided by the staff, and in my time it started at 94p a week, and slowly worked up to £1.15; and I think there was one week when I got £1.20. That was when I had been very good, and done a lot of extra cleaning. After another week, when I had been very bad and not done as I was told with my exercise books, my money was sharply reduced as a result. The whole thing was quite impossible. Canteen was a highlight of the week, however little money we had to spend there. Prisoners on remand had to spend every penny of their money every week, as the authorities did not like us saving it. Convicted prisoners are allowed to save. To make it possible for every penny to be spent, the canteen used to sell large chews for 1p and small ones for ½p, so that any amount outstanding when the major purchases had been made could be used up.

My mental arithmetic is not what it ought to be, and so I used to spend some time on a Thursday evening working out what I was going to buy with my money. At least I had a choice; those who smoked had none. They had to buy as much tobacco and as many cigarette papers as they could get for their money. The centre did provide soap and shampoo – horrible government issue types – but if you smoked you could not afford to buy decent brands at canteen. I used to keep myself supplied with soap, shampoo, handcream and toothpaste from canteen. Although I had private money, I saw no point in using

99

it unnecessarily to buy such things on private spends. Any money I had left over I used to spend on Mars bars, and make up the total with small packets of mints, or chews. Just occasionally, if I ran out of soap, shampoo and handcream all at once, I did buy on private spends, but I got a good deal of fun out of working things out so that I did not have to.

As time went on, I spent the extra money I 'earned' each week on chocolate. The longer we were locked up, the more obsessed we became with Mars bars. It was compensation eating, no doubt; outside I would very rarely buy sweets, but in there all we could think about sometimes was chocolate. We used to hoard it away in our lockers and have secret binges. Gillian used to make hers last until Sunday afternoon, but I rarely got to the end of Saturday. I suppose I was getting through about fifty pence worth of chocolate a week. We rarely shared canteen things with each other, as we all had the chance to buy things. It wasn't like having things brought in on a visit, or even buying things on private spends, where people who had a lot of money had an unfair advantage over people like Josie who had none or very little.

I had come in with about twenty pounds, and I left Pucklechurch for Styal with about ten pounds. That will be the first and last time in my life that ten pounds has lasted me five months. Fifty pence a week! Everything else I had, my food, and the salaries of my jailers, was all at public expense. I think it was a totally unwarranted waste of public money. Stories differed as to exactly how much it cost the state to keep each of us on remand per week, but it was probably around three hundred pounds. In my opinion, it would be a lot more beneficial to use that money to provide establishments more suited to the needs of the majority of people than remand centres are.

Private spends happened on a Wednesday afternoon. On a Tuesday, you had to get and complete a form giving details of what you wanted. This form had to be posted under the canteen door before 9.30 on a Wednesday morning, which in practice meant that it had to be put on our breakfast trolley – since we would not be allowed near the canteen before we went through to class, and that was liable to be much later than 9.30, or even not at all. The nurse who saw the trolley back to the kitchen would then post the slips under the door for us. The canteen officer obtained permission from the governor for us to have the things we had asked for, and went shopping to get anything special. (The wording of the slip said, 'I respectfully request permission to spend my private cash on the following items'. Name and number.) Why 'respectfully', we wondered? Were we convicted and in prison already? We might as well have been.

In theory we were allowed more or less anything on private spends – fruit, squash, chocolate, tobacco, cakes, biscuits, or whatever. The officer would buy tights on our behalf, but there was a notice in canteen saying that she would not buy other clothes, for which I don't blame her. I have a feeling that she was probably supposed to buy anything reasonable, to make up for the fact that we were not allowed out to spend our own money. Most people had things sent in on a visit, and did not therefore need to bother with exotic things on private spends; but if you never had a visit, like Josie or Elsie, it was the only way you could do any shopping.

The most important thing I bought every week were stamps for letters, and for these I would use private spends if I did not have enough at canteen time. Otherwise, you were limited to the single weekly letter sent at state expense. As I have said, we could have an almost unlimited supply of letters, provided we had the stamps for them. So every week, my first order at canteen was always two, three or four 'own stamps'. We never actually saw the stamps, but the canteen officer would make a note in the book that I had paid for three or four stamps, and I would therefore be entitled to that number during the next week. Gillian, who wrote letters by the dozen every week, spent a fortune on stamps. Stamps could also be brought in on visits, and my solicitor also generously provided me with some.

Not only did we never see the stamps, we never saw any money either. The £1.15, or however much I earned every week, was recorded on paper. It was considered too risky to let us have any actual money. We were told week by week in canteen how much we had to our credit, and we could buy up to that amount. The whole thing was a paper transaction. Presumably a certain amount of money was received from the Home Office for prisoners' earnings, and the goods in the canteen were bought with it, then given to us according to how big our share of the earnings was. The new twenty pence piece came out while I was in Pucklechurch: I never saw one until I went to Styal, where we were allowed to have money as if we were human beings.

Visits from friends and relatives occurred in the afternoon. I usually had mine on a Saturday, but when my daughter was at home before going on her European tour, she came to see me as many afternoons as she could. Visits were events to be longed for and dreaded. I was not the only one to find them intensely upsetting. As we were on remand, we could be visited every day, but as the visit only lasted for a quarter of an hour, this was not a great concession. We could apply for an extended visit, but were not likely to get it except in special circumstances. A quarter of an hour is a rotten time for a visit. You have just about got over the initial feelings of strangeness and begun to talk, when it is time to go. I would have much preferred to see my children less frequently, but for longer, than to have these rushed fifteen-minute visits, when either we were hurrying to say everything, or sitting wondering what to say to break the ice. I must say that very often the officer on duty was generous as to when she stopped the visit, and a nominal quarter of an hour would often stretch to twenty or even twenty-five minutes, but you could never be sure of it. It all depended who was on duty, and how many people were due for a visit.

Visits took place in the visits room, and we were escorted out of the wing, along the admin. corridor, and through to the complex of rooms used for visits. There were two small rooms, used for visiting solicitors and probation officers, and a larger room (but not much so) used for general visitors. There were half a dozen little tables, each with three chairs, one for you, and two the other side of the table for the visitors. You were not supposed to touch the visitors, but everybody did, and the visitor was not supposed to put anything on the table. We were body searched before and after every visit, in one of the little visiting rooms. That was a good test of whether the nurses saw themselves primarily as nurses or as jailers. The nurses hated the search and didn't do it properly, but the jailers were very thorough. I found this a hateful and degrading experience.

There was a little table for the officer on duty, and at weekends there was usually more than one. If someone from the hospital wing had a visit, she was accompanied by a nurse, presumably in case she had a fit. At first, the sister in charge used to accompany people to visits. I am sure this was to get a look at the relatives: no doubt useful background information. When she had sized up my home situation, she gave up accompanying me. Because of the size of the room and the number of staff there, it was next to impossible to have a private conversation. This was very inhibiting. It was very difficult to talk to my family, and in the case of my husband I simply gave up trying. I needed a long time with him and privacy, if we were to sort ourselves out in any way. Neither was forthcoming, and so I gave up attempting to say anything meaningful at all. For the children I was able to make a greater effort, but on the whole I hated visits, and they always upset me for the rest of the day.

We did not have to see anybody who came to visit if we did not wish to do so. In the first days, when I was not at all in control of myself, I had to refuse to see several people. I always felt guilty, as they had gone out of their way to travel the long distance to Pucklechurch, but I simply could not face anyone other than my family. On one occasion, I went actually into the visits room, thinking the visitor was my daughter, but it turned out to be two colleagues from school who had got time off to come and see me. I panicked, and pushed my way back past the nurse and out into the corridor. I could not face them, I could not face anybody. After that, I made certain that I knew who the visitor was before I went down for the visit. My next door neighbour called once, as did the chairman of the school governors. I was sorry to seem rude, but I could not see them. The only person apart from my family whom I did see was my fellow deputy. He came early on, before I had actually broken down. I saw him because I felt it was the least I could do for the school, as there were things I had to sort out with him. Then he himself had a breakdown, and never came again. The headmaster, to whom I felt accountable, never came for his account.

The word got round that I would not see anybody. People stopped coming and left me alone, which is what I wanted. As my trial approached, the nurses tried to persuade me to see people again, and I was able to see two of my female colleagues for a couple of visits each. I was very grateful that so long after I had vanished from their lives, people were still prepared to come and see me. They were difficult visits, but I managed, and it was a milestone along my road to recovery that I was able to swallow my shame and see people again. I always felt, and indeed still feel, that unless I could tell the whole story, I would prefer to say nothing, and let people think what they like. I have no doubt that some lurid stories were in circulation at school – I got some surprising letters from people who had obviously got hold of entirely the wrong end of the stick, but I was not prepared to enlighten them. After my trial, I wondered whether it would not have been better to tell my story first, rather than let people find out via the press a wholly distorted version of events which I suppose they now believe to be the truth; but at first I could not, and then I would not.

More constructive and less shattering were the visits I had from my solicitor. He came shortly after I was admitted to Pucklechurch, and then arranged for a young female clerk in his office to come and get the whole story from me, as we both felt it might be easier for me to talk to a woman. She came three times, and I did indeed find it easy to talk to her. It was a long and complicated story, but then I suppose they always are. She took down details of my life, and asked sympathetic but probing questions. It was actually a relief to be able to talk freely. She made sure that she had understood the ramifications of the story, and I know that at the end she believed me. She knew the truth when she heard it.

Then there was a long period while I was being remanded every week when my solicitor did not come to see me, because I saw him each week at court. Later, nearer the trial, he brought my barrister to meet me, and then twice again to discuss the case. These interviews were always held in the little visiting rooms, and there was no time limit. A solicitor could see his client at any reasonable time, and for as long as he liked. Once, he and my barrister appeared after tea. A nurse or an officer always sat outside the room, and I am sure this was not necessary. The theory was that they were protecting our solicitors from unfounded claims that we had been molested. You could not have a man and a woman alone in an office without observation, not even a solicitor and his client. As the doors did not shut, I am sure that they could hear a lot of what was said, as well as being able to watch us through the glass top half of the partition.

On one occasion, my solicitor asked me to sign something. I was just bending to do so, when the officer who had been keeping watch outside, flung open the door said: 'Don't you dare sign that!' David could not believe it, and remonstrated with her. He also told me to sign. The officer told me not to, saying she was protecting my interests. I could not understand how she could be protecting me against my solicitor who was acting in my interests, so when he told me to sign again, I did, though doing something I had been forbidden to do by an officer was a very odd feeling. The argument between my solicitor and the officer continued, and eventually he demanded to see the chief officer. Both of them went off, leaving me sitting in the room with another officer to keep an eye on me. He came back after a long while, having, I think, received the apology of the chief and the officer, and he said loudly enough for the officer to hear that if I was victimized in any way as a result of the incident, I was to let him know. I was not in any way victimized, either then or at any other time.

I had other 'official' visits. Quite early on, the psychiatric social worker who had been looking after me came in. He looked quite ill and appeared to be very concerned that there was nothing he could have done to stop me doing what I did. I don't remember much of that interview, as it occurred at the time when I was not myself. He neither came back again, nor contacted me. He did have a talk with my husband, during which he was apparently more concerned to point out that whoever else was responsible for what had happened, he was not. I imagine he then marked my file closed, and that was that. They have a terrible workload, these people.

Before my trial, my solicitor arranged for me to be seen by an independent defence psychiatrist. That was just as well, as the centre psychiatrist spent two hours with me during all the five months I was on the hospital wing, and never finished taking the story down. I had no confidence whatsoever that any report he might make on me would have any validity at all. He did not know me, he did not know what had happened, he did not care why. So long as I kept quiet and gave no one any trouble, that I assumed was all he cared. At first, I had hoped that this man might be able to help me, but I soon found out that he was not there to help people. The whole thing was purely a holding operation. Being surrounded by people who needed help, and not being able to spend enough time with any of them, must have been a very unsatisfying job for him. Yet he was a kindly man. He was also hopelessly overworked, and had to concentrate on the people who were really ill, and on those who had been remanded for the specific purpose of having a psychiatric report carried out on them. In fact, all they usually got was an hour with him just before they went back to court, despite being held for three weeks for the purpose of that report.

I used to wonder just how much of the reports were actually the work of the sister in charge, based on the observations of her nurses. And if so, whether this was as it ought to be. The nurses, with a couple of exceptions, were all good and well-meaning people, some of whom were a tremendous help to me, and whom I shall remember with gratitude as long as I live. But they did not all seem to be particularly interested in this kind of work, and had by no means all bothered to take extra qualifications to fit them for it. Indeed, not all were nurses anyway, though they wore uniform and we called them 'Nurse'. Three of them were only nursing auxiliaries. We had a lot of agency nurses as well, especially during the summer holidays. Some of them were so appalled by what they saw that they did not stay long. I believe there was extra money for working at Pucklechurch, and while I am quite sure that they earned it, especially when one of the madder prisoners was on the rampage, I am also sure that 'nursing' in a prison or a remand centre has nothing to do with psychiatric nursing as that profession understands it.

There was one nurse whom I shall call Sister Smith. She was very strict and was always having a go at me about something. We used to have the most incredible conversations frequently at cross-purposes with each other. I remember one argument about my weekly letter which made me wonder if I had lost the art of communication. The whole story was not very complicated, but I found it impossible to explain to Sister Smith, who I think had it firmly in her head that I was somehow trying to get one up on the establishment. We had many similar conversations which left me shaken; but one good result was that I became so angry that I could hardly speak. This was beneficial, as if you have lost most of your grip on reality as I had, there is nothing like anger to get your perspective back again.

Sister Smith was always on duty. She never seemed to have any time off as the others did; she never went on holiday. She was always there. She could knit like lightning, always perfectly, and without looking at her fingers. She used to sit with us in class, knitting away, and never taking her eyes off us. She always refused to allow me to take my knitting bag to my place with me, but only the needles and wool I was actually using. Then she used to go through my bag to see if there was something that should not have been there. I used to pretend that I had not seen what she was doing, because I minded very much having anyone going through my things. Sister Smith would never give me my knitting to have in my room if we were being locked in, and soon I stopped asking when she was on duty.

My conversations with Sister Smith caused my friend Gillian much amusement. When we had our little contretemps about my weekly letter, it was in class, where everybody could see and hear. Sister Smith never told me off privately. When I turned back to my seat, Gillian was purple in the face with the effort not to laugh. So we helped one another, for with Gillian beside me in helpless hysterics, it was difficult to be upset for long over so trivial a thing.

One day there occurred the incident of the great exercise book drama, as a result of which some of my pay was docked. The whole episode is, I fully realize, too ridiculous for words, but it was exactly the kind of thing which used to happen at Pucklechurch, where a perfectly innocent happening would be blown up out of all proportion. Most of us had exercise books, which we obtained from the teacher and took back to our rooms to use to while away the hours during which we were locked up. (Needless to say, we had to ask Chief's permission first.) I had not bothered with an exercise book until August, because I did not want to write at all at first, and then I could not face having whatever I did write read every Friday as I went to court. I probably wouldn't have bothered otherwise, but we were told that there were not likely to be any classes during the month of August, and I thought I had better get some books in case we were to spend August locked up. (In fact this did not happen.)

So I asked the teacher for two exercise books, and was given them. This, of course, was all wrong and should not have happened. What should have happened was that first of all I got Chief's permission, then I got one exercise book from the teacher, which had all its pages numbered, and a rubric written on the cover: 'It is an offence to write on the covers or tear out pages from this book'. When that book was full, I could get permission to have a second book. The idea that you could just ask for an exercise book, and get it, was too simple. I should have known. I had been in Pucklechurch long enough.

So there was I, with two exercise books at once, neither of them with their pages numbered, neither of them with my name and number on, neither of them with the rubric about not tearing out pages. I kept the books quite happily for ages, totally unaware that I had broken the law. Every Sunday morning we had a locker check, every Sunday morning the books were seen by one or other of the sisters, and nothing was said. I never knew what happened, but I surmise that the teacher, who was in fact leaving at the end of July, had handed out books as if she were in a school rather than a remand centre. Many people had acquired books illegally, and were tearing out pages like a snowstorm. This was a serious offence, because notes can be written on exercise books, and notes were strictly forbidden. The authorities must have found too many of these notes, and come to realize that there were dozens of illegal exercise books in circulation. So they must have complained to the teacher, and on a day in September we were suddenly instructed by the sister in charge to take our exercise books with us.

So we did, me included. We were not told why, or what was happening. The teacher told us to put the books out on our tables, which we all did, me included. Then towards the end of class, she went round and collected some of them and put them in the cupboard, saying that we could not have them in our rooms until we had asked Chief's permission. But she did not collect mine. I had no idea then what was going on, and indeed the explanation I have given as to what was happening is sheer guesswork. I did not much fancy having my books in the cupboard with everybody else's, so I put them back in my knitting bag.

It became obvious to me that the staff went through my knitting bag behind my back, because on the following day I observed my exercise books on Sister's desk. Now I knew that I ought to have handed the beastly things to the teacher and asked her if she wanted them, but they had been out in full view on my table, and she hadn't taken them. But I had a guilty conscience, and so I said nothing except to tell Gillian that the books were on Sister's desk.

I went off to class, and from time to time during the morning I wondered how Sister Smith was getting on. She had obviously thought that the reason I had hidden my books and not handed them in was that there was something incriminating in them. One book was filled, one half full. What would be in them? Rude comments about the staff? Names and addresses of the other girls? Accounts of all the nefarious things I got up to?

Oh, poor Sister Smith! What did she make, I wonder, of what she found? Long, long copied extracts from the Bible. Lists of books I had read. Odd quotations which appealed to me, such as 'Don't spoil history with facts'. A few, a very few, strictly factual accounts of Pucklechurch, most of which are printed here. And above all, poems. Hundreds and hundreds of poems, long poems, short poems, extracts from poems. Poor Sister Smith! I bet she was bored! I bet she was so bored that she didn't read the poems properly. And yet, if only she had known it, those poems contained all the evidence she was looking for. A word changed here, a line there, and the poems safely held some comment I wished to make.

As the time for my trial drew near, I began to panic about whether all my reports, not just the psychiatric ones, would be done before the trial. Sometimes, when the trial is over and the jury have convicted you, the judge asks for reports before he sentences you. I had been in Pucklechurch long enough to have seen many people sent back on judge's remand for reports. I could not imagine what those people must have felt, knowing they were going to be sentenced, but having to wait days and sometimes weeks for the reports to be done. I wasn't going to let that happen to me if I could help it, and began to pester my solicitor to get the arrangements for the reports made, so that I could be given my sentence on the same day as I was convicted.

So the last official visitor I had in the little visiting room was the probation officer assigned to my case. She was about my own age, and

I found her instantly a sympathetic friend. Not in a gushing way, for she was much too wise and too professional to do that, but in the sense of being someone I felt I could talk to at the time and afterwards. She told me that strictly speaking I should not have a report done on me at this stage if I was pleading not guilty. I was by no means sure that I would be pleading not guilty, as the attraction of pleading guilty, so as to get everything over quickly and comparatively quietly, was very great. And indeed I was to pay heavily for my eventual plea of not guilty. But although I was not guilty of the charge, I had undoubtedly committed a crime, and was expecting to be punished for that. I was still at this stage hoping that the prosecution would agree to let me plead guilty to the lesser charge of which I was guilty.

So I persuaded the probation officer to go ahead with her report. That meant that I had to tell the whole sorry story all over again, and I think she came three times before we had it finished. I was getting better by this time (September), and I did not want to tell the story again. I really didn't. I am by nature shy and reserved, and all the talking about myself that I had done, to nurses, psychiatrists, solicitors, seemed to me to be a symptom of my illness. I found it more difficult to talk to my probation officer about it all, because I had again begun to rebuild my wrecked shell about me and I didn't want it broken again. Whether I was talking to my probation officer or the barrister and my solicitor, I had to face up to the fact that the trial was really very close now, that the story would have to be told again, and this time in public. So the last few times I spent in that little visits room were upsetting ones for me.

One way and another, the pattern of the afternoons was never the same. There was always something happening for somebody, and sometimes for most people. Letters, visits – official or from friends and relatives – and Chief's Aps all added to the interest of life, particularly when there was nothing but sport on the telly . . .

5   Pucklechurch Evening

The afternoons came, eventually, to an end. We returned from watching TV, and were free to hang about waiting for tea at five o'clock. Again it was time for me and whoever was with me to prowl up and down the corridor, up and down. The others sat on chairs at the end of the corridor and smoked. I hated it as there was nothing to do but kill time. Yet it was difficult to go into my cell, even if it was unlocked, which was by no means regularly the case. When unlocked we all wanted to be out of the cells, even if it was just to wander around in a corridor.

Quite often one or other of the sisters would come upstairs and sit with us, not so much for friendship's sake, but to keep an eye on us. If it were one of the sisters to whom I could relate, we sometimes had quite good conversations. They were interested in whatever we had to say, and I have no doubt it went down in their notes afterwards. Gillian used to hold herself aloof from all the staff, saying that they could not be trusted, no matter how nice they seemed. She had the belief that the remand centre was in league with the police, and what was said to the one would be reported to the other. I am still not sure whether I believe that or not.

At last, some time after 5.00, and often very late, tea would appear on the trolley, and down we would go to collect it. There was always bread and butter and, as at breakfast, one item cooked: a tinned tomato and a piece of ham was the regular Sunday tea. There was never cake, because we had cake for supper. We would return to our rooms with our plates of goodies, and be locked in. Sometimes we would not be unlocked again that night except for a quick wash. I developed a craze for bread and sugar, and used to tip my red plastic eggcupful of sugar ration on to my bread. I would never have done this in public, bread and sugar being very hard to eat in a civilized manner, but when eating alone in one's cell, all kinds of manners went

111

by the board. I learned that there is something to be said for dressing for dinner come what may. If one thing is no longer considered to be important, then the whole network of customs and manners which at once divide and connect people's social life are liable to dissolve. Before this experience I would have doubted that there is a direct connection between eating peas with a knife and giving up bathing. Now I am not so sure. I used to tell myself that as my dignity and personal worth were every minute under attack in this place, I ought to be doubly careful to keep my personal standards high; but it did not really seem worth the trouble. So I ate peas with my knife, and dropped sugar all over me from my bread, and I understood the fragility of the hold that a civilized being has on civilization, and how much easier it is to relapse. And I understood how people can give up washing.

When the tea things had been collected, we were left to ourselves until at least six o'clock. During this time I would listen to the radio while I tidied my locker, or I would read or, after I had acquired them, write in my exercise books. About half way through my time at Pucklechurch I had recovered sufficiently to notice that there were some jigsaw puzzles in a room used as the store room. I became the jigsaw addict of the wing, and I always had a puzzle on the go. After I had done all the available jigsaws once, I did them again, making myself work from the bottom up – then again, from the top down. I found this activity entirely suitable to my needs, as it occupied the brain in a way which stopped thought, but did not demand the concentration of reading.

One of these puzzles, of the Eiffel Tower, was very difficult indeed, in that the sky which formed the bulk of the puzzle behind the tower was almost impossible to do. It took me ages and ages, and much of it was achieved by the laborious business of trying one similar piece after another until it seemed I had the right one. This took hours and hours, but then I had hours and hours. All the puzzles had pieces missing, but I didn't mind that. I got exceedingly fed up with them, however, by the time I had done them for the third time. Two of the nurses kindly brought in puzzles for me from their own homes, which they should not really have done. I could have had puzzles sent in, and had I stayed much longer there this is what I would have done.

It was part of my evening routine to put the puzzle away. They were big puzzles, of 500 or 1000 pieces, and I used to spread them out all over my bed in the morning after I had made it. This was partly because the table was too small to hold the puzzle when made, let alone when I was in the process of completing it; and anyway, I liked the table cleared for my meals. So, every evening I had to transfer the pieces of completed puzzle to the table, and then gather the remaining pieces into assorted piles, and store them on or under the table. At home, having to do this every night would have driven me mad, but here I didn't mind. It was another way of passing the time. People were always amazed at the way I transferred the puzzle, but it's easy when you know how. I did drop it sometimes, but so what? There was no shortage of time to do it again.

When I was first at Pucklechurch, we were unlocked every evening at six o'clock, so that I thought it was an inevitable part of the day's routine. In fact, I even felt aggrieved that just as it was time for the six o'clock news on the radio, I should be unlocked and sent for my bath. Later, we were not unlocked so regularly, and later still we spent more evenings 'in' than 'out'. At first when we were out, we used all to be unlocked together, and it was left to us to work out how we fitted in our baths, washing our smalls, and watching TV. The hospital wing had its own portable black and white television, and we used to arrange the chairs, together with those from our rooms, in a long row against the wall opposite the set, and there we were allowed to sit until just before eight o'clock.

I used to arrange always to be on the extreme end of the row. This suited everyone else, because the person on the end (or people, if there were a lot of us) had a poor view of the set. It suited me, because I was upwind of the smokers, there being a steady draught down the corridor which blew the smoke the other way. As the set was almost always tuned to ITV, and as the programmes were not very good, I did not in the least mind missing them. The one night when you could be sure the set would be on BBC1 was Thursday, for 'Top of the Pops'. Many a Thursday ended in a near riot when the set was turned off before eight o'clock and the playing of whatever was number 1 of the week. Most times, I must say, the staff were kind to the young ones and let them have the programme to its end. 'Coronation Street'

113

also tended to be watched to the end, mainly because the staff were also watching.

A number of people used to establish themselves in front of the television as soon as they were unlocked, to ensure a chair with a good view. They would go for their baths reluctantly, and with much 'saving' of places by their friends. I preferred to have my bath as soon as possible, because the earlier one bathed, the cleaner the bath was. Most people did not seem to mind getting into a dirty bath, and never thought to clean it after them. Only a few odd-ones-out like Gillian and me would not bathe until we had obtained the Chemico from the staff, and cleaned the bath. The staff never actually refused to give us the Chemico, but some of them made it clear that they could not understand why we made such a fuss. I am sure none of them would have got into one of those baths without cleaning it, and it was yet another little indication that they thought that we, no matter what our background, were in some way inferior, and therefore should not mind a dirty bath. It was sad to see how many people in fact lived down to that opinion, and did not mind. Young Josie was another who would not have a bath unless the bath was clean, and she was in many ways genuinely the toughest of us all.

The Pucklechurch washrooms were functional places. On the hospital wing there were two, one on each floor. Each contained two basins, one toilet and one bath. There might be more than a dozen women on the wing, and sometimes nearly twenty. There were no locking doors. The bathroom door had a gap above and below it; it was easy to see over the top, and there was no privacy at all. Tenure of the bathroom was indicated by clothes thrown across the top of the door so that they hung down the other side. From the clothes one could tell not only that the bathroom was occupied, but who its occupant was. One thing I will say for Pucklechurch is that the water was almost always hot, and it was possible to have a good wallow. We could not buy bubble bath at the canteen because it was considered in some way to be dangerous, but we were allowed to buy Radox which, if you ignored the drying effect it had on the skin, provided a pleasant smell and the illusion of a luxurious bath.

Sometimes the pleasant smell was much needed because, as I have previously explained, people had little chance to use the toilet, and the evening was one of the times when you could go with a reasonable chance of being uninterrupted. That was tough on whoever was in the bath. With both doors having gaps, top and bottom, there was no way in which the smell could be contained. Opening the little toilet window only blew the smell more forcibly out into the rest of the washroom, besides freezing people trying to bathe or wash. My inhibitions would not let me use the toilet if anyone else was in the washroom, so I was never the cause of ruining someone else's bath, though I often had to suffer in that way myself.

After a short time in Pucklechurch it ceased to surprise me that grown women should be walking round in their nightclothes ready for bed at six or seven o'clock in the evening. Everyone was supposed to be washed and in her nightclothes by the time supper arrived at 7.30. Most of us had no nightclothes of our own, and were dressed in prison-issue nightdresses and dressing gowns. An effort had been made to choose pretty materials, but they had been washed and worn so many times that all were shabby, and most in need of mending. The few people who had their own things stood out from the rest of us. I used to think that never did we look more like prisoners than when we were sitting in our shabby nightdresses in a sad long row in front of the television.

At first, I sat for most of the one and a half hours between having my bath and being sent to bed. Later, when the amount of sitting down had become unbearable, I spent time fiddling about in front of mirrors, doing my washing, and just staring out of the upstairs window at the gardens. As the year drew on, it was pleasant to stand and watch the beginning of the sunset. I would turn all the top corridor lights off, and watch in the gathering dark. The trouble was that other people, also fed up with the television, would come up and find out what I was doing, and a peaceful minute was destroyed. They would always put the lights on, which began increasingly to annoy me. It was one of my little treats, to stand alone in the dark and watch the sky.

From time to time, there was a purge, and we were not allowed upstairs by ourselves, but had to go down and sit in front of the television whether we wanted to or not. This rule was usually enforced whenever there was anyone on the wing who was liable to steal, and this was quite often. One evening, though, just before my trial, nobody was downstairs and the television was talking to itself. This was a time when there were few people on the wing, and most of them were long-term people whom the staff knew well and could trust. The couple of doubtful cases were ruthlessly locked in downstairs, and we were all told to go upstairs. I can say nothing about the two sisters who were on duty that night, because I want to do nothing which might identify them and get them into trouble. Greatly wondering, we went up, closely followed by a sister bearing a tray on which were biscuits and *coffee*. A great, steaming jug of strong, aromatic coffee. Only someone who normally needs her coffee to get through the day and then finds the supply totally cut off could realize what that meant to me!

The coffee was poured, with milk for those who preferred it. Biscuits and a packet of cigarettes were handed round, and we had what amounted to a party for half an hour. The sisters were on tiptoes listening out for any sound from below: supposing the chief had decided to stroll through as she sometimes did? We knew the drill, the door of an empty room had been unlocked, and had anyone come upstairs, the tray and the coffee would have vanished, and we would have been found sullenly on our way to bed. But nobody did come. We drank coffee, we laughed as one of the characters on the wing, a Bristol prostitute in for the hundredth time, related some of her hilarious experiences in her typically dry manner. The sisters told stories of their own. For half an hour we were human again, treated as human beings and not as subnormal and inferior forms of life.

I could not say at the time what that meant to me; the fact that those two sisters had taken what was certainly a risk with their jobs to do such a simple but forbidden thing as sharing a cup of coffee with the prisoners. I hope that they will read this one day, and understand what that half hour meant to those of us who were beginning to think that we were losing our status as human beings. To have that one evening of near normality demonstrated that the usual way in which we were treated was quite unnecessary.

One of those two sisters, seeing my delight at being given the coffee, saw to it that on both the mornings of my trial when she was on duty, a mug of strong sweet coffee was waiting in the kitchen, which she put into my hand instead of filling my own mug with tea. In such an inhuman place, a small gesture like that was tremendously important.

According to the rules, we had to be locked in for the night at eight o'clock. This meant that medicines had to be given out before then, and occasionally, if supper was particularly late, we even got medicine before we ate. Supper consisted of a large jug of tea and a plate of cakes of an indescribable texture. There was one cake (bright yellow in colour due to the use of that bright yellow baking powder which I suppose must be cheaper than the ordinary kind) for each of us, but for nearly all my stay there I never ate mine. It was only as my trial approached that I began to eat all the time, and then I would sometimes eat not only my own but Gillian's as well if she didn't want hers. I rarely drank the tea either, as if we were going to be locked up all night the less fluid I had last thing the better. Mildred was the compulsive tea drinker, and would return again and again to the jug, which usually stood on top of the television, and drink cup after cup until there was none left. That was why in the morning her pot was full to overflowing, but she never seemed to connect the two things, or to restrict her fluid intake in any way.

After the big event of supper, those of us not interested in the television strolled away to brush our teeth and make last visits to the toilet. Nobody went into her cell until the very last minute, except one woman who came in at the end of my time. She was a sort of replacement for Mildred, and it was she who would always push into the meal queue. She was tall and terribly thin, just like Mildred, and seemed hopelessly neurotic. She could not cope with remand centre life at all, and was reluctant to come out of her cell, creeping back into it again whenever she could. She seemed to spend most of her time just lying in bed staring into space. The staff seemed to have little sympathy for her, and it emanated from them that she was a fraud, behaving like that for her own purposes. She also was 'in for murder'. At one time it seemed that everyone was.

The rest of us had to be shepherded into our cells by a nurse moving slowly up the corridor locking people in from the stair end up. Gillian and I, in the two end cells of the corridor, would stand outside our doors until the very last minute, then dive in as the nurse came to the door. The nurses knew that they would have no trouble, that Gillian and I would in fact go in when the moment came, but not a second before we had to. I suppose we were making some kind of harmless protest, though at the time it seemed more like a game.

Only once did I see someone refuse to go into her cell at night. This was Laura, Josie's young friend, who had been brought to Pucklechurch the day after her seventeenth birthday, having been held in a secure unit for young offenders until then. Laura had certainly committed murder, though the story she told us was not the same one that came out at her trial. Laura was hugely overweight, and thought a good deal of herself. She had a man friend in another prison with whom she corresponded regularly, and told us all she was engaged to him, though he was a hardened criminal and much older than she was.

When Gillian was allowed an interprison visit with her husband, this greatly upset Laura, who kept on at the authorities until a visit with her 'fiancé' was arranged. This annoyed the rest of us, who felt that Laura, unaccountably to us, was spoiled by the staff. We all hated her thoroughly. She seemed to be a hard, spoiled bitch, caring nothing for anyone else at all, and she treated everyone like dirt, including poor Josie. Josie did at least realize that she had done something wrong in murdering the man who molested her. Laura clearly felt that her victim, her flatmate, had been in the way, and could justifiably be disposed of by murder. As Josie and Laura were about the same age, it seemed natural that they should become friends, but Laura only talked to Josie until someone more interesting appeared, then she dropped Josie flat.

The situation was complicated by the fact that Josie was a lesbian, while Laura was prepared to be what was known as 'nick gay'. When another youngster, also 'nick gay', came in, the situation was fraught with all manner of complications. Josie came out of everything worst because she was sincere, while the others were simply amusing themselves. It seemed to be the fashion at Pucklechurch that summer for people who were heterosexual on the outside to form lesbian relationships on the inside. There was much discussion about it, and the feuding and feeling it led to. I think the staff probably thought it was all talk, but it certainly was not, and the three youngsters very often organized opportunities for physical relationships right under the noses of the staff.

Laura also tried to get her own way by organizing an accident. She had been annoyed that when the visit with her fiancé was arranged, the man had been brought to Pucklechurch, whereas she had really wanted a trip outside. So she said to us that she would arrange one. Laura was cunning, and a good actress. She 'fell' in the washrooms, damaging her ankle. She had told both Josie and Gillian that she was going to do so. I thought that she would never get away with it (after all, these were trained nurses), but she did. An ambulance came and took her to the casualty ward of a Bristol Hospital. And the rest of us had to be locked up so that a nurse could go with her. She fooled the doctor as well, and came back with her leg in plaster, and had to be pushed around in a wheelchair for a fortnight. Laura thought it was extremely funny, and the annoyance that the rest of us showed only added to her pleasure. The staff were very sympathetic towards her, and full of reproaches for those of us who refused to push her wheelchair, which included me. I would have told them what had happened, only I knew it was useless. They had their faces to save, and a doctor had ordered the plaster, so it must be genuine. When the staff weren't looking, Laura would dance along the corridor like an elephant. How she had the barefaced gall to do it, and to continue the pretence for so long, I do not know.

The sight of Josie pushing Laura's chair round the garden on exercise, while Laura sat there like a queen with an unpleasant smirk on her face, really annoyed me. Gillian named her 'Miss Piggy', which was very appropriate. Later, Laura actually did twist her ankle, falling off her high-heeled shoes, and I am not ashamed to admit that this gave me much pleasure. Laura had a large supply of fashionable clothes and shoes. She was in the care of the social services, and it seemed she only had to write to her social worker and anything would be sent in for her. She had a mini skirt sent in, and the sight of Miss Piggy's fat thighs was too much even for the staff. After a while Laura saw the doctor and was put on a reducing diet, which lasted a day, and was then supplemented by chocolate, biscuits and Josie's puddings till the doctor took her off the diet again.

Of course, I do not know Laura's background, but if one could believe what she said, it was pretty grim. But young Laura is a manipulator. She has the gift of making authority feel sorry for her, and she got away literally with murder. She rather enjoyed her trial, as she was the centre of attention, and she was 'let off' with a suspended sentence. It was not long before she was back in Pucklechurch for GBH. Laura will spend her life in and out of prison, and of course I am sorry for that. But what I still cannot sort out in my head is why she should arouse such sympathy in those in authority, when others of us did not. Was it simply because she was so young? Because they believed they could save her in some way?

If I disliked Laura, she disliked me equally. She disliked both me and Gillian because she knew that we saw through her, and were not impressed. She disliked me most because, personal relationships not being my strong point, I did not even bother to pretend that I regarded her with anything other than contempt. Gillian, better than me at social skills, kept up some kind of relationship with her. Indeed, Laura used to seek Gillian out when she had quarrelled with all her young friends, if 'friends' is the right word. Laura also disliked me because I used to get the radio turned down.

That radio was the bane of my life. It lived – where else? – on the table at the bottom of the stairs, and it was tuned all the time to Radio 1. When we were locked up, the staff would often put the radio on, in the belief that it soothed troubled minds. Intolerant of meaningless background noise at any time, I found this radio particularly aggravating. After inhabiting various rooms, Laura decided that she wanted the room right at the end of the upstairs corridor, opposite mine and Gillian's. This was so that she could indulge in her pseudo-lesbian affairs with the maximum of security. Being Laura, she got what she wanted. The trouble was that at the end of the corridor she could not hear the radio as loudly as she wanted. So, before she went into her room when we were locked up, she used to nip downstairs and turn the radio up very loud. Incredibly, she was always allowed to go down and do this. None of the rest of us would have been.

The nurse would lock me up first, then Gillian, then Laura, and then pass my door on her way downstairs again. If it were a reasonable nurse, I would always ask for the radio to be turned down, and as most of them were my age and shared my view of Radio 1 at top volume, it was usually turned down. When we were out there was always so much noise, with voices, footsteps on uncarpeted floors, keys jangling, water running, that the radio made little impression. When we were in, the silence made the radio seem twice as loud, as it was the only major source of noise.

Laura asked her social worker for a radio of her own, which she got. At first she used to play it at maximum volume, but then she found that the batteries ran out faster than she was prepared to buy them. (Batteries could not be sent in – they are potentially dangerous in a well-run prison and we could only buy them from canteen.) But by that time I had been moved to another room.

The volume of the radio was yet another trivial thing which became an obsession in the world of the remand centre. There were times when it made me so unspeakably angry and frustrated that my head felt about to burst. I could easily have justified my charge and murdered somebody then. It was made worse by the fact that for about half my time in Pucklechurch the radio was scarcely ever switched on; it was only really when Josie came that the torture caused by Radio 1 began. It was a torture for me to be shut up with it going on and on and on, and no way of escaping or turning it down.

I used to sabotage the set. I would surreptitiously alter the tuning or the waveband. It was interesting that people often did not notice for a long time that the music had stopped. They were not listening to it at all, they merely wanted a noise in the background. It was plugged into a socket just inside the cleaning cupboard, which was supposed to be kept locked so that we could not electrocute ourselves: there were no sockets anywhere in the place except in the staffrooms and in this cupboard. The cupboard was often unlocked, so I used to switch it off and push the door so that the Yale lock engaged. Then, only a nurse could unlock and switch the thing on again. However, switching that socket off also disconnected the socket in Sister's room. So there was a row when they found out it was me daring to interfere with the electricity supply. After that, I simply unplugged the set.

All this led to bitter rows between myself as spokesman for the people of my age who did not want to constantly listen to Radio 1, and the young ones who did. I asked the young ones if they were prepared to listen to Radio 4 for a fair percentage of the time, as there were only three or four of them and eight or ten of us. But no, they would not have that. Eventually the atmosphere got so heated that the sister in charge stepped in, and it was decreed that the young ones should have the radio as loudly as they wanted on Sunday, but that blessed quiet should obtain for the rest of the week. However, it still depended on which sisters were on duty as to whether or not that happened. The reason that Sunday was decided on is that Radio 1 broadcasts the Top Forty for two solid hours on Sunday afternoons. By this time Laura had got her own radio, and if the one downstairs was on for Josie, whose room was nearly opposite it, I could hardly hear it. This struck me as being fair. I never wanted to deprive them of Radio 1 completely, though never once was the radio tuned to Radio 4 for my benefit. Accepting that I was in a minority, I would not have expected it to be.

When there was a move one night to refuse to go to bed, it was young Laura who was the instigator. I still think that all she wanted was some drama, and to get some of her enemies into trouble. I would have nothing to do with it, and nor would most of us. When it came to it, it was only Laura and Josie who sat firmly in their chairs at the end of the upstairs corridor and refused to move. Gillian and I had begged Josie not to join in: she was always in trouble anyway, and seemed unable to get through a day without an explosion of some sort. She was on report about once a week, and always losing privileges. But Josie saw it as some kind of test of her loyalty in a them-and-us situation, and stood by Laura when she refused to move.

Sensing the potential danger of the situation, the sisters on duty had the rest of us locked up in double-quick time. They then went back and tried to reason with Laura and Josie. It had now become difficult for Laura and Josie to back down: everyone on the wing knew what was happening, and the atmosphere had become charged with that electric sense of drama and forthcoming violence which always accompanied trouble at Pucklechurch. The riot bell was not in fact rung, but the officers were sent for, and there came the tramp of heavy feet in sensible shoes ascending the stairs, and the jingling of numerous keys.

The officers tried to reason with the girls, but Laura had it all nicely calculated. Her leg was still in plaster at the time, and she thought that they would not hurt her. She could stand out for as long as she liked. Young Josie finally saw some sense, and was led downstairs to her room, screaming protest all the way, but not actually being dragged. On the earlier occasion when she had been taken away to the silent strips soon after coming in to Pucklechurch, it had taken half a dozen officers to handle her, and I had seen her being dragged along the corridor.

Laura sat her ground, apparently believing that they would not hurt her. She was most amazed when two of them grabbed her, and dragged her, plastered leg and all, down the corridor. I averted my eyes from the disgusting spectacle going on outside my door, but Gillian was looking through her peephole, and told me afterwards that Miss Piggy, for all her boasting, was a great baby. Two officers had her down on the floor, with all her clothes off and dressed in a strip gown, in just thirty seconds. Other officers were quickly removing all the furniture from her cell and storing it in the corridor outside the cell. They left her mattress, and then she was inside her cell with the door locked as easily as if she had gone of her own accord. Another reason for Laura's dislike of me was that she thought I had been witness to this humiliation, but in fact I had not. I couldn't help hearing, though, and when Gillian remarked loudly the next morning that the trouble had amounted to hardly anything, I agreed, and was bitchy enough to add that if poor Laura's leg had not been in plaster, no doubt she would have sorted them out as she had promised!

By the time I said that, however, poor Laura's leg was not in plaster. She had got her revenge by sitting on her mattress and picking off every bit of the plaster. So she had again to go to hospital in Bristol to be replastered. And Laura was not disciplined for this incident, as any of the rest of us would probably have been. I'm sure Josie, for example, would have got some punishment, but Laura could get away with anything. The officers had taken the unusual step of putting her into her own cell, converted into a strip cell by having the furniture removed, rather than get her downstairs with her plastered leg. If only they had known that there was nothing wrong with her leg after all!

123

Apart from this one occasion, I never saw anyone actually refuse to go into their cell at night, although we went with heavy hearts and there were often complaints.

When they had got us safely locked up, the nurses had to take the medicine trolley round to the other wings. During the day, the women came over to the hospital for their medicine, but at night it was taken to them. They did this for the space of an hour, and cleared up whatever administrative work had to be done, before we were handed over to the officer on night duty.

Not all Pucklechurch evenings were spent unlocked. There were many evenings when, either from shortage of staff or some other reason, we were not unlocked. I learned to dread the appearance on duty of a certain sister who would never unlock us if she could find an excuse not to, and who almost never unlocked us in the evening. The more of us there were, the more likely we were to stay locked up. I suppose from her point of view it did save a lot of trouble having us all tidily locked away. It meant her evening could be spent in the staffroom rather than keeping an eye on us, and it also meant that she did not have to cope with the stress of the possibility of violence, which was a reality for us all.

When we were in for the evening, what usually happened was that we were unlocked in ones or possibly twos, since there were two bathrooms, to have our baths. That tended to be a battle between the prisoner, who wanted to spend as long as possible out, and the nurse, who wanted one to get finished quickly so that she could let another woman out. Poor Josie had a terrible time when this happened. Once out, she was very difficult to get in again, and was likely to spend half an hour in the bath – a bit antisocial, since there was only just over an hour for all of us to get through. So poor old Josie was often left till last, which she found very hard to bear, and our baths on many evenings were accompanied by Josie's yelling and banging. Josie could behave like an irrational child in these circumstances.

On some evenings we were not even able to have a bath or a proper wash, but were unlocked just to go to the lavatory and wash our hands, while the nurse stood outside the washrooms to hurry us up. This didn't happen very often, nor did the occasions when a nice sister on duty, leaving Gillian and I to be unlocked last, would then 'forget' to lock us up again. We would sit in the chairs at the end of the corridor, and gossip in whispers so that no one would know we were out. Somehow, I can't remember how, Josie got to know that this happened. From then on, whenever she was locked up, she was suspicious that we were unlocked, and would accuse us of having been unlocked even though we had in fact been locked up just as much as she had been.

During the peak holiday months, when I suppose there was a real staff shortage, we spent most evenings locked up. I developed a routine for these evenings. First, I listened to the six o'clock news. Then I wrote in my exercise books, until I saw that I was capable of getting through several hundred if I did not restrict the amount of writing I was doing. I slowed up by doing my best to write neatly instead of with my usual scrawl. I would sometimes be allowed my knitting when we were locked in, or I would read a little. Sometimes I would be let out for my bath, and that could take twenty minutes. If I hadn't tidied my puzzle away so thoroughly that I couldn't get at any of the pieces I was working on, I might do a bit of that. The time soon passed until 7.30 when supper arrived below, and would be brought round to us one by one. Very often Josie was allowed to go round with the nurse and pour our tea from the big jug while the nurse proffered those indescribably yellow cakes, and Josie collected all the ones which people didn't want.

After supper, I did more exercises, with the object of making myself tired in the hope that I would sleep. If we had been out for the evening, my exercise time was reduced, perhaps to only a few minutes, though I always tried to do something. If we were in, then I might have up to an hour, during which I would alternate violent with gentle exercise, not forgetting the hideous grimaces with which Gillian said I must exercise my facial muscles so that I did not get horrible lines of sadness on my face. Sometimes the whole thing was too much for me, and I would collapse in helpless laughter at the thought of the spectacle I would present to any nurse looking through the peephole, with my face twisted into the parody of a smile while I tried to follow Jane Fonda's way of working out. Remembering what I had been told at some time, I made sure that I did some fierce running on the spot, so that I was out of breath and my heart was racing. The trouble with this is that the more you run, the more you have to, in order to get the desired effects on the cardiovascular system, and by the end of my time at Pucklechurch I was having to go really fast for a long time before I got out of breath.

When I thought I had done enough to prevent my heart and lungs seizing up, and to get me to sleep, I organized my things around me and got into bed. I had to have my radio, not so much for the evening, but for the following morning. I had to have my book, my handcream, and most importantly of all, my biro and the two pieces of illegal paper I kept. The first was my chart of days. Not to cross off, because I did not know how many days I had to do. If I had known when I went in in May that I would still be there in October, I don't know what I would have done. But I collected days in neat rows on the back of an envelope, and after the rows of weeks had become months, I thought I must be half way now. This was something I began to do only after I had stopped going out to court every Friday. At first I was not well enough to care, and I suppose it was a sign of recovery when I did begin to do this. I would sit in bed and stare, mesmerized, at these rows of days, and wonder upon which of them would be my trial. At first I only put down the days until the end of August, but I had to extend it to the end of September, and then into October.

The second illegal bit of paper was my 'lists of things'. I could not trust my memory in the slightest, even for the simplest things, so I used to write everything down as it occurred to me, and things mostly occurred to me during the night: requests to Chief; what I wanted to say at my next visit, or put in my next letters; something to tell my solicitor; something to tell Gillian; personal things which came back to me after a long lapse which I did not want to forget again; the list of poems which I knew well enough to be able to alter to contain a message, and the actual alterations I could use. When one bit of paper was used up, I would tear it into small pieces and put it in the incinerator, so that nobody could ever find it. I used to do this with my letters as well, and could never understand why the sister in charge, who caught me doing this once or twice, seemed to think it was a sinister way to behave. My letters had all been read before I got them anyway, so why did I need to shred them into such very small pieces and burn them? Why could I not throw them in the bin as everyone else did? Everyone did not, actually, but Sister certainly thought that my behaviour was disturbed. I didn't; I always shred and burn any paperwork which is in any way personal. I never put it in the dustbin to be blown off the dump for anyone to read.

I do not know what had gone wrong with my memory. Like my concentration span, it had shrunk to nothing. Whether it was the drugs, or merely a side-effect of the shattering experiences I had gone through, I have no way of knowing, but it sometimes seemed that I could remember hardly anything during the day. At night, things would come back to me, as I lay between sleeping and waking; and that was why I had to have my biro and my lists of things at hand, so that when I suddenly woke knowing something, I could write it down at once. If I left it till the morning, it would be gone again.

Having organised all my things around me, I then began reading. The night officer would look in at about nine o'clock; by which I mean that she would peer through the peephole. Once locked up, as I have already explained, we were not supposed to be unlocked except in a life-threatening emergency. If it were a kindly officer, she would exchange a few words with each of us, but some of them merely looked in and went on without a word. The officer was checking on who was where, and it was her responsibility to deliver the same number of women to the day staff as she had received.

The senior officer on duty came round yet again to check the fire door at the end of the corridor: yes it was there, yes it was locked, yes it did open. They were very strict about unlocking it and relocking it, though as it was checked three or maybe it was four times a day, I should think they got heartily sick of the precaution. All the exits had to be checked in this way, and everything had to be reported as correct before a shift could go off duty.

Finally, at last, the corridor lights were turned off. The sounds of departing officers faded away, and Pucklechurch began another uneasy night.

127

6 Pucklechurch Night

Most of us slept badly. Everybody in the place had grief and worry to contend with, the innocent and guilty alike. Everybody had a trial to prepare for. Many women had families to worry about. By day, you could sometimes forget what had happened, but with the night came the thinking and the suffering. Whatever our backgrounds, whatever we were charged with, we were there because something had gone seriously wrong with our lives, and guilt about the past and fear of the future haunted us all.

There was no real darkness, and no real silence, in Pucklechurch. I had plenty of light to write with at night, because the bright sodium lights illuminating the walls and gates so that we could not escape shone into all the cells, or at least into the five cells that I occupied. But, in addition to this, for those of us on the hospital wing was the orange light. The light fitting in the middle of the ceiling (sealed shut, and very high up, so no escape that way) contained two bulbs, one ordinary and one orange . The orange bulb could only be switched on and off from outside the cell. It was switched on by the night officer, sometimes as early as nine o'clock, and frequently it was switched off again by me when I was unlocked the following day.

This light was because we were considered to be risks of some kind: suicide, disciplinary or, very rarely, medical, though with some of the drug addicts I suppose it was medical as they went through the process of compulsory withdrawal. So, for one reason or another, we had to be kept under constant supervision. For the most part we were looked at regularly during the night, but there was one officer who never came round at all, except first thing in the morning. If I had been planning an escape, I would have tried it when she was on duty, knowing that my absence would not be discovered until morning.

In the interest of close supervision therefore, we had to sleep with the light on, which is something I cannot abide. At first, I was too ill to realize, but as I got better it began to annoy me increasingly, until it became one of the things I hated most at Pucklechurch. I got more and more steamed up about the orange light as the darker nights came with the autumn. I complained about it all the time, but there was no way in which I could stop them switching it on. Some of the night officers were considerate, and would wait until I had got to sleep before switching on the orange light. One or two would 'forget' to switch it on at all when they realized how much it distressed me. But most of them switched it on automatically at nine or ten o'clock, and that was that.

On one occasion this orange light nearly got me into serious trouble, and on another it caused me to be rude to an officer for the only time while I was there. On the first occasion, I devised a method of making a tent with my blankets, so that once inside the tent, I was shielded from the light. I had even thought seriously about getting under the bed, so that the light would be completely dimmed out. As it was, I made my tent, and lay there happily while the night officer raged outside. Of course, if I could not see the light, she could not see me. She fetched a senior officer, and they stood outside discussing the matter, while I lay 'doggo' in my tent, pretending to be either dead or asleep. Then it occurred to me that if they thought I was dead or not there, they might come in, and the whole thing would develop into a major incident. So I yawned a mighty yawn, and moved about a bit. They evidently came to the conclusion that I was just avoiding the light, and left me to it. In the morning I was told that if I ever did such a thing again I would be on report at once, as prisoners must at all times be visible!

On the second occasion, it was a sultry, thundery night, and it would have been difficult enough to sleep anyway, without the orange light as well. Just after midnight, I gave up lying there, and stood on my bed, so that I could get close to the window for some air. There was no rain, but lightning was playing across the sky, and I stood there for some time watching it. Then I was called from the door by one of the officers from the centre, who had seen me standing there, and had taken the trouble to come all the way up to speak to me. She asked what the matter was, and I am afraid that, made irritable by the weather, by my approaching trial, and above all by the orange light, I told her in no uncertain terms. I hope that I am not often rude to people, but once started, I deliberately use my superior command of the language to be very rude indeed, and so I was to this poor officer. She remained unfailingly kind and courteous to me, and when she went away I had the rest of the night to regret what I had done. I apologized the next time I saw her, and she was very good about it. I know that the officers often came in for abuse, but I never foresaw that I would descend to the level of getting things off my own chest by abusing someone who had come to see if she could help me.

No doubt both incidents found their way on to my file. I am sure the second one did, because Sister said to me the next morning, 'You had a bad night then?' and I explained that I was very sorry I had been rude to the officer, but that I was finding it more and more difficult to tolerate the orange light. And of course the more I hated it, the more I came to dread it, and the more screwed up about it I became, the worse it was. By my last night in Pucklechurch, the orange light had become a real torture to me, mitigated only by the fact that by then I had been moved into a double-bedded room, and I had the bottom bunk where it was possible to lie so that the light was not visible. Poor Gillian had the top bunk, on the grounds that she hardly ever slept anyway, and she preferred to be where she had the light to read by.

Nor was there blessed silence during the night. It was like a hospital, in that the place was always awake. Always movement, always people talking, and walking and maintaining the place as a twenty-four hour a day establishment. Some of the officers could not be bothered to keep their voices down, as if it did not matter whether we slept or not; but then the same can be said of some nurses in hospitals I have known. There was not the ceaseless traffic of the day, of course, especially not the coming and going through the gate to the outside world. By day there was a long procession of vehicles and people coming and going through the gate: lorries delivering bread, milk and other food; the van which travelled backwards and forwards from Pucklechurch to Leyhill; the groundsman's tractor and various trailers; police cars, Black Marias, the occasional ambulance; the lorry which acted as dustcart, collecting the old skips full of rubbish and bringing the new ones in; and people – officers, the governor, solicitors, social workers, psychiatrists, doctors and, at the appointed times, visitors. The first cell I had was on the ground floor facing the gate, and I used to watch this traffic in wonder.

To gain admission, one had to ring the bell at the main gate. This would then be opened, and entrance was gained into a kind of airlock, or pen between the gate in the wall and the second gate in the wire fence. This was of course to prevent us from escaping and contaminating the outside world with our criminal selves. The hut where visitors waited was within this pen, or airlock. It was like being in a state of limbo, for those who were no longer part of the free world, since they had come through the gate, but were not yet part of the remand centre world. Here, credentials were checked, and then the visitor went to the gate in the fence, large for cars, small for pedestrians, which was opened and locked behind you. To get out, the procedure worked in reverse: there was a bell for pedestrians to push, while cars relied on the sound of their engine to alert the gateman. If this did not work they hooted. During the day it seemed that one bell or the other was ringing continuously. At least this traffic stopped at night; and the gate was not often opened between the departure of the day shift at about 9.00 p.m. and their return at 7.00 the next morning. The scraping of those gates as the gateman opened them several hundred times a day is one of my abiding memories of the place.

The worst offenders against the silence of night-time were the inmates themselves. Although it was not allowed, girls would call to each other through the windows, conversations of unbelievable triviality which went on and on and on. Often there was singing; and always if someone was leaving the following day. I had not heard of the tradition of 'singing out' but I know all about it now! 'Good luck, good health, God bless you' over and over again. Various superstitions abounded about being 'sung out'. Some people were not allowed to sing, on the grounds that anyone they sung out always came back again. Others were much in demand, on the grounds that no one they sang out had ever come back in again. I learned these and other fascinating facts in the late evenings at Pucklechurch, when I would much rather have been asleep.

The worst offenders for shouting out of windows were those of the women who were most disturbed. They could find no way of passing the time which did not involve talking. I suspect that many of them could barely read or write, so what else could they do with their time but talk? The most outstanding of them all was a girl called Sarah. Sarah was not actually a girl at all, but a young woman in her early twenties. She had an illegitimate daughter, who was cared for by Sarah's mother, as Sarah was not capable of looking after herself, let alone a baby. She was quite pretty, and did not look like an inadequate person, except that her clothes were never very clean. Her mother looked after her well, and saw that Sarah had new clothes when she needed them. I suspect that in the intervals of her life when Sarah was outside prison, her mother did her washing whenever she could. This could not have been often, for Sarah was a great traveller. There seemed to have been few places in Britain that Sarah had not visited at one time or another, hitching her way round the country, living rough and sleeping wherever she could, usually in someone else's bed.

Sarah had dark brown eyes, which would have been pretty had it not been for the look of animal cunning in them. Cunning is the only word to use, but it was cunning almost devoid of intelligence, more based on instinct. Like a little child, Sarah lived completely in the present. She had no conception of cause and effect, and seemingly no ability to learn from experience. She had been in every remand centre and most prisons in the south of England, several times in some cases. She spent more time in than out, as was inevitable because she had no conception of right and wrong, no understanding that there were some things she must not do.

This time she was in for abducting a baby. The baby was not harmed, and in the event Sarah was not punished for this, as the judge gave her a short sentence which meant that, having already served so long on remand, she could go free. The judge used her case to make a complaint about the lack of places he could send her, there being absolutely no facilities in England to provide care for someone like Sarah, who was not mentally ill, nor a vicious criminal, but just a hopelessly inadequate personality. Sarah's case achieved publicity in the national press as a result of what the judge had said, and she was immensely proud of this. She had to return to Pucklechurch on a technicality for about ten days, and was moved from the hospital wing to A wing, where she was supposed to be kept locked up for her own protection under rule 43. Somehow the other girls got to her, and beat her up heartily, feeling that she had not been sufficiently punished for the theft of a baby, which touched women at their hearts. It was my first example, though by no means my last, of child molesters, abductors and murderers being punished by other prisoners. There might seem to be a kind of justice in this, but whenever I saw it in operation I was never happy about it. Too often it seemed like a excuse for women who were pretty near the bottom of the pile themselves to take revenge for their own problems on one of the few people they could feel were really worse than they were themselves.

I would not have wanted to have a go at Sarah because of what she had done, since she was so obviously not able to control her own actions. I did sometimes wonder, though, what I would have done if I had been sent to Durham and encountered Myra Hindley there, though later at Styal I met several people who had known her and said she was not as bad as she has been painted. I expect it is after all simply a matter of *tout comprendre, tout pardonner*. Who am I to judge?

Sarah had a habit of moving her fingers. Always, every minute of every day her fingers would move. She would touch the tip of her index finger against her thumb, then the other fingertips, in order, and then back to the index finger again, and so on. She never stopped, unless she had a cigarette or something in one hand, but then the other would still be moving. Only on the rare occasions in class that she was occupied, using both hands, did she stop. She used to stand with the defensive attitude of a child, her arms stiff and by her sides, and her fingers moving, moving, moving. One of the nurses told me that she had been interested to know if Sarah did it in her sleep, and had been quite disappointed to look through the peephole and find that Sarah's fingers were still.

Sometimes Gillian and I used to try to talk to Sarah, to get her to adopt a better attitude towards her mother, whom Sarah treated badly. She used to long for her mother's visits, but not to see her so much as for the cigarettes she knew her mother would bring. I remember one occasion when Gillian had reproached Sarah for her attitude, as you would a child, and had said that nothing upset her

133

in the way it should, not her own troubles nor anyone else's. Sarah replied all in one breath: 'Everything upsets me can I have a light please'. This last to a nurse who had just appeared. The only thing that upset Sarah was not having a cigarette when she wanted one.

Sarah was a real cross to bear at nights. She would shout and call and sing out of the window until really late, and she would not ever stop, nor learn from experience. Several times she was put on report and punished for it, yet she continued to do it. The girls on the other wings were just as infuriated as we were with Sarah: everyone disliked her. Yet she would not stop shouting out of the window; and if no one would talk to her, she talked to herself, or worse, sang. The only person of whom Sarah might occasionally take notice was Melanie, a tall, thin, highly neurotic girl in her late teens who was almost always in the strips because the staff did not trust her. Melanie had a terrific voice, and when she had had enough of Sarah, her tremendous '*Shut up!*' would echo along the whole wing, and Sarah would occasionally shut up.

I liked Melanie very much, and would have given a lot to be able to help her. She had been to Bullwood Hall, the notorious Borstal, and was now facing a Borstal recall which she dreaded more than anything. I used to call her my pink panther, because she wore pink pyjamas in the evening. But I fear there is no helping Melanie, and I recently read in the paper that she has now been sent to prison for terrorizing the inhabitants of her little market town with a knife attached to a broom handle while under the influence of drugs. I think she also went in for arson in her spare time. So Melanie will be another one who spends more of her life inside prison than out. Why?

It was Melanie who nearly got me put on report one day towards the end of my time at Pucklechurch. Another girl was in with us, with whom Melanie had become friends. This girl, Sheila, was a convicted prisoner serving three weeks for shoplifting. She was held with us remand types under observation on the hospital wing, officially because she was pregnant and had nearly lost the baby, but really because she was a policewoman, or rather an ex-policewoman. It was thought that if she went on to B2 with the other convicted girls, she might well be murdered, as she had had a hand in putting some of them inside. Sheila was very pretty, very expensively dressed, and as tough as nails. She did not seem to feel any shame at all about having stolen so much (she used to tell us that she was expensively dressed because it was all shoplifted stuff. I believe it). I knew she was not telling us a tale, because I had heard on the radio that she had been convicted, and so had a lot of people. All Sheila cared about was her forthcoming wedding.

Sheila served her sentence and went, and Melanie was at last moved from the hospital wing, which she said 'did her head in', a common prison expression. She went on to A wing, whose windows were on the ground floor overlooking our exercise garden. One day, we were going round and round in our usual enthusiastic way, when Melanie appeared at her window. I often used to talk to her as I went past, as so long as I kept moving the nurses turned a blind eye to our strictly illegal communication. On this day, Melanie said that she had a postcard from Sheila, and did I want to see it. I said yes, and completely without thinking, I took it, as you would take something handed to you. At once I knew I had done wrong, and that impression was confirmed by the way the nurses on duty began to converge on me. I held the postcard in clear sight all the time – I didn't want a strip search – and quickly read what was on it. The nearest nurse pounced on me and took the card away. I explained that I was very sorry but that even after all this time I still had natural reactions such as to take something proffered to me, and only after I had taken it had I realized that I should not have done, communication being forbidden between the wings and the hospital girls.

The nurse just told me to continue exercise, while she went off with the card and the story to the sister in charge. I walked round and round convinced that I would end up on report, but it was decided not to put me on report, information which was given to me only at the end of the exercise period. Melanie meanwhile was demanding to have her postcard back, which she did get back eventually, but not until the card, and presumably the story, had gone to the governor. I think that had it not been me, but someone regarded with suspicion by the staff, this trivial incident would have been blown up out of all proportion. Sometimes it was very hard indeed at Pucklechurch to remember that I was innocent until proved guilty.

So, peace often fell at night after Melanie's tremendous 'Shut up!' from A wing had quietened Sarah. Sometimes I used to bribe Sarah, as I might a child, that if she were quiet that evening I would give her a Trebor mint the next day. She would come up to me in the morning saying, 'Where is my mint, Audrey, I was good, wasn't I?' Bribing her to be quiet only worked once in a blue moon though as, like a child, Sarah was more concerned with present desires than with possible future rewards. I came to accept that there would be no going to sleep until the officer on night duty had shouted at Sarah often enough to shut her up, which might be midnight or later. Fortunately sleep was not necessary for the kind of life I was living. It was not as if I had to use my brain in any way the next day.

Just once or twice I would not have missed Sarah's conversations out of the window at night for anything. When she first came in, I was still in my room downstairs, and Sarah was put in the room above me. A diagnosed schizophrenic was in a room two away from me, and on this particular night when Sarah leaned out of the window to ask, 'Is anybody there to talk to me?', she got an amazing answer from the schizophrenic. A conversation ensued, so abundant in misunderstandings and sheer lack of comprehension on both sides that I just lay there shaking with helpless laughter. It had to be heard to be believed.

Sarah was soon moved from the room above me, as she would not stop calling out to the men on the gate, and to any visitors who happened to have the misfortune to come in while Sarah was in her cell. She was moved to another room on the opposite side of the upstairs corridor, where she only overlooked A wing. Sarah was one of the few people who went straight upstairs: she had been in Pucklechurch so many times that the staff knew her well. She caused endless trouble, but was neither violent nor suicidal, so was safe upstairs.

Sarah went out and came in twice more in the time I was there. At Styal I heard that she had been in Holloway after that, so for those eight months when our lives ran parallel, Sarah had had about three weeks of freedom between re-arrests. What on earth does society think it is doing with girls like that? I heard a rumour later that Sarah had died a particularly unpleasant death, being run over by young motorcyclists in a car park. They had persuaded her to lie down while they rode close around her: too close at the end. I do not know if that is true or not, but I can well believe it of Sarah. It is exactly the sort of situation she would get herself into.

Shortly after I had been moved upstairs, I was also moved to a room on the opposite side of the corridor, not because I used to shout at visitors but because Delia had come in and been given Room 5 which was under mine. Delia was an example of total non-cooperation. She was young, and quite pretty, and on the couple of occasions when she was persuaded to go with the rest of us to association, she sat quietly, with a smile on her face. She looked intelligent and pleasant, but she was, however, an unholy terror.

Delia used to spend her time on remand making everyone's life as unpleasant as she possibly could. This took the form of noise and filth. Delia would throw the contents of her pot into the face of a nurse opening her hatch to give her food. She would pass water up against the door so that it trickled under the door into the corridor. She smeared her cell with food, and faeces which she passed in the corners of her cell like an animal. She made herself sick, and coughed up phlegm which she also smeared over the cell. Needless to say, she was in strips, and she would deliberately foul her strip gown. The smell of her cell was truly awful, and when she was there, for two long spells when I was there, the smell hung over the place permanently. Later, as a convicted prisoner, I had to clean that cell, so I know exactly what she did in it.

At the time, however, it was the noise more than the filth that got us all down. Delia never seemed to sleep. All night, every night she would keep up a constant banging of her pot against the radiator, which echoed in everyone's room round the whole wing. If they took the pot away, on the grounds that she never used it anyway, she would bang with her bare hands. I simply do not understand how she could keep it up day after day, night after night. But she did. She shouted and screamed as well, on and on and on, keeping the whole wing awake. Sometimes, as a variation from banging the radiator, she would bang the door of her cell – throwing her whole body against it so that a mighty crash reverberated round the wing. I would not have believed that one little person could have made so much noise.

She could not use her buzzer, because she was in Room 5 which was the room where the buzzer could be switched off. She must have caused the staff great aggravation too, but at least they could go off duty and get away from it. We had to live with it all the time.

Delia vanished mysteriously one day after she had had an adjudication – a disciplinary hearing before the Board of Visitors. I don't know where she was taken, presumably for punishment elsewhere, but in a few weeks she was back again and the noise and smell began again. Sometimes at night Delia was taken over to the silent strips to give the rest of us a bit of peace and quiet, but often she was considered unsafe to move, so we just had to put up with it. I do not know why she was in Pucklechurch, or what happened to her eventually, but I do know that the rest of us should not have been subjected to the added discomfort of her presence. Poor Josie, always precariously balanced anyway, suffered tremendously from the constant noise at night.

One night Gillian and I got no sleep at all, not because of Delia, but because of another woman. They had thought her to be only mildly potty and so she was upstairs in the room opposite mine. One night she went berserk for no apparent reason and wrecked her cell. The noise brought the officers up, and all night they seemed to be standing outside my door, trying to remonstrate with the mad woman and prevent her from doing any more damage. Like Delia, she threw the contents of her pot under the door and soaked the officers' shoes. I was not amused when I had to clean the corridor the next day: we didn't have goings on like that on the top corridor, and I did not see why she should not be told to clean up her own mess, or why I had to do it – considering that I had not yet been convicted.

The mad woman continued all night, destroying everything in her cell that was destructible, and throwing it out of the window. This included all her clothes, her bedclothes and mattress. The mattresses were only foam rubber, and easy enough to destroy if you wanted to. The next morning the flower bed outside her window was littered with rubbish which had once been the contents of her cell. It was to stop behaviour like this that the strip cells were used, but if someone suddenly went berserk in the night, there was little the officer could do. It was not a life-threatening emergency, so the door could not be unlocked, although senior officers from the centre came up to assess the situation.

What with a berserk woman and officers tramping and talking all night, neither Gillian nor I got any sleep. I dozed off at about 4.00 a.m. but it was only fitful dozing, not sleep. An officer was outside all night keeping an eye on the mad woman, and in the intervals between talking to her, would talk to me or Gillian, for a bit of comparative sanity I suppose. We were sorry that the duty officer that night was about the nicest officer in the whole remand centre; she always had time for a pleasant and sympathetic word, despite having some nasty family problems of her own.

One way and another, night-time at Pucklechurch was hardly something to be looked forward to. Even if by a miracle the place was quiet, there was always the orange light. If by an even greater miracle it had not been turned on, there were still those thoughts which came at night and would not go away. Life always looks worse in the middle of a sleepless night. In the middle of a sleepless night in Pucklechurch, it can look so bad as to make you wonder why on earth you go on with it. Best not to think, but at night, alone in your cell, there is nothing you can do to stop thinking, until sleep comes at last, and with it dreams which are sometimes worse than the thoughts which preceded them.

7　The Trial and After

As my trial approached, I became more and more nervous, as did everyone, naturally. It was like a greatly magnified visit to the dentist: I wished both that the trial would come to get it over with, and hoped that something would happen to put it off for another week or month or year. The sister in charge told me that many people tried to stay on remand for as long as possible, as they could take advantage of remand privileges for the maximum possible time, and for most short-sentenced people, time spent on remand was deducted from the sentence to be spent in prison, so that it was possible for someone to walk out of court free, having been sentenced for a length of time already served on remand.

I believed what the sister in charge was saying at the time, but now, having experienced both being on remand and in prison, I cannot imagine why anyone would wish to extend the time spent in the highly restrictive remand centre. If I had been able to do all of my eight months at Styal, I would have been a lot happier. The privileges of a remand prisoner consisted of being allowed a daily visit (of only fifteen minutes!); being allowed to have food and cigarettes brought in (a fairly meaningless privilege, except to the smoker, I suppose); and theoretically being under the presumption of innocence. Such privileges did not outweigh the disadvantages, such as being locked up for so much of the time.

The stress a prisoner feels as the trial approaches is not difficult to imagine. From my point of view, not knowing the exact date of the trial was as bad. I had been on remand for four months before I was given a date for the trial; this date was then altered, and then changed back to the original. All this information was given to me by my solicitor. I do not know whether he withheld it from me to reduce the stress of waiting, but I do not think so. It all seemed very inefficient to me, and so cruelly long-winded.

The trial was to begin on a Wednesday, and that was something my solicitor certainly did keep from me: the fact that the trial would last for more than one day. The other women who had gone to trial, Corinne, Caroline, Mildred, Elsie, had all known on the same day what their fate would be. I had assumed that my trial would also take one day, and then it would all be over. But, of course, they had all pleaded guilty.

For a long period of time I had insisted to my solicitor that I was going to plead guilty as well, both because then it would all be over in half an hour, and because I could not see how I could plead innocent and have a full trial without the presence of the other person being involved. Under no circumstances was I going to accept that, even if it meant my sentence would be harsher. I expressed myself forcibly on this point to my solicitor, and only when I had his absolute assurance that the other person would not be called to give evidence did I agree to plead not guilty. This of course weakened the case I could offer, and meant that my barrister had to leave out evidence which might well have resulted in a different verdict had it been presented to the jury, but I was adamant. Nor do I think now that I was wrong to do as I did.

Great pressure was put on me to plead not guilty, not only by my solicitor, but by my family, my probation officer, some of the staff in Pucklechurch, and other people who believed in my innocence. I don't know whether I did the right thing or not. It is in fact a lot easier to plead guilty to something you have not done, than to plead not guilty, endure the trial, and then end up being convicted. My solicitor always only gave me a fifty-fifty chance. He thought it was worth the gamble; I was not so sure. He also said that I would probably get a non-custodial sentence, and was as shocked as everyone else that I was in fact sent to prison. David still maintains that it was right for me to plead not guilty, and that I would have got a much longer sentence had I not done so. Perhaps he is right.

My actual guilt or innocence seems to be beside the point here. I have learned that there are two separate kinds of innocence and guilt: there is the actual truth, which is known only to the person concerned and to God; and there is the legal decision. Once found guilty in a court of law, one is effectively guilty, no matter what the

141

truth may be. Had I been found innocent, I would have been accepted as innocent by society, though possibly with some reservations along the lines of smoke and fire. Having been found guilty, I am considered to be guilty by society, with precious few reservations at all. Yet, just because twelve pudding-headed Bristolians said that I was guilty, this does not make me guilty. However, as nobody but myself and God knows the truth of the matter, there is little point in worrying at it.

I felt that I did not see my barrister very much before the trial. This is not intended to be a criticism of either my solicitor or my barrister. It is merely to record that one of the things I find amazing about the English legal system is that the man who is to present the case relies so much upon what the solicitor has prepared, and so little upon contact with the defendant.

The days of the week before the trial passed very slowly for me. In class I could not settle to anything in particular. I would have liked a really good long walk, and the perpetual sitting down in class and everywhere else was even harder to bear than usual. I began to eat much more: obviously a sign of stress. I ate all my own food, and Gillian's too. It happened that about ten days before my trial, Pucklechurch began to get very crowded, and the more people there were, the more the tension built up. The staff became uneasier, and we spent more time locked up. We did not have class at all for many days, and I was rather relieved about that. I was beginning to find class more of a strain than to be in my room alone. My temper and my ability to tolerate other people were getting worse every minute!

On the evening before the trial I was handed an urgent communication from my solicitor. He wanted me to write down in detail what had happened on a certain day just before my arrest. I was grateful for something to do, and was allowed to go upstairs, while the others were watching television, to work on this request. I could not bear to sit in my cell and do this, so I pulled my table and chair out into the corridor and worked there. I took my time about it, trying to do it perfectly, concentrating on the task and trying to clear my mind of the steadily rising panic within me. What I wrote was hardly mentioned during the course of the trial, so I am still not sure whether it was necessary, or whether David was just providing me with something to do. It certainly did seem rather strange that he should have left it to the last minute.

I was allowed a sleeping pill that night, as was everyone on trial. I did get off to sleep all right, but I awoke in the early hours, feeling extremely ill, and got no more sleep after that. I thought at the time that the terrible stomach upset I was suffering was due to nerves, and only discovered the next morning that all the women who had eaten chicken curry for lunch were suffering an attack of food poisoning. Fortunately for me, I had not eaten very much curry, so my attack of food poisoning was mild compared to some people's, but it was still a very unsettling thing to happen just before the trial.

I could eat no breakfast, but that strong, sweet coffee slipped to me on the quiet by Sister was marvellous! Because of my previous behaviour on court days, and because of the strain I was obviously feeling (though I never did break down and throw a fit, which I thought was an achievement, and a sign of how much more in control I was at the end of my time in Pucklechurch than the beginning), the sister in charge kindly agreed that I could go to court from the wing and not through the reception procedure. This was a great privilege, often allowed to people on the hospital wing who were considered to be a risk either to themselves or each other, or to the smooth running of the reception procedure. Josie was never allowed, as far as I can remember, to go through reception, because she was such a potentially explosive person. Josie was very annoyed about that, as she wanted to have the opportunity to meet other girls from the other wings. I was highly delighted not to have to go near the place.

My clothes and belongings had been taken from me the previous day, for checking and packing as usual, except certain things which I left with Gillian. By this time I had come to terms with the fact that the trial was not going to be over in one day, and that I would be returning to Pucklechurch that night. If, by some miracle, I had been allowed to go free, I would not have cared about my possessions, mostly toiletries to which Gillian was welcome. The clothes I was going to wear in court were brought to me after the breakfast things had been collected (until then I only had my night things to wear, as was usual).

I was able to dress peacefully and in privacy, and I was not

143

subjected to the horror of having to display my naked self to an officer. If I could be trusted on some occasions, why not on all? I was kept locked up while the others went out on exercise and began to clean their cells. I had nothing to do. I was re-reading *To Kill a Mockingbird*, but I could not concentrate. All I could do was wait, fighting to control myself, until the officers came for me a little after 9.30. The others had gone to class by then, Gillian having wished me luck as she went.

I was put into the taxi, and driven out through the gates for the first time since that Friday in July when I had finally been committed for trial. It felt a little odd to be out, but as I was naturally in a state of increasing apprehension, I did not register much of what was going on about me. I have no memories at all of those three journeys from Pucklechurch to the court, except that on the second day one of the officers with me (there were two officers each day, and a sister in case I threw a fit) opened her newspaper and I saw the headlines concerning me. She should never have done this, and it naturally upset me. I remember that and nothing else.

If I had thought about it at all, I suppose I assumed that I would be taken to the same building which had housed the magistrates' courts; but I was in fact taken back to the scene of my first night in captivity, the police cells. I was put into a cell opposite the one I had been in all those months ago. After a while, my solicitor and my barrister came together to see me, trying to exude confidence, and giving me a couple of shrewd looks to assess my nervous state. I was still feeling queasy, the officers explained about the food poisoning, and my lawyers went to arrange with the judge that if I felt ill I might leave the courtroom.

After what seemed an interminable length of time, I was unlocked, taken up to the court and the trial began. Those three days were unlike any in the rest of my life. I counted it as fortunate that I had done a long spell of jury service in the past so that the courtroom formalities and procedures were known to me. Had that not been the case, it would have been all the more overpowering and frightening than it was. It was agony to me to be in the dock, hating the limelight at all times, and I found it unbearable to be the centre of attention. I dared not turn my head to look at the public behind me, but it sounded as though there were an awful lot of people there. The vultures of the press were much in evidence, and unfortunately I could see them clearly, licking their pencils and their lips, waiting to make money out of another person's suffering. I remember how they all rushed out of court at the end of the day, as though we were in a bad film. How once, when my eyes met those of one of them, he looked away, as a cat does. How they were lying in wait for me when I was taken up to the car at the end of the day, and I was given Sister's coat to put over my head, and how I sat in the car with my head on my knees while they let off flashlights at me. How they persecuted my family, as if my family had not enough to bear, and laid siege to my husband in our house so that he could not open the door for fear of the photographer lurking outside.

Something must be done about the press. I understand that in a free country there must be a free press, but to capitalize as the gutter press does by gloating over those who cannot hit back, from the Royal Family to a prisoner on trial, is another thing. In addition, they have unfair power. Because I was mercifully shielded from them by the strong walls of Pucklechurch, and my family would not talk to them, they went round the village and the school, picking up gossip and tittle-tattle. Most of it was trivial in the extreme, much of it was utterly untrue. This they printed, and everyone who read it probably accepts it as the truth. The newspaper cuttings of the case were sent with me to Styal, I suppose in lieu of a proper report. I saw them on my file in the psychiatrist's office at Styal. Those cuttings had become the 'facts of the matter', which they certainly were not.

Worse, when I was summoned to the Department of Education and Science to account for myself, I was asked questions which surprised me. When I said, 'Where did you get that from?' I was told that they had studied the newspaper reports of the case. Marvellous. So now the DES has it on file, to take one example, that I used to leave school early on a Friday, to pick up my husband from the station. In fact, quite the opposite is true. Working in London, my husband used to arrive at Stroud station at anything after six o'clock, depending on how late the train was. I used to hang about at school when everyone else had gone. In the summer I sometimes played tennis, in the winter I used to hope that there would be the usual Friday group of people

145

in the staffroom with whom I could chat till one by one they left. I wonder which of my colleagues could possibly have told the press that I went early on a Friday. So many people know that to be untrue, yet that is what the DES has on file, because this is what was reported by the press.

It was not just the gutter press which amazed me by its reporting. The good lady who reported the case for the *Observer* went so far as to criticize my clothes, commenting on the fact that I wore the 'same drab coat' for the three days of the trial, in contrast to the 'pretty clothes' worn by my daughters. The fact is that my daughters were in their early twenties, and I an ageing forty-five-year-old, and that one of my daughters appeared on one day in a bright red skirt which I considered totally unsuitable for her, never mind for me. As to the same drab coat, what ignorance of the remand system that phrase reveals. We were allowed one set of clothes for court. We were allowed one coat. All my other clothes were 'packed', that is to say screwed up in those dreadful white plastic bags which accompanied me backwards and forwards from court for the three days. And 'all' my other clothes were the two other sets of clothing we were allowed. Perhaps the reporter would have preferred me to appear in court in jeans and a shirt? Nor did I think the coat was drab when I bought it at great expense for a special occasion some years before. But even if it was, what on earth has my dress sense got to do with the point at issue, which I thought was my guilt or innocence of the crime of which I was accused? Sometimes I wonder about the *Observer*.

It had been the publicity which I had been dreading more than anything else, not so much because it would hurt me, but because it would hurt my ex-colleagues and my family. Which it did. My ex-headmaster went to all the trouble he could to stress that he was just that: my *ex*-headmaster, and that I had nothing whatsoever now to do with the school. He had asked for my resignation in July, and I had of course given it. The press, however, without caring about the effect on the school, gave its name with glee. What purpose that served, I cannot imagine. I still cannot come to terms with the fact that what I did was more interesting to the press because of who I was. I was hardly ever referred to by my name alone, always my ex-title was used as if that somehow made the whole thing more shameful. I do not know what I think about that, even now. I never thought of myself as being a position first and then a person. I thought of myself as a person who happened to hold a certain position in order to earn the money necessary for living. The fact that I loved my job, was good at it, and always felt grossly overpaid for being so happy seems to me beside the point, which was that there was a separation between me as a person and me as a teacher. Was this wrong? Ought I to have been at more pains to become a teacher first and a person second?

So the disgrace I felt was the disgrace of me, the person. But the press found it much more dramatic to present it as the disgrace of a teacher, as though teachers were somehow unlike other folk and should be judged by different rules. I am by no means convinced that what happened to me in any way hurt my young ex-pupils. If anything I imagine they were given the benefit of an instructive lesson upon aspects of life which might not have previously occurred to them. That it hurt the school I am very sure, and I bitterly regret. That it made life very difficult for my colleagues I am also sure, and also regret. One of the sisters once said to me abrasively that I should have thought of that before I did it. There was no use replying.

The first day of the trial passed in the selection of the jury and the presentation of the evidence against me. By the time that was over I was both certain that I would go to prison for a million years, so vile a criminal had I been portrayed; and also furious at the slant that had been put on the evidence. I had said to my solicitor that I did not think that I could go into the witness box, which he had dismissed with 'We'll see how you feel when it comes to it'. Wise man. I had been so vilified on the first day that I was determined to have my say. Whether they believed me or not didn't matter. I was merely determined that I was not going to tolerate all that without replying.

From my point of view one of the best things which happened on that first day was being allowed to have a long time with my daughters at the end of the day. The officers didn't lock me up, I was allowed to sit right away from the cells in a little cubby hole, and both my daughters were allowed to stay with me until my transport back to Pucklechurch came. I felt almost free. I was able to hand over a lot of my things, because technically when I was at court I was not subject to the Pucklechurch rules of having to ask Chief's permission. When at court, you were in a kind of limbo, neither free nor in a remand centre, so long chats with relatives and the handing over of things to be taken home were allowed.

I remember the trips back to Pucklechurch from the court because of having to face the photographers the first day, and being afraid of having to on the other two days. But in fact they were only there the once, and they never did get a picture of me. I cannot at all remember whether or not I had to go through the reception process. I know I went into reception, because I remember them tipping out and checking my money while I sat at the table, and I saw a twenty pence piece for the first time. I remember being shut in the horse box for nearly an hour on one occasion, but I can't remember at all which day it was. I know that by the end of the hour I was on the verge of screaming. The officer kept going by and saying 'Sorry, Audrey, not long now. I'm being as quick as I can.' But I had my watch on, and I know how long I was shut up for in that horse box which was three feet wide and about five feet long. There were some magazines, but as they had my glasses outside that wasn't much help. Anyway, I didn't want to be shut up like that after a day in court. I think I was allowed to go on to the wing without the bath and hairwash routine, but I can't really remember much about it.

I know that when I finally got back to the safety of the wing, the staff were really kind to me, and allowed me to go into Gillian's cell and be locked up with her until it was bathtime. That made the world of difference to me, being able to talk to Gillian about it on both the first two days. I was expecting to have to tell her everything, but the local radio had been issuing full bulletins, and she knew how far the trial had got. She let me talk, though, and I think she was really genuinely interested, especially in the way things were done. She, of course, was facing a much longer and more complex trial than mine. She wanted to know what it was like in the dock, what the jury were like, how often the judge looked at me, whether I could easily attract my solicitor's attention: things like that. Telling her was very good for me, and I hope it helped her prepare her mind for her own ordeal.

I was no more restless on those trial evenings than on other recent evenings. On the first night I slept really well, because I was allowed a sleeping pill again, and also because I was exhausted not only by the events of the day but also by the broken night I had had the night before as a result of the food poisoning.

On the second day, I was in the witness box most of the day. I wish I could say I was telling my story, but of course the law does not work like that. You are not allowed to tell your story, you can only answer questions put to you. Before I was put on trial I had great faith in the English legal system born of total ignorance of it. We assume that the courts work hard to elicit the truth, and to deal with defendants accordingly. I no longer think that they do. I think that there have been, probably in recent years particularly, a very large number of travesties of justice played out in our courts. I think that at this moment there are a very large number of completely innocent people suffering punishment in our prisons for crimes which they did not commit. As pressure builds on the police to secure a reasonable number of convictions in the present situation of steadily rising crime rates, the aim seems to have become to secure a conviction, almost regardless of what the truth of the matter really is.

I do not understand the law, or the rules by which the game is played in the courtroom. I only know that the original intention was that the two parties should be brought together before twelve of their peers, that the two stories should be heard, and that the jury should decide between them. This no longer happens. There are incomprehensible rules of evidence. Although my barrister gave me ample opportunity to tell the parts of my story which he thought ought to be told, at no time was I allowed to tell the whole thing in my own way. This is not a criticism of my barrister; this is how the system works. Yet I think that all those people to whom I have been allowed to tell my own story in my own way have believed me.

I am sure that if the jury and I had been allowed to communicate with each other in a human way, without the barrier of the mystery of the law coming in between, they would have believed me too. I do not think that the jury system is effective in present-day circumstances. Recent cases have demonstrated over and over again how a jury is capable of convicting against common sense, or on the basis of insufficient evidence. This may be the law, but it is not justice. I do not think juries are capable any longer of doing the job they are supposed to do. The procedure has got too complicated, too technical, too professional for the ordinary common sense of the ordinary man to be able to deal with, which is surely the idea behind the system.

I have been pretty disillusioned with juries ever since I served on one. I know how they work. When we deliberated, one woman got out her knitting and took no part except to agree with everything that anyone said, regardless of how contradictory it was. One juror with a dominant personality had made up his mind that our man was guilty, and he steamrollered anyone who ventured the opposite opinion. Our deliberations wore on, and one woman who clearly thought the man was innocent kept looking at her watch and worrying about her children, now home from school. In the end she declared 'guilty', more, I am sure, because then she could get home than because she had been so persuaded.

The concept of trial by jury should therefore in my opinion be reconsidered. I am not in the least perturbed that I was found guilty by mine; it only serves to show that juries can often be wrong. I think of my jury as being twelve pudding-headed Bristolians, but that may be being unkind. They were probably so overawed by the technical expertise of the police that they could see no further. And, as I have said, my barrister did not have a fair chance because I would not let him use all the available evidence. I am sure I had as fair a trial as anyone gets. I am not complaining about my trial in particular (and I did not appeal after it), but I do think that it is high time that the legal profession reformed itself. If it does not, like the sixteenth-century church and the twentieth-century trade unions, someone else will eventually do it for them. Meanwhile, the innocent suffer. That I know; and I suspect that the guilty also get away.

I found giving evidence very hard, both because I did not really wish to discuss my private life in public, and because I hated having to stand there all alone, and being absolutely the centre of attention. I was nervous the whole time, and had to keep moistening my lips with my tongue in what I had hitherto thought was a classic sign of a guilty conscience. I was plagued with people insisting on trivialities: the prosecution at one time produced, like a rabbit from a hat, a piece of evidence – that I had access to my children's money – so amazingly trivial I could not believe that they could be trying to make the point that they were. Whether I had or had not made absolutely no difference to anything as far as I could see, and being pushed about so trivial a point when there were far more important things to talk about upset me. On another occasion the judge himself intervened: there was quite a little disturbance as to whether I had described someone as 'tired and old' or 'tired and ill'. As the person in question at the time in question looked both old and tired and ill, again I could not see what earthly difference it made, but I had obviously offended some legal sacred cow.

From time to time I looked at my solicitor for some guidance as to whether I was doing as I should, but his face remained utterly impassive throughout. Once I looked up to the public gallery in search of moral support from my family. They looked tired and old and ill too, all three of them! I did not look again. Out of the corner of my eye I could see the press scratching away, which in itself was enough to put anyone off. The prosecuting counsel had a particularly baneful stare with which he fixed me from time to time. I kept getting the feeling that he was overacting, and would burst into laughter at any minute. I was tired with standing up for so many hours after having to sit down all the time for so long at Pucklechurch.

I was very glad indeed when it was all over.

The third morning of the trial was devoted to the judge's summing up, and a long boring morning it was too. It was me he was talking about, and I couldn't get very interested in what he was saying. I wasn't really listening, so when my family discusses how fair he was (or in their view, was not), I cannot add very much, because I was just sitting there wishing he would finish so that we could get to the only bit which interested me by then: was I going home or to prison? I only hope the jury wasn't as bored as I was. The officers beside me had the fidgets too.

At last the judge sent the jury away to consider their verdict, and I was taken down to the cells again to await their pleasure. Ominously, I had been put that morning in exactly the same cell as I had been given when I was first arrested. One of the officers with me was the same one who had seen me into Pucklechurch on my first day there. I did not know whether all this was a neat rounding up, the end to be similar to the beginning, or whether it was a quiet warning to me that the cycle was going to begin again. I was expecting to have to wait quite a long time, and so were the officers, who got out their thermos flasks and settled down to a leisurely lunch. I suppose I was given lunch, but I can't remember. I had eaten on the two previous days, and I had enjoyed it. Food in the police cells is rather better than food in Pucklechurch.

To my horror, the jury were out for only just over half an hour. I knew then, when I was sent for so quickly, that they were going to find me guilty, and I could not stop myself crying at the unfairness of it. We went up to the dock, along the dreary corridor with an immensely high ceiling, painted a hideous shade of green. There was a slight altercation on the way up the stairs to the dock between the two officers and the sister accompanying me. Previously the sister had sat next to me on one side, with one officer also next to me, and one beyond the sister. Now the officers could see that I was getting upset, and they wanted to change the seating so that there was one of them on each side of me, and the sister on the end of the row. The sister could also see that I was getting upset, and wanted to stay next to me, but the officers would not let her. Goodness knows what they thought I was going to do. I don't. I was far too old and out of condition to make a break for it. But, like the early days, I could not stop crying.

Everyone took their places and the jury filed in. Not one of them looked at me. I knew anyway that they were going to convict, and I watched them come in. A jury will never look at a prisoner it is going to convict; that is old prison lore. They made me turn and face the jury, and the officers took firm hold of me, whether to stop me collapsing or to restrain me, I do not know. But I found it very comforting. I kept telling myself over and over again that it didn't matter, whatever the jury said, they could not make an innocent person guilty, except legally. Morally, nothing they said could alter my position. I had done what I had done, and I had not done what I had not done, and if the whole world rose up and shouted 'guilty', I would still be innocent. None the less it is an awful thing to stand in the dock and hear yourself pronounced guilty.

Somewhere behind me, I could hear the sounds of ill-restrained sobbing. I knew it was one or other of my family. My younger daughter later apologized to me for it, but I couldn't blame her, as I couldn't stop snivelling myself. I wish I had been able to. I wish I could have stood there with my head up, and, like Sidney Carton, faced with pride that I was there because I was shielding someone else. But it didn't seem like a far far better thing; it seemed like a sordid miserable mistake. I heard my barrister's plea in mitigation. He concentrated on the fact that I would never work again, I had destroyed my career, my life, everything. It didn't seem to matter much; I felt as though he was talking about someone else. I did not really expect to be sent to prison, because my solicitor had been so positive that I would not be.

But with judges you never know, and I was sent to prison for two years, one year suspended. Even as he was saying it, I was working out that this meant only another three months, as I had done five on remand, and I would get four months' remission for good conduct. As the sentence was passed, I can't remember feeling either relieved or dismayed. My life had been out of my own control for so long now that it seemed natural in a way that I should be going back to Pucklechurch. On the other hand, I had very much wanted to go home. Three months was not a long time: I knew I could 'handle it' inside.

I was helped by two things. First, the knowledge that my life had been ruined anyway, long before any of this happened. The worst time had been the year before I was arrested. Going to prison was a minor thing compared with the shattering emotional collapse I had suffered, and from which I was still suffering. Nothing really touched me, nothing really mattered. I was sorry for the guilt and shame, but I had been hurt so badly before that my soul was scar tissue, and scar tissue, though it may be ugly, at least has the benefit that it cannot feel. Secondly, there was the knowledge that at the end I had done the decent thing, and I was going to prison now because I had refused to drag another person through the courts to save myself. It still didn't make me feel like Sidney Carton, but it helped.

I was put back into the cell. My solicitor and my barrister came to me together, and I am ashamed to say that I greeted them with 'Why did you not let me plead guilty?' It seemed to me that the whole thing had been a quite useless three-day charade. Here I was going to prison anyway, so I might as well have pleaded guilty on the first day and got it over without all the publicity. Then I recovered myself and thanked them. They had done their best, but mine had been an impossible case, since protecting myself had not been my first priority. I must say that they both looked genuinely upset and unhappy, as if they really cared about having lost the case. I think they were more distressed than I was. I was just reacting emotionally to the stress rather than deeply disturbed by what had happened.

I never saw my barrister again. David continued to be a good friend to me up to and after I was released. He came to see me after the trial, when I was still at Pucklechurch, and I saw him in his office after my release. I had been told by people at Pucklechurch that he was a very good solicitor, and certainly if I were ever in trouble again I would go to him. To a large extent I see now that he saved me from myself by pressurizing me to plead not guilty, thereby allowing myself the opportunity to present at least some of the case so that the judge would have the chance to make his own estimate of my character and sentence me accordingly.

Given that I had to go to prison at all, I certainly got a very light sentence. One of the officers told me that the last person she had known convicted of the same offence had got eleven years; and only the week before, a man who had been on trial at Reading was sentenced to seven years. So it is a tribute to my lawyers that I was given effectively only another three months in prison. Sometimes now I wonder what I would have done if I had got a longer sentence. The answer, I suppose, is that I would just have got on and done it. Once I got to Styal, I found that most people there had longer sentences than mine, and you just stayed there until the required time had gone by. It was not a bad life: I could have handled a longer sentence. We are all in one prison or another anyway. At Styal, my freedom to go away from the place was curtailed. Now I can go, geographically speaking, wherever I want to, but I am still in a prison of another sort. Limitations are still upon me as they are upon us all. I could no more visit Bali now than I could visit Blackpool then. An interesting word, freedom.

When my solicitor and barrister had gone, my family was allowed to come down and see me. They had all been crying. It was made worse by the fact that I was kept locked up in the cell, which was a shock to them. They had not seen me literally behind bars before. I sensed the unspoken horror on my daughters' part that Pucklechurch might look like this, and I assured them that it did not; the cells were locked, but they were only little rooms, and there were not even bars on the windows, just exceptionally strong and narrowly spaced glazing bars. They seemed very relieved to hear this. There was not much to say. I knew I was allowed a reception visit, so arranged that they would come to see me tomorrow, if they were able to. Then male officers arrived, seemingly anxious to get my family out of the back way because of the photographers lying in wait in the front. They did not look after my family very well, because they were seen and chased half way round Bristol by the press. I think that some better arrangements should be made to protect the innocent families of convicted prisoners from this sort of harassment.

In due course I was whisked off back to Pucklechurch in a taxi. I felt absolutely shattered. I felt betrayed by the legal system. It was too early for anger, though that was to come. But I felt better than I had often done when I came back from a session at the magistrates' court. At least I was no longer crying. I arrived back in the middle of the afternoon, while everyone was in association. The staff treated me with kid gloves, as though I might explode any minute. I have a clear memory of the sister's face as she came forward to receive me on to the wing. She was so clearly wondering whether I ought to be put straight into strips, that I said, 'It's all right, Sister, I'm not going to have a fit'. So she took me to my cell and locked me in. I seem to remember that all my things were still in reception, and I had nothing to do but lie on the bed and think. I was very tired, and I think I dozed off at one point, but was awoken by the officer bringing my things up from reception. That gave me something to do, to tidy everything up and put it away in my locker. My locker seemed very empty now that all sorts of odds and ends had gone home with my family. I really did have the irreducible minimum now.

The others came back from association, and Gillian came straight to see me. No need to tell her what had happened, the radio had already done that. Gillian said that it had even been on the television that afternoon, but that Josie, as soon as she realized what they were going to say, had leapt to the set and changed channels in a sweet attempt to safeguard what was left of my privacy. I asked Gillian to see if she could get me unlocked (we were talking through the peephole in the door). The staff seemed a little reluctant to let me out, but at last they did, and I was absorbed again into the Pucklechurch routine as if I had never left it.

There were differences though. For one thing, everyone now knew what I was 'in' for, and their attitude to me altered subtly. I think that most people had assumed that I was in for some harmless offence; as I have said before, they were all far too occupied with their own crimes to worry about mine. But now they had seen the extensive press coverage, and they looked at me as if they couldn't quite believe it. Neither could I, so that was all right. Miss Piggy in particular changed her attitude from indifference to a grudging respect, but then Miss Piggy would. She liked a bit of drama and notoriety, did Miss Piggy! Knowing that I had been a teacher had a sobering effect upon the young. How right I had been to suppress all the facts before!

There were other differences too, notably those brought about by the sudden increase in Pucklechurch's population. The wing became more and more crowded, and at the weekend Gillian and I were moved from the single rooms we had had for so many months to a double room at the staircase end of the corridor. They put us in together because they knew we would give no trouble, though of course they should not have done, as I was a convicted criminal now, and Gillian was still under the theoretical presumption of innocence. We used to joke about the unsuitable company innocent remand prisoners had to keep, but I was getting quite bitter about it. Every cell door had a card slipped into a little holder which reminded me of the card holders by the clock in a factory. On this was written mostly 'Unconvicted Prisoner' and details such as name, date of next court appearance, type of court. But my card now said 'Convicted Prisoner', and that upset me every time I set eyes on it.

Gillian and I got on well in our shared cell, though obviously in some ways it was better to be alone. But it was nice to have someone to talk to, particularly as it looked as if we were in for a lot of locking up with so many people on the wing. I would have hated to share with someone I did not know, but Gillian and I were all right together. We did not stay alone together for long though; I think that we were only in the shared room for two or three nights when we were unlocked one evening and told to move again, this time to an even bigger room with four bunks in it. We shared with another person, and then later on the fourth bunk was also filled. The wing was bursting at the seams and this was very worrying to me, because I was afraid that I would be transferred away from the hospital wing on to B2 with the other convicted girls, and I dreaded this more than anything.

When I had seen the chief on the morning after my conviction (she automatically saw everyone who had been to court the next day), I had asked to be allowed to remain at Pucklechurch for the few months I had left to do, and also that I might remain on the hospital wing. This was along the lines of better the devil I knew than that I was particularly fond of the hospital wing. If I had to be transferred from Pucklechurch altogether, I had asked to go to Styal, as my younger daughter lived in Manchester and could visit me easily. The chief said that she would have put me down for an open prison, which meant that they trusted me to behave, but I preferred to go closer to my daughter, as I had heard grim tales of the travelling involved for relatives visiting at Drake Hall Open Prison which is where I would probably have been sent.

So I found all the new people on the wing not only unsettling, but also a personal threat, as I could see very clearly that I was number one on the transfer list. As it happened, it was better for me to be moved to Styal, where I was a lot happier than I had ever been at Pucklechurch, but at that time I was dreading transfer, either to B2 or away altogether.

In fact, I was only to stay at Pucklechurch after my trial for eighteen days, and each of those days was spent wondering and worrying about when I would be moved. We were very crowded in our room, with four of us in there, especially at mealtimes, when there was not really room for us to eat at our little tables. I still had a part-constructed jigsaw on my table, and there it had to stay, so at mealtimes I put a 'tablecloth' in the form of a sheet of newspaper over it and ate on top of that. Apart from mealtimes, we mostly settled on our bunks in true 'Porridge' style, because there simply wasn't room for four people to move about the cell. There was nowhere to put anything, especially

157

wet washing, and I hated having other people's knickers dripping off the radiator on to my bunk. I had the bottom bunk below Gillian, which provided a merciful release from the orange light, but also meant it was dark to see to read, and I used to lie the wrong way round on the bunk to get as much light as I could from the window.

Not that there was much peace and quiet, either: with four people in one room someone was usually talking. The fourth person was very young, and seemed to come from a good family: certainly she had unbelievable amounts of food brought in at her daily visits, which she shared out well with everyone. As I was the one who usually told her to shut up, because she went on and on and on all day and most of the night, I never took any of her goodies. Having had my cover 'blown', and been exposed as a schoolteacher, I found myself behaving like one again. It had been a great relief to be able to lay down the mantle of authority which I have lugged round all these years; now I found it a protection to take it up again, and I almost consciously began to speak as I would at school, especially with the young ones or with anyone who annoyed me. My husband says that this habit of addressing people as though they were schoolchildren is one of my less endearing traits, and I can well believe it. It works, though. People tend to leave me alone, which is what I wanted then.

For the first few days, I was allowed to follow the normal routine with everyone else. We spent a normal weekend, and on Monday and Tuesday we had class and association as usual. On the Tuesday afternoon, the stress which had been building inside me came to a head. There was one woman there whom I had hated long before my trial. She was ill and could not help herself, but that did not make her easier to bear. Her illness took the form of talking and behaving as if she was in a position above even the staff, and certainly above us. She used to tell the sisters publicly that the standards of their work and cleanliness were not high enough, and the sisters found her a terrible trial. She was given to throwing all her possessions out of her cell window, and then complaining because her clothes were damp. Hitherto, she had left me alone, apart from causing me the one sleepless night already mentioned. Had she continued to leave me alone, I would have silently put up with her phoney airs and graces, her phoney tone of authority, her pretence that she had worked as a state registered nurse in a hospital, her insistence that she was not a prisoner like the rest of us, but she had been asked to stay in Pucklechurch by some elevated personage like the Home Secretary to make a report on the place. When we pointed out that the card outside her door said 'Convicted Prisoner', she got very upset, took the card out, tore it up, and refused to have a card at all, which was an offence. The sister took to putting her name on pieces of ordinary paper, but she wouldn't have them either, and tore them up too. What she had done I have no idea, as she told so many stories, not one word in twenty of which was likely to be true. She was quite potty.

On this Tuesday afternoon, she was sitting fairly close to me, going on and on in her false upper-class accent about the lack of hygiene in the place, and getting on everyone's nerves, not just mine. I was sitting on the other side of the table, trying to get on with my knitting and feeling less and less in control of myself. She suddenly said to me, in the haughtiest of tones, 'And you. You there. You do not take your knitting out of class in the mornings, you are to put it in the cupboard as everyone else does. You are not to bring it in here ever again.'

I intended to injure her if I could. I have never lost control so completely, and I can only repeat that in normal life I am not a violent person. I put my knitting down, and I went for her. Only two things stopped me: the table between us, and the fact that Gillian had realized that I meant business and caught hold of my arm. The sisters knew an emergency when they saw one, and one of them came to help Gillian with me while the other went to the cause of the trouble. She had seen her end in my eyes and had fallen silent. I am very ashamed now to have to admit that I had to be forcibly restrained from fighting another woman. It is probably the thing I am most ashamed of in all my life.

I often think about that episode now. I know all the excuses that can be made for me, all the pressures and stresses I was under. Yet I still feel that to lose control to that extent was unpardonable. It frightens me, for, I repeat, I am not a violent person. I also like to think that I am a civilized and sophisticated person. Yet on that occasion I was within an inch of getting involved in the kind of disgusting physical brawling which in real life I regard with horror.

Nor do I think I can claim to have been 'brutalized' by my experiences. I think it was worse that that. I think that, without my knowing it for all these years, there are things in my makeup which do not bear close examination. And of all the explaining of myself which I shall have to do if I meet my parents the other side of the grave, this will be the hardest. Going to prison for something I did not do will not worry them too much, but intending a physical assault on someone else will! It worries me.

I had no chance of hurting her of course. She was younger, bigger and stronger than I was, and no doubt would have sorted me out very quickly had we actually come to blows. But that is immaterial; the point is still that I intended serious violence. In the event, the sisters realized full well that she was the cause of the incident: never would I have sought to attack her had I not been provoked. It was she who was taken out of the association room to be locked up in her cell, and I was left, having apologized to the sisters for my behaviour.

That was the last time I entered that room, either for class or association. The following day the sister in charge came back on duty after her days off, and I was told that in future I was to be the wing cleaner and work for my living. I had expected this. All convicted prisoners were supposed to work, and at Pucklechurch there was little work to do apart from cleaning. I had worked it out some time earlier that I would be wing cleaner. Fortunately, I was only there for two weeks. I say fortunately, because although there were definite advantages of being wing cleaner, there were definite disadvantages too, and on the whole I was pretty sick of cleaning corridors and washrooms.

The advantages were that I could work in peace by myself. I was also unlocked and out of our overcrowded cell for most of the day, as cleaners were unlocked most days so that the cleaning could be done. The others were in fact locked up a lot during that fortnight, though not every day. When they were over at class, I had the place to myself, and very peaceful it was too. The reputation I had acquired of being a 'good little worker' meant that the sisters mostly left me alone, and assumed that I was doing something somewhere. In fact I spent a lot of time having extended breaks in the chairs at the end of the corridor, indulging my favourite pastime of staring out of the window. I had decided that if this was to be my life for three months, I was not going to kill myself trying to keep the whole place clean. I preferred to work really hard for a time and then have an extended rest.

The disadvantages of being cleaner on the hospital wing were that some of the jobs were downright disgusting. There were two people who deliberately fouled themselves and their cells while I was cleaner, and it was my job to go in once a day while the person concerned was having a bath, at court or otherwise out of the way, and clean up the mess. One girl used to pull all the plaster off the walls of her cell, and crumble it up into the general 'goo' of spilled tea and urine on her floor. This mess was indescribable, and of course I was not allowed to use anything other than a broom and a scrubbing brush. No long-handled mops were allowed: it was down on the floor on hands and knees. I think that this was excessive, and should not have been asked of anyone. The second girl, Delia, made an even worse mess, because she added faeces, spittle, phlegm and vomit to the urine, and she did not pull off the plaster to soak it up, so that her cell was often awash. To be fair, some of the nurses would sometimes go in with their long-handled mop and wipe the floor first, but then I would have to go in and finish it off on my hands and knees. I used to do the first bit standing up, cleaning a place big enough to kneel in, and then working slowly outwards. I was allowed rubber gloves (if I asked for them) and a kneeler. Knowing that the buckets, cloths and kneelers in the cupboard had been used to do this sort of work, I had long hidden the things I used to clean my cell with where other people couldn't find them. The thought of doing the floor of my cell with a cloth that had been used to clean out a filthy cell upset me, and yet that was something else the staff didn't care about. I bet they wouldn't have had the Pucklechurch cleaning materials anywhere near their own floors, but we were not supposed to mind.

I rebelled one afternoon. Emboldened by the knowledge that I was to be transferred to Styal the following day, I refused to clean this particularly filthy cell unless I was given clothes other than my own to wear, as I did not want to go to Styal with dirty clothes which had been worn to do a job like that. The nurses agreed with me: many of them thought that we had a raw deal cleaning on the hospital wing.

161

I was given a set of clothes from reception, and I got on and did the work. I did complain to the nurse on duty though, which much surprised her, as I never usually objected openly about anything. I said that I thought that nobody should be told to do such work, and she said that in the past they had sometimes got the work done by asking for volunteers from B2 and rewarding them with cigarettes. I said that I hoped that in future this work would be done by volunteers, and added for good measure that I was sure it was against the Geneva Convention and the European Community's Declaration of Human Rights to force convicted prisoners to do such work. I was by no means sure of any such thing, but it sounded impressive, and I was quite enjoying my totally uncharacteristic role as shop steward and troublemaker. It happened that Gillian was with me that afternoon, as there had been so much work that she had been asked if she wanted to help. Unconvicted prisoners could not be made to work, but often it was regarded as a treat to be allowed out to do something, especially if there had been a lot of locking up, which there had been that week. We had a constant background of wails from Josie that Audrey and Gillian were out again, and it wasn't fair . . .

Gillian was lugging mattresses about from one cell to another, and she passed me in the corridor. I was dressed in some fairly incredible purple trousers and a top which was at least size 22 (I am size 10), and I was leaning on my broom haranguing the nurse about the Geneva Convention, while the stench from the room I was supposed to be cleaning surrounded us. Gillian got a fit of the giggles and dropped the mattress. Then, being Gillian, she offered to do out the cell for me. But I was only making my point, and then went in to do the job. Nobody was going to say of me that I was too lily-livered to get my hands dirty with some real work. Afterwards, I went and had an illegal bath in a bathroom I knew was clean because I myself had cleaned it. I thought that if I was off to Styal the next day, I could behave as I liked for a bit.

I was having quite a good day for complaints. Only that morning I had led the protest to the sister on duty about a girl who had been moved into what used to be my room. She had a mania for cleanliness, and washed her pot out every morning. The trouble was that she washed it out, not in the sluice which was there for that purpose, but in one of the washbasins in which we would have to wash our faces. We had all complained to the girl concerned, and as that had got us nowhere, we had then tried to stop her from doing it. As she was a big West Indian woman with a reputation for violence, we didn't get very far, but the resulting racket brought Sister up to see what was going on. I was the spokeswoman and stated that it was not reasonable to expect us to wash ourselves in a basin with bits of faeces in it left over from this girl's pot washing. Sister was more concerned about preventing violence than with our complaint. I was the one who Sister shouted at, which I thought was very unfair. Again, because we were remand prisoners, we were not supposed to have finer feelings like that.

This was before I had known that I was to be moved, though I had suspected it. I had been sent for by the chief, and it seemed to me that all she could possibly be going to say was that I was moving. Had I just been going to B2, they would simply have told me to pack my things and an officer would have fetched me. Seeing the chief meant transfer out. And so it proved. Heaven knows why, I don't, I was so upset, but I stood there again crying while she told me I was going to Styal the following day. I think I did more crying during those five months at Pucklechurch than in all the rest of my life put together. I was very ashamed of it, but I could not stop. We were always told just the day before if we were to be moved, the theory being that then we would not have time to arrange a rescue. It led to problems, though. We were given one transfer letter which we could write and which they guaranteed would be posted that day. I wrote to my solicitor and asked him to let my family know.

I had been half-prepared for a move for so long that my few things were organized and ready to go when the officer came to take them to reception for the last time. My last Pucklechurch day passed very quickly. I now had a proper piece of paper with all the days marked on until 12 January 1983, and I crossed off my last Pucklechurch day, Tuesday, 26 October, just before my things went down to reception, although the day was only half way through.

I slept quite well that night. Now that it had happened, and I was going to have to move, I was able to come to terms with it. I was even

163

quite glad that the uncertainty had ended, though I was very apprehensive indeed about what life would be like in a real prison. I wish I had known then what I know now: how glad I would then have been to be moving.

In the morning I was 'woken' very early, although I was in fact already awake. I was marched off to reception, and not one of the nurses on duty came out of the staffroom to say goodbye and good luck, or whatever. Not one of them. I went through the beastly reception procedure for the last time at Pucklechurch, but at least I did not have to hang around until half past nine as I had been used to doing when going to court. We were to travel to Styal in a minibus it seemed, and it was not long after eight o'clock when I left Pucklechurch for the last time as a prisoner. The officer on the door chanted the litany 'Who are you and where are you going?', and I was able to reply with my name and 'Transfer to Styal', which of course she knew anyway. Into the minibus, and away out of those gates for the last time.

8 Transfer to Styal

I quite enjoyed the trip in the minibus as far as Drake Hall Open Prison. There was one other prisoner, who was bound for Drake Hall itself, and, I think, three prison officers. It was a bright sunny day, and after being cooped up for so long in Pucklechurch it was very pleasant to be out driving. The only unpleasant part was when we went past my house, clearly visible from the motorway, up on its hill. My daughter was there, probably still in bed that early in the morning, and my cats. I cried a little, in spite of trying very hard not to. But I recovered, and enjoyed the trip up the motorway I know so well from frequent trips to Manchester.

I did not think much of Drake Hall as we turned in the gate. I was impressed by the lack of security after the Colditz-like entrance to Pucklechurch. No fence, no wall, just a hedge. No high gates, just a half-barrier. But the prison itself appeared to be a series of huts in the grounds, resembling nothing so much as an army camp. The girl who was to stay there was taken away, and I was taken to the punishment block, which was the only place they could lock me up while I waited for the escort from Styal.

I was put into a cell and left there, with nothing to do, and no lunch. I had to wait a long time, nearly two hours, before I was unlocked at last. I had had nothing to eat, nothing to do, and there were no toilet facilities in the cell. I was very glad to hear the key turn, but soon revised my opinion when a very substantial officer from Styal strode into my cell. I found out afterwards that she was in fact quite popular, and was known to be willing to go out of her way to help, but that afternoon she created a very bad impression with me.

She said that she would have to search me. She took my coat as I was taking it off, went through the pockets, and dropped it on the floor. This made me instantly furious, but of course there was nothing whatever that I could do about it. I swallowed back the tears of anger and the words I might have wished to speak. She then did the same with my skirt and jersey, and at this point I caught the expressions on the faces of two of my Pucklechurch officers who had appeared in the doorway. They obviously thought it was a bit much to treat me like that. I had expected with such an officer to have a complete strip search, but fortunately she left me my underclothes. 'Right, get dressed', she said, and I ostentatiously picked up my coat from the floor, and laid it carefully on the bed before getting into my skirt and jersey again.

I still cannot see what the point of that performance was. I had been in the custody of prison officers all day; I had been strip searched at Pucklechurch before I left. What on earth did they think I had picked up, and from where? No doubt I would be searched again at Styal. It is unspeakably galling to be treated in such a way, with no attempt made to discover what sort of prisoner I was. To be helpless before authority wielded in such a way is like having to return to the helplessness of childhood. After a while, it dissolves one's adulthood, but the process is a painful one. I was never able to accept that I was not trusted to think for myself and do for myself, but must do as I was told by other people. I had ample opportunity to ponder the nature of their authority.

I was told to go and stand outside the cell in which I had been locked. I was expecting to be alone, and was somewhat shocked to see about a dozen other women. As usual, they looked me over and dismissed me as if I did not belong. I stood at the back of the line, and wanted only to be left alone. The girl next to me tried to start a conversation, and I wished later that I had been a bit more forthcoming, because it turned out that I was to share my first room in Styal with this Irish Maureen. At the time though, I was tired and hungry and extremely fed up. I had not been asked if I wanted to go to the toilet, and I was afraid to draw attention to myself by asking. I felt, and was behaving like, an eleven-year-old on her first day at the big school. These other women had come from Holloway, on transfer to Styal, and it was because their coach had arrived so late from London that I had had to wait so long.

We were sent outside to get on the coach, and there was a mad scramble for the back seat. The coach was more than half empty, with only a dozen of us and three officers from Styal. The first thing they did when they got on was to move people from the back to the front, separating a couple of groups. I had found a seat alone by the window and was left there. Then one officer went to sit at the back, and we were off. I decided that Styal was going to be exactly like school, and that it was maybe poetic justice that I should now be on the receiving end of the kind of discipline I had handed out for so long. We were being treated exactly as any teacher would treat a group of fourth formers on a coach trip.

Styal when we reached it looked more like a prison than Drake Hall. A groan went up from the many prisoners on the coach who had been there before, and who had spent the journey swapping stories with each other and the officers. It was getting dark, so I could not see all that much of the place. We were taken from the coach to reception, which was in an old building with large rooms divided to make smaller ones, but still with an impressive height of ceiling.

The reception officer dealt first with the people she knew, and in fact I was left until last. Then it was the usual performance: take all your clothes off, put the dressing gown on, leave all your clothes, go back and wait. Clothes are searched, you are searched, body, feet, hands. Right, get dressed again. Go through the property, trousers, jeans, shirts, three bras, three pants, and so on. I had many letters which had been sent to me at Pucklechurch after my trial, and which I had not yet been able to answer. I asked if I might take them, but was told that I could only have two recent letters; that the rest must stay in my property. I was very glad that I had used the opportunity of the trial to give most of my belongings to my children to take home. I had really very little with me now. My radio was, of course, taken away to be checked. They have some kind of obsession with checking radios, whether for secretly hidden drugs or because a radio can disguise a bomb, I never discovered. Both theories were currently rumoured among the prisoners.

Every prisoner entering Styal is issued with a bundle. This contains the blankets, sheets, toilet things and towels which accompany you round the prison thereafter. Into this bundle at reception you have to put the clothes and personal items you are taking with you. It becomes a very heavy and very unwieldy thing to carry. When I was through reception, a group of us started off with our bundles, under escort of course, down to the Assessment House.

Styal is not one building, but a campus of houses. Each house can accommodate about twenty-two inmates. They have changed the system now, but when I went there, every new prisoner went to the Assessment House for about a fortnight, where she was more broken into the Styal regime than assessed, though I have no doubt some of that went on as well. On the basis of that assessment, a woman was then transferred to one of the other houses, and given work. I had heard the old-timers on the coach pleading to be allowed to go to other houses straightaway, and I understood that Davies House was a place to be avoided. I could not avoid it though, and was taken up to a two-bedded dormitory which I was to share with Irish Maureen. She at once helped herself to the bottom bunk, which surprised me slightly, as I had always thought the top bunk was the desirable one. Not in prison, though. It is a lot easier to get back into a bottom bunk in a hurry, and avoid being caught out of bed by the night patrol.

The long delay at Drake Hall meant that it was now teatime – five o'clock. We were told to unpack quickly, and go down to tea. We also had to make our beds, and I made mine in a normal neat manner. Irish Maureen, muttering to herself, was performing amazing convolutions with her bedspread. A girl who had been at Pucklechurch with me shot in and asked questions about old friends still there. This girl, Susan, had been sent to Drake Hall initially, but had recently been transferred to Styal because she had had a parcel of drugs tossed over the hedge for her to pick up. Rumour of this had already reached Pucklechurch, so I knew all about it. I remember during a recent prison disturbance, in which men in several prisons all stopped work at once, some television pundit remarking that he could not see how men in geographically separated prisons knew what was going on in other prisons. We always knew most things of any import. Prisoners being transferred are a useful source of information, as also are new people coming in, who have been in contact with other people who have just come out.

Perhaps people outside forget that there is very little to do inside except talk. Information is important, and people spend their time exchanging news and gossip about their prison and other prisons. There is a witness to most things which happen – prisons are crowded places and news spreads like the proverbial wildfire. Visitors are also an important source of scandal, news, and hearsay, which always seems to have more than a little truth in it.

It is also worth mentioning that the criminal world does not seem to be very large. It was a constant source of surprise to me to see how many people knew each other. It was like an old girls' reunion at times in the common rooms at Styal. Everybody seemed to have been in with everybody else at some time in the past, and there were many occasions in which I felt thoroughly out of it. Irish Maureen was typical – she knew Holloway and Risley from being on remand in both; and she had been imprisoned several times in both Styal and Holloway.

We went down to tea. There were two dining rooms, each with a long table. We queued outside, and when all were present we were given our food by the officer, and told which dining room to sit in. This handing out of food by the officer is standard procedure: it ensures that the cook cannot get away with giving more or better food to a crony. (But there were ways round that, as I was to discover when I became a cook.) I stuck close to Irish Maureen, and did as she did. She soon became involved in a series of 'old girls' conversations with the others at our table. I sat quiet, and concentrated on my tea. It was only fish fingers, peas and chips, but it had been properly cooked, and I was surprised at the quality. The plates were the familiar red and blue plastic, and sugar came in eggcups as it did in Pucklechurch: the same red plastic eggcups, stamped EIIR on the bottom.

I was ill at ease about eating in public after eating for so long alone in my cell, and was afflicted with the nervousness which I sometimes get which makes my hand tremble so much that I cannot lift food to my mouth. I have often had to leave food uneaten for this reason, and of course it had been so bad at Pucklechurch that I had to request half a cup of tea only, or I would not have been able to drink at all. The others added to my nervousness by asking directly 'What are you in for?' I later found that it was a question which was not often asked, but I suppose in my case they wondered what on earth such a misfit could have done. I had been afraid that they would all have read the papers and would know what I had done, but I was to find for the most part they did not care. They had probably read the papers, but they were not really interested in other people's crimes, and the name meant nothing. The only people who were looked out for and quickly identified were those who had committed a crime involving children. Anyway, there was always the grapevine, and although I never told anyone what I had been convicted of, I was made aware, when I moved to Size House, that everybody knew.

On this occasion I mumbled that it wasn't serious, and I had only got three months to do, and they left me alone, probably dismissing me as a middle-aged shoplifter. I was older than the others, who were all in their early twenties, by about twenty years. If the question 'What are you in for?' was asked and evaded, they never pushed. The understanding was that people had a right to their privacy. Most people wanted to talk about what they had done sooner or later, and when people wanted to talk there was always someone to listen. But until you wanted to talk, you were left alone. Only the child beaters, child molesters or child murderers suffered from the nasty remarks, the refusal to sit 'next to her, Miss'; the deliberate exclusion from the companionship of the common room. Some of these women tried to say that they had done something other than what they had done, but it was no use: the papers had been read, the name noted, and the truth was spread abroad.

I was given a breakdown during my first exercise period of the child murderers we had in Styal, exactly how they had murdered their unfortunate children, what jobs they did, and what they looked like. The woman rumoured to be one of the worst offenders had a solitary job in the library, and would deliver newspapers to the houses each day. I must admit that I did not much want to talk to her either, once I had been told what she was supposed to have done. There was no open violence that I ever saw against any of these women. They were just ignored and shut out. A life sentence with that sort of treatment must be very hard to bear. No allowances whatsoever were made for anyone's state of mind at the time of the deed: if you harmed a child, that was that. No excuses.

Other murderers were more readily accepted. 'That's old Mary:

she did her old man in. She says she didn't, but she did, you know.'
The IRA terrorists, two of them new arrivals from Durham, seemed
to be accepted fairly well, though there was a feeling that they should
not be allowed to go free. The ritual for serious female offenders is
a long spell in the maximum security prison at Durham, then a
transfer to a closed prison like Styal, somewhat quaintly described as
a 'training prison' (though what on earth the training was escapes me),
then open prison, perhaps at Drake Hall, then freedom. All this could
take a number of years. The chief grievance at Styal about the IRA
girls was that they were the cause of fairly frequent scares when we
were all confined to our houses, as the IRA was rumoured to have
sworn to get the girls out by blowing a hole in the fence. These two
were serving sentences imposed after the Birmingham pub bombing.
We also had one of the people responsible for the Guildford pub
bombing. She was not much more than a girl when she had committed
the offence, and was held 'On Her Majesty's Pleasure', which is the
cruellest way to hold a prisoner. We all knew our release date; she did
not. We could count the days until the time of our release; she could
only wait, hoping at some time in the future she will be allowed to
go, and allowed to request a release date every few years.

After tea, as it was Wednesday, which was locker check night in
Styal, all we possessed had to be taken out of our lockers and laid out
on the bed for inspection. Never mind that I had just come in from
reception, Wednesday night was kit check night, and that was that.
So I unpacked again. The time spent waiting for the officer to come
and do the check was filled with washing the locker, and washing
meant washing. Every part of it had to be thoroughly cleaned. The
first time I did not mind, as at least then I knew that my things were
in a clean locker, but, as kit check succeeded kit check nearly every
other night on Davies House, it got a bit wearing. The officer on duty
would feel into all the most inaccessible parts of the locker, to make
sure that they were wet, and check that visible parts were shining
clean. It was 'bull' for the sake of 'bull', and nothing else.

When all my belongings had been checked against my card and
found to be present, I was taken to task for the state of my bed.
Immaculately made by any ordinary standards, it didn't do for Styal.
The blankets had to be put on in such a way that the coverlet could

be tucked round them with hospital corners at the bottom, and the pillow folded neatly into it at the top. Had the coverlets been six inches longer, it would have been an easy matter to produce the desired result. However, either by accident or design, they were just that little bit too short, so that to produce hospital corners at the bottom and a correct fold round the pillow at the top was extremely difficult – and I am by nature a neat person!

Now I understood what Irish Maureen had been muttering about as she struggled with her bed before tea! It was also another reason why the bottom bunk was preferable to the top one in Styal, for it was the top bunk where neatness or otherwise was at once apparent to an officer coming into the room. Irish Maureen used to have terrible troubles with her bunk. We did them together, first hers then mine, and you could always tell which side of the bed I had done and which she had struggled with. I was always getting told off for her efforts with my bed. But it was easier to share the making of the bunks, particularly the top one, so I held my peace and did not complain to her. Sometimes I used to catch myself becoming really agitated about this matter of the bunks, and it was easy to lose all sense of proportion over it. When I moved into Size House I discovered that it was only on Davies House that the staff were obsessional about the bunks. The same rules applied throughout the prison, but it was up to each house officer how she enforced them.

What was the reason behind the attitude of the staff on Davies? I could never work out whether they were just petty-minded (well, bastards is the word which springs as readily to my mind as it did to many people's lips then); or whether they were simply implementing a policy of the prison that life in the Assessment House should be made as difficult as possible for the inmates. I was on three other houses during my time at Styal, and on none of them were the staff so petty-minded. There were usually three officers to a house, and the three on Davies were grim. One was a foreigner, who had a Germanic obsession with unnecessary cleaning. Another was small, pretty, and as hard as nails. She spoke with a very pronounced Scottish accent, and had me in perpetual fear that I might misunderstand what she said and do something wrong. It was she who was on duty my first night. The third was rumoured to have had a bad love affair, and was certainly the most miserable officer I ever knew. Her speciality was to make us go out on exercise whatever the weather, unless specifically told by the centre that there was no exercise that day.

When my efforts at producing a bed up to Styal standard had at last met with grudging acceptance from the officer, I joined the other members of the new intake in the dining room, sewing labels on all our clothes. These labels were merely pieces of tape with our initials written on by the officer. They were far from long-lasting, and the initials soon faded. Sitting sewing labels on clothes with the warning that there would be no telly until all of us had all our clothes labelled added tremendously to the boarding school feeling which had begun to haunt me irresistibly. I suffered from the poor light and not being able to thread my needle, but I managed not to delay the television for too long, and sewed rapidly once my needle was threaded.

We were interrupted half way through sewing by being called into the office. Here we received the housemistress's pep talk. We were told that if we made trouble we would get trouble, that if we buckled down and got on with our work and did our time without trouble everything would be much easier for everybody. We were given a booklet of rules to read, but neither verbally, nor by means of the booklet, then or at any other time, were we given a list of deeds which would be punishable by being put 'on report'. The thing I found hardest in the early days was the uncertainty of never knowing what innocent act could result in such punishment.

There was a reason behind every one of the rules at Styal. Later, a more sympathetic house officer on another house was to explain some of them, although even she could not give an explanation for them all. Once explained, they made sense. I would have been prepared to obey the rules even without explanation, but what upset me was that at no time was I told what the rules were, never mind having them explained to me. It is supposed to be very easy to get put on report in Styal, and perhaps that is why – if you are not told the rules, how can you know when you are breaking them?

For instance, it was a reportable offence to be walking on the grass – any grass. Only at the end of my imprisonment did I learn the reason. It was because the area close to the perimeter fence was grassed and obviously the authorities did not want people there. So to avoid arguments about what grass was in or out of bounds, they simply said that walking on any grass was a reportable offence. Fine, but they never told me. It was also an offence to go into a house kitchen beyond a certain point. Again, the reason is fair enough: there are knives in kitchens, and these should not be accessible to all and sundry. But again, nobody told me. I found that one out in my second week when I was talking to the cook. I came forward into the kitchen past the imaginary line, and the cook turned on me, shouting 'Get out, get back. It's twenty-eight days for me if you are caught here.' I was so shocked that I could not help but cry. I was suddenly returned to my small childhood, being shouted at by furious adults for some transgression which I did not even know was a transgression. The fear of doing something wrong has been with me all my life, and now here I was in the situation I had feared all my life, where there are no secure boundaries, and an ordinary situation can turn into nightmare in a second, for no reason. Fluid madness.

Other reportable offences were such things as smoking upstairs, being out of bed, lesbian activities, refusing exercise, going upstairs without permission, leaving the house without permission, refusing to work, insulting an officer, causing trouble of any kind, and being near the main gate. I never did get put on report, though I was threatened with it twice – once for going across to the hospital for my medicine without an escort, and once for being near the main gate. This was when I did not know the layout of the prison, and stumbled upon the gate by accident.

Going upstairs was the only one of these offences that we were given any warning about. There was a notice at the foot of the stairs in some houses saying 'Stop. Have you asked permission?' Again, the reason for this being an offence is fair enough: people kept their things upstairs in unlocked lockers, and petty theft was rife. It was clearly in everyone's interests for most people to be downstairs most of the time, but, oh it was wearisome having to ask every time you wanted to go upstairs. Time and again this rule was broken, by me as well as by everyone else. You simply took a chance. But to break a rule knowing what you were doing was a lot less of a strain than the constant fear of breaking one by accident.

The report system is a powerful weapon in the hands of the prison authorities. When 'on report', the inmate is taken to the punishment house, usually at 8.00 in the morning, by two officers. Called Alderley House, this house is known to all in Styal as 'Bleak House'. I never saw the inside of it (walking past the outside of it was another reportable offence!), but it was reputed to be very bleak indeed. You waited there for the governor, who made a daily round to hear cases, and from his decision there was no appeal. Among the punishments handed out were 'behind the door' (solitary confinement), loss of pay, loss of privileges, and, most awful of all, loss of remission. Frequently these punishments were dealt out together: thus you might get five days behind the door, loss of one week's pay, and fourteen days' loss of remission.

This loss of remission confused some people, who were convinced that the governor had the power to add to their sentences, but of course he only has the power to take away the remission one earns for good conduct. As this is one third of the sentence, his power is quite considerable. If someone commits a really serious offence, they are known as 'waiting for the VC'. This is the Visiting Court, or magistrate, who equally does not have the power to add to the sentence, but can impose another sentence for another crime, assault for example. To many of the women though, even those who had far greater familiarity with the system than I did, it was the governor who was responsible for 'adding to her time', and the governor was feared accordingly.

For me, the worst punishment would have been loss of remission, and in my first weeks in Styal I was so sure that I would end up on report and lose all my remission because of some unwitting offence that I gave up thinking about my 'early release' date, and trained myself to think that I would come out in May, having served the full year. I was quite surprised to learn that for other people the most feared punishment was loss of pay. This was because they smoked, and for a smoker to be in prison there is an extra dimension to this punishment. Loss of pay meant loss of cigarettes, and to many women this was the worst punishment they could face. Those who smoked suffered enough in the ordinary way from never having enough money to buy tobacco to last them the week, without having what little they did have taken away from them.

This is about the only way I can think of, apart from the restrictions on visiting, that the convicted prisoner is worse off than the prisoner on remand. On remand, you can have as much in the way of cigarettes and tobacco as you can persuade people to bring in for you, but once convicted, the only tobacco you may have is that bought with the money you earn. This system irons out the unfairness experienced on remand where some have much tobacco brought in and some have none at all. It does mean, however, that those who do smoke are made to suffer the extra punishment of never having enough tobacco. In Styal, we went to canteen on a Thursday, and by the following Wednesday or even Tuesday, most people would have run out of tobacco, and the tension in the air would be worse than usual because of all the smokers who could not smoke. I thought it was odd that very few people made any effort to cut down or give up smoking. They all smoked the whole allowance every week and that was that.

As it was a Wednesday when I first came to Styal, the atmosphere of tobaccoless gloom hung over the common room when, labels safely sewn on and checked, we were allowed to join the others with the telly. The common room was quite an attractive and comfortable room, with a carpet in the centre of a wood block floor, pictures on the walls, and comfortable modern chairs arranged in long rows along two of the walls. There were large, unbarred windows with curtains. After the gruesomeness of Pucklechurch, the place came as a very welcome change. I could not believe the lack of security: the door was not locked and the windows opened normally. The obsession with locking up and unlocking which I had known at Pucklechurch was entirely missing here. It was civilization again, to be sitting in a comfortable chair in a pleasant room, with unbarred windows and an unlocked door.

It was also surprising to find that we were not driven off to bed before 8.00. Instead, we had supper at 8.00, a cup of tea and a couple of pieces of toast, and then went up to bed. Lights out was at 9.00, and again I was amazed to find that the doors of the dormitories were not locked. After I had been at Styal a short time, new regulations were introduced which meant that we did not have to go to bed as soon as supper was over, but could go back into the common room and watch TV until 9.00. Lights out then was at 9.30, although on every house except Davies the lights were not turned out by the officers but by us. We usually settled down at about 10.00, which was quite late enough for me when we were getting up at 7.00 or, when I became a cook, 6.30. The whole regime seemed to be infinitely more tolerable than at Pucklechurch – or at Risley, where the girls had fared the same. I cannot understand why life in the remand centre is made more intolerable than it is in prison.

I did not get a bath that first night, as there was a system of booking baths by getting your name in the 'bath book'. That had to be done by about 4.00 or you were too late, and at 4.00 I had just come into reception. Later on, in spite of a certain amount of aggravation, I got a nightly bath because I was a cook. The baths were considerably cleaner than in Pucklechurch. Those girls who were not having baths washed in the communal washroom, where there were half a dozen basins, separated by shower curtains, so that you could have privacy. Luxury!

As soon as the lights had been turned out and the officers had gone, Irish Maureen was out of bed, out of the dorm and lighting up a strictly illegal cigarette. Smoking upstairs was absolutely forbidden, but everybody did it. Tobacco tins had to be handed in after supper, and on some houses we were also given a rub-down search, but that never stopped the smokers from smoking. They hid dog ends, matches and a 'strike' (the strip of the match box which actually ignites the match), and every night they had their good-night smokes. There was not much else other than illegal smoking which went on on Davies House, because the night patrol were based there, and when they had gone round the other houses they would be returning to Davies. It was very convenient, as it gave just enough time for a quick smoke and a talk with the other girls (although an officer once stayed behind when the others went on patrol, and Irish Maureen fled back into bed considerably quicker than she had left it, and I understood why the bottom bunk was the favoured one!).

On this first night, though, there were no problems for the girls, and they were able to gather in the toilet and have their smoke and a chat. I was grateful that being a non-smoker gave me the excuse not to have to join them, as I was very tired, and anyway not at all sure that I had much in common with any of them. The bunk was comfortable enough, and I slept well.

I shared the room with Irish Maureen for about a week, and then she was moved to her other house. The girls who had been in before, and were therefore known, were usually moved from Davies before people like me, about whom the authorities were not sure. Before she left, she told me a bit about herself. She was in her late twenties, older than she looked, and was married with two small children, although she never saw them and hardly ever saw her husband. In all the years of her marriage, Irish Maureen reckoned that she and her husband had never had more than six months together at any one time, because one or the other of them was always in prison. Her husband was at present doing a long stretch for a burglary, and Irish Maureen did not seem to be looking forward to his release, because she said, 'He takes the drink, and then he beats me black and blue'. They never wrote when one or the other of them was in prison. Irish Maureen had no home, she lived in a squat at the back of King's Cross, on social security and prostitution. She had been arrested, again, for drug offences.

Irish Maureen knew one of the other girls on Davies by sight, because she also made her living from prostitution around King's Cross station, and they used to compare their past clients. They had a deep contempt for men, who would pay good money for unbelievably perverse practices. They clearly had a different perspective from my own, as their tales of past clients would send them into hysterical laughter. I suppose I wasn't shocked, but it didn't strike me as funny. It struck me as very sad, both that men should seek such services from such women, and that women should mock them for doing so, and also defraud them. For the idea seemed to be that you took the man's money and then got him so drunk or drugged that you could get away without actually having to do anything at all but provide the alcohol or heroin. The only thing I did wish was that they would not tell their explicit stories at mealtimes, but I knew better than to say anything. It seemed to me that while obsessed by sex, these girls had never in their lives experienced the tenderness and passion of a really caring relationship, and sex to them was just smut. To me, this seemed a grave pity.

There were two other women with me on Davies who you might

have been surprised to have seen there. One was the daughter of a clergyman, and one the daughter of a policeman. Both of these women were to be with me throughout the time I was in Styal, though we never became friendly, because, in spite of their background, they were both in fact used to prison and had little in common with me.

Jenny, the policeman's daughter, was in her early twenties. She had a little daughter of three, who was in care. By what she said, she came from a good family in Manchester, and her repeated arrests had broken her mother's heart. She had been told after her previous arrest that if it happened again her family would disown her, and for a long time she got neither letters nor visits from them. As Christmas approached they thawed, and Jenny did have a visit from her father, but her mother still could not bring herself to visit her daughter in prison. Jenny was articulate and intelligent, and had a younger brother who was at university. She herself had left school at the earliest opportunity, and had drifted into a series of dead-end jobs, and into a social life which introduced her to heroin. She kept saying that she wanted to be allowed to go to Lifeline, the organization which helps drug addicts, but I do not think that she had any real intention at all of coming off heroin. It was a pity, because she was a lively girl with a good sense of humour, and it was dreadful to see her in the process of quite deliberately destroying herself.

Jenny was pretty, and well dressed. Her skirts and jerseys had obviously cost money, and she treated them casually as if she was used to expensive clothes. When she first came in, she was much too thin, because of the heroin, but as time went on she began to get her figure back, and ended up being quite plump. I was frequently surprised to see how well the drug addicts coped with being without their supplies, but of course the worst effects of withdrawal had been undergone in the remand centre, where addicts were put on a steadily decreasing regime of Methidrine, and weaned forcibly off the drug in just under three weeks. That could be a bad time for them, as I had learned in my Pucklechurch days. It does seem, however, that being deprived of heroin is not as stressful a situation as I had been led to believe, and people like Jenny seemed to cope quite well. They knew that there was no way they were going to get a fix, and that was that.

Jenny had an interesting personality. With her roots in one way of life, she never seemed quite to belong to the prison situation, and yet she was popular with the others, and often the centre of things. Dawn, the clergyman's daughter, was a different case altogether. She seemed absolutely to belong in Styal, where indeed she seemed to have spent most of her adult life. She had no connection at all with her family, never got a letter or a visit, and was completely on her own. She was in her thirties, but looked younger, and although she had once been married, she had no children and had lost touch with her husband. She was a lonely person, and not at all popular with the others, though she seemed to be 'well in' with everyone, and was given to displays of extrovert behaviour, during which the others would laugh at her rather than with her.

Dawn was doing three years for a particularly nasty social security fraud, of which she was inordinately proud. She had the press cuttings of her trial, which she showed to me the minute I walked into the common room that first evening, as she showed them to everyone else. Dawn had arrived at Styal the day before I did, and spent her time greeting the officers as they came on duty as old friends, and yelling out of the windows to the lifers and other long-term prisoners, all of whom knew her. I think she had been out of Styal for about six months on this occasion. Clearly, Dawn was a hopeless recidivist.

I could not like her, as she was a thoroughly nasty piece of work. But I did feel very sorry for her; she was so alone and so unpopular. Something really awful must have gone wrong in her life, and she was now caught in a web apparently beyond her strength to break. She will be in and out of prison all her life: indeed she seems to have no life at all outside, and is only really safe when in prison. Yet she must have had a good upbringing. How could she have sunk to the state she was in when I first met her, when she was in the kind of high mood of excitement at being back with all her friends, like a girl beginning a new term at boarding school? She knew the place and the people, and was like an older girl with a new girl to me.

I suspect that Dawn had more intelligence than she showed. She would never say a word about her background, so I do not know how far her formal education had gone. Certainly she was possessed of a kind of low cunning. It was Dawn who read the papers avidly, and noted the names of child murderers, so that when they appeared at Styal she could lead the hue and cry against them. She always knew what everybody had done, and I am sure that it was dear Dawn who told everybody what I was in for. I think no one else would have been bothered, but Dawn had to know, and having found out, would tell everyone else. When I was moved from Davies to Size, one of the worst things about it was that Dawn was on Size, and I am convinced that she was behind the worst episode I had to endure there, when one of the other girls suddenly began asking me loudly and always in public what I had done. I think Dawn had put her up to it. I handled it as well as I could, but having Karen repeating every evening in the common room, 'What have you done, Audrey, come on tell us what you have done' reminded the others that they did not actually know what I had done. Dawn sat in the corner and smirked silently to herself while my ordeal continued. At last I told Karen: 'Incitement'. She was content with that, but I suspect Dawn wasn't, because the next evening Karen was at it again: 'Incitement to what, Audrey, come on tell us'.

I thought I had better find out if Dawn was behind this, so I said to Karen, in a really evil voice, 'Incitement to *murder*, of course'. Karen didn't believe it, and kept on. I got up and went out, saying to Dawn on the way, 'There, I have told her the truth and she didn't believe me'. And Dawn looked as if she knew perfectly well that I had told the truth. She also looked guilty, because she realized that I knew that she was behind my being victimized. Karen asked Dawn, 'Was it, Dawn? And how do you know?' To which Dawn replied that she had asked Susan, who had been in Pucklechurch with me at the time of my trial, and probably did know.

So I bet a marvellous version of what had happened to me was doing the rounds, though as I have said before, unless stirred up by someone like Dawn, most girls did not care what anyone else was in for, particularly older ones like me. They were far too preoccupied with their own affairs, and if someone did not want to talk about themselves, their privacy was respected.

I was later to discover that it was known not only what I had done, but that I had been a teacher. The grapevine in prison is an amazing thing and so is the tendency of women with not enough to do, and no excitements but what they can create for themselves, to gossip. Yet after this incident, Dawn and I got on better, strangely enough. There was something to her, somewhere, but it needed an awful lot of straightening out!

9   Davies House

I was to remain on Davies House for exactly a fortnight. The routine of the days did not change, and yet no day was like another. There were differences all the time. The early morning routine was the worst, as I never find it easy to get up early. The 6.30 start was awful. The officer (who must have got up even earlier) came round the dorms switching on the light and saying good morning. We then had until 7.15 to get ourselves up, washed and dressed, and to stack our beds in the approved Styal manner. We had to get down in order to sign the time book before 7.15. It was a reportable offence to be late more than three times. As we signed the time book, we also checked whether we were on one of the chores – 'wash up', 'sweep up' and 'duty cook'. We then went and sat in the common room in weary gloom, until everybody was down.

The chores were done by each of us in rotation. 'Wash up' was exactly that: on top of the normal work, you had to wash up after every meal of the day. Two people were always on this together. 'Sweep up' was the job of clearing the tables after each meal, stacking the chairs and sweeping out the dining rooms. You also had to sweep and tidy the common room last thing at night. The worst chore of the lot was 'duty cook', for this did not really mean cooking. It meant peeling a great bucket of potatoes for the next day's meals, washing the kitchen floor, and making the tea for supper. Only if we had toast for supper did the duty cook have to do anything resembling cooking, but supper was usually a biscuit or piece of cake which had been cooked by the house cook during the day, and only had to be put out for supper. All this was in addition to a normal day's work, and one of the things I most appreciated about becoming a house cook was that cooks were excused from these extra chores.

At 7.15 we would all be sent back upstairs to wait by our beds for the officer to come round and inspect the stacked bedclothes. This was an incredible experience. It was not enough merely folding your bedclothes neatly; they had to be folded according to a rigid pattern. First the bedspread had to be folded lengthways four times, and laid across the bunk. Then a folded blanket was placed over this, so that its edges exactly coincided with the edges of the bedspread. Next came a sheet, again folded so that it coincided exactly. Then another blanket, the second sheet, and any further blankets, all to be perfectly folded. If that sounds simple, you try doing it against the clock at 7.00 a.m. on a winter's morning! Lastly, the bedspread was folded up and around the folded blankets to make a perfect stack, without a corner out of line, or an edge poking through anywhere. It was exactly like being in the army.

At first I simply could not believe that anyone could really be going to take this stack business seriously, but they did. However we tried, the stacks were never right, and of course poor old Irish Maureen suffered every morning because her stack was the worst on the whole house. Again, I found when I moved off Davies that other house officers were not as fussy about the stacking of bedclothes. It was clearly being used on the Assessment House as yet another method of breaking us in, and was as much as anything else responsible for the desire of those who knew Styal to get off Davies as fast as they could. I used to watch the officers closely to see if I could detect a hint of them realizing the ridiculousness of what they were doing, but as I never could I resisted the urge to laugh. They must have been amazingly dedicated, those three, or else extremely good actresses. I never once caught a glimpse of a sense of humour. Imagine spending your early mornings telling people off because they had not got their second sheet to the tenth of a millimetre in line with the blanket below it. My God!

I often wonder whether the way Davies was run was a deliberate policy, or whether it was just the accident of having three like-minded house officers on duty there. Either way, I wonder what the underlying philosophy was. I do not think that Styal had decided whether it was an institution in which people were held to deprive them of their liberty, or whether it was an institution in which people were punished by being treated in a petty way. Perhaps society does not know what its prisons are for, nor what exactly the punishment awarded by the judge should consist of. Is the mere fact of being deprived of liberty enough, or should life also be made deliberately uncomfortable, and if so, in what way? And how uncomfortable? Who decides these things? At Styal it seemed to be more or less up to the individual prison officer how they interpreted their duties, and some clearly believed that loss of liberty was not enough; people should be made to suffer in other ways for what they had done.

When the officer was at last satisfied with our stacks, we were allowed back downstairs. The smokers were allowed to have their tins, though often it was breakfast-time by then. When the routine of the day was altered soon after I arrived, we were woken at 7.00, and had to sign the book by 7.20. This led to a lot less hanging about first thing in the morning, but on the other hand it was a wild scramble to get through and down to sign the book in twenty minutes. Not that it much concerned me, for as a cook I had to get up earlier than everyone else anyway, and would be reporting for work at 6.55, before everyone else was woken up.

Davies food was unbelievable, especially after Pucklechurch. Because of the system of houses at Styal, each one of which had its own kitchen, the food was always freshly and almost individually cooked. Those in the know said they were vegetarians, because then their food was individually prepared, there being only two or three vegetarians per house. When I was on Davies, there was a really marvellous cook. About my own age, Petra was in for drugs, and was later to have her sentence reduced on appeal from four years to eighteen months. She had been a professional cook outside, and she loved cooking. I was her assistant cook for a month, and I am still not sure exactly what she did to the food to make it taste so nice. She had only the same basic ingredients to work from as any other cook on other houses, but Petra's food always tasted special.

I think it is simply a gift. Petra would just put the breakfast sausages, or whatever, on to grill, but her sausages were always caught at exactly the right moment, when they were done to perfection. Her cakes, puddings and pastry were out of this world. Her scones melted in the mouth. The only extras she used were cheese and mixed herbs, so that her macaroni cheese for example was really cheesy, and her meat dishes had that something extra. Petra could not have cooked badly if she had tried.

The first breakfast in Styal was as good as the preceding night's tea. The rations were little different from those at Pucklechurch: porridge, one grilled sausage, toast and margarine, scalding hot tea. Yet it was all different. The sausage was beautifully grilled, the toast was freshly made, the porridge even smelled good, and was of a reasonable consistency – not the solid dollop we got at Pucklechurch. At first in Styal I did not eat the porridge, but later on I did, and it was to become my secret vice thereafter. There was plenty to go round, and there seemed to be no sugar shortage, as little eggcupfuls of sugar appeared from behind curtains and on top of window frames. At Pucklechurch I sometimes had bread and sugar, but here if you did not eat your sugar, you were expected to contribute it to the general fund, so that those who had sugar in tea could have it all the time, not just at breakfast and tea, when the official sugar ration in one red eggcup was issued.

There were also strange plastic cups which appeared from time to time full of jam or marmalade. A cook would sometimes have jam left over and would pass it round like this; or it might be that not all that was put out officially would be eaten. Instead of throwing it away, it was jealously hoarded, and reappeared to enliven our bread at another meal. We used to keep the cups full of illegal jam in the cupboard with all the other cups, so an officer would just see stacks of clean plastic mugs, and not realize that the bottom one contained jam, marmalade or sugar. I am sure that the officers knew quite well what was going on, and turned a blind eye to it. In other houses it went on quite openly, and goodies not eaten at one meal were left on window ledges for the next.

After breakfast we went upstairs to make our beds, and again there was the doomed wrestling with the bedspread to provide the hospital corners at the bottom and the pillow tucked into the top. My second effort was little better than my first. The officer who checked the beds also checked that lockers were tidy, and then we could go downstairs and wait in the common room until 8.30 and time for work. If one was on wash up, this time of the day was impossible because we were supposed to have the washing up done as well as the bed made, all at the same time. If in addition you had to see the doctor, as once happened to me, both the washing up and the bed had to be left as soon as the summons came to go over to the hospital, and then you were in trouble on your return for having left the washing up and having not made the bed. You just couldn't win in this situation, and the only way I could keep sane was by telling myself that the whole point was that we were not supposed to win. No attempt at justification would do; the prisoner was always automatically in the wrong, and if it wasn't one thing it would be something else. All we could do was to say nothing and do the best we could, knowing that the whole system was against us, and was supposed to be so. A bit like life really.

The idea at Styal was that convicted prisoners must work. This served three useful functions. Firstly, the work had to be done, and it might as well be the prisoners who did it. Secondly, it gave us all the idea that life was about working, and they hoped we would carry this bright new ideal out with us when we left. Thirdly, it gave us something to do and, they thought, stopped us from getting bored and rebellious and having to be locked up. It might also teach us something about contributing to the community, pulling our weight, mucking in together, and other such worthy, socially desirable aims.

Work at Styal came in several kinds. Every house had to be cleaned, and every house therefore had people whose whole day was spent doing housework. Each house had a cook and an assistant cook. There was a party of girls 'on the bins' who went round collecting the refuse every day from every house, burning the rubbish, and putting the swill ready for collection for feeding pigs, I think on a prison farm elsewhere. There were girls working in the gardens, and a party of toughies formed the 'works party' and did things with drains and pots of paint. Two girls worked in the stores, and two more trundled the supplies of bread, milk, potatoes and groceries round to every house kitchen. Then there was the workroom, a horrible little factory, where the majority of people in Styal were employed and at the same time things required by the government were produced. When I was there they were making shirts for use in nuclear power stations and other establishments where the government has to provide a considerable number of shirts for one reason or another.

I got to know about the types of work available by listening to the women who had been in before discussing the work they hoped to do. The work that appealed to me most was the gardening, but in October there was not much to be done, and though I would have preferred to be outside in the open air, I wasn't sure that I wanted to commit myself to three months of it, especially three winter months. The gardening girls were sweeping up leaves and cutting the grass for the last time when I arrived at Styal. Later in the winter they were to be seen in shivering groups sweeping paths with brooms, or working in the polythene tunnels by our exercise yard, which they said was much warmer, but not as warm as an inside job.

Anyway, it was not much use trying to decide what I wanted to do, as of course it was not my decision. Within two or three days of a new inmate's arrival, they were seen by the assistant governor responsible for the house. There were two assistant governors, one male and one female, and they shared between them responsibility for the houses. While I was there they swapped, I am not sure why, and the houses which had 'belonged' to Mr Hutchinson became the responsibilty of Miss Dawson and vice versa. Initially it was Mr Hutchinson who was in charge of Davies, and so it was he who interviewed me on about my third day there.

Not surprisingly, he found it difficult to understand why I had ruined my life as I had done, and he gave me some kindly advice about how to get through what he thought would be a distressing experience for me. Little did he know how much better I was finding Styal compared to Pucklechurch. But as I was only going to be there for three months, what the girls called 'bed and breakfasting', I was not really one of his major problems. He seemed to know a lot of the girls well and was a humane and approachable person, liked by all the women in his care. He knew who I was when he met me again from time to time, and towards the end of my sentence he came into the kitchen where I was working and wished me well when I was released. If ever there was the right man in the right job, it was Mr Hutchinson, and I hope if he gets promoted he will not lose the kindly approachability which made him able to use his personality to so much good effect among the women with whom he worked.

He discussed the various types of work with me, and said he would do his best to put me into as congenial a job as possible. Being a cook was regarded as a good job, and several people were envious of me when I was given that job. It obviously had to go to people who were responsible and trustworthy, and there were many people who kept asking to be a cook but were clearly never going to be entrusted with such a post. I was alarmed at first, as my cooking is of the slapdash and temperamental variety, but I need not have worried. There is a cook and an assistant cook on each house, and as assistant it was mostly my job to do as the cook told me and peel the vegetables. So no degree of culinary skill was required.

But before I got into the kitchen I had to serve my fortnight on Davies House doing nothing but housework. Every morning at 8.30 the list would go up on the board outside the office of which dormitories and corridors we each had to clean that day. At least we had a change every day. Sometimes the dormitories were empty and had not been used since they were last cleaned, but they had to be cleaned all over again from scratch. There were instructions as to exactly what had to be cleaned, and how it had to be done. For instance: 'Floor, sweep and scrub; lockers, wipe and polish; outside window ledges, wipe'.

These jolly tasks took us all morning; and we were persecuted as we did them by the officers, depending on the time they had available and the mood they were in. Sometimes, the officer with a reputation for obsessive cleaning would come silently up the stairs holding her keys in her hand so that they did not jingle as they usually did when left loose on the chain all officers wore attached to their belts. She would appear behind someone who was wiping the floor with a cloth instead of scrubbing it, send them back to the end of the corridor and stand over them while they did scrub it. If you protested you could end up scrubbing the floor all over again.

Or the officers might emerge from a room which someone had finished, claiming to have found dust on a skirting board, or outside a window, and back you would have to go to do it again. Never in my life have I lived in so clean a place as Davies House, and I hope never have to live in so clean a place again. The whole house, every corner, every cupboard, would be scrubbed out at least once and sometimes twice a day. And then it was someone's job to clean the buckets, brooms and cloths which we had used to do the cleaning. All windows were cleaned inside and outside every day, sometimes twice. The dirtiest place on the house was certainly the kitchen, which was only cleaned once a day, though I heard after I had left Davies kitchen that the new assistant cook was being made to do the floor during the day in addition to the duty cook doing it at night, so that brought the kitchen into line with everywhere else.

It was soul-destroying work, akin to digging a hole and then filling it in again, or moving rocks from one side of a road to the other and back again. Of course the house had to be kept clean, but it was so obvious on Davies that we were being made to do this work for the sake of doing it, not for the sake of keeping the house clean. Any housewife who kept her house like that one would be in need of psychiatric help! It was all part of the punishment, and the others always used to set out to get away with doing the absolute minimum that they could. I well remember one day going past one dorm on my way to clean another, and there was Jenny lying flat on her back on the bed, reading. Had I been an officer, Jenny would have been in serious trouble, as it would have been construed as refusal to work, which was, of course, a reportable offence.

Jenny used to laugh jokingly at me because I could not bear to skive about in the way the others tried to. I reckoned that time passed much more slowly if you were always trying to do as little as possible than if you got on with it and did the job as it was supposed to be done. So I would scrub my floors, and wash my window ledges, and empty and refill my fire buckets, not because I was trying to conform but because dinnertime came along quicker that way. But by the end of the fortnight I was so utterly sick of housework that I felt I would scream if I were not given another job soon.

We got a smoke break at ten o'clock, and then it was back to work until dinnertime at midday. Sometimes, but very rarely, we were able to extend the smoke break from the permitted ten minutes to a quarter of an hour. Most people had finished their work before twelve, and then it was a matter of keeping out of the way of the officers, because if you were caught doing nothing you would be given something else to do, or told to do again what you had already done.

Sometimes we dared to go into the common room, but it was dangerous, as the officer might well appear in the doorway and demand to know what we thought we were doing sitting around at only ten to twelve. It was better to appear busy somewhere else.

At 12.00 we all lined up for dinner, and invariably it was one of Petra's successes. People ate a lot because the food was so good, but the quantities were limited and there was a good deal of trading of rice pudding for chips and so forth, which was of course forbidden. We were left more or less to ourselves at mealtimes: the dining rooms were at the oppostie ends of the corridor from the office, and we had to stay in the dining hall for twenty minutes without leaving it, as that was also the officer's meal break, and she was usually content to leave us alone at that time. However, when Irish Maureen, waving the brown sauce to illustrate a point, accidentally decorated the wall with brown smears, the ensuing outcry brought in the officer on duty in double time.

There was little time left after the meal to sit and do nothing, as the workroom went back to work at one o'clock, and we were all supposed to be doing something at that time. Usually, it was exercise. I didn't mind exercise, except in the rain or when it was really cold. On a pleasant autumn day, it was quite nice to be able to walk in the fresh air. The problem was the same as it had been in Pucklechurch, that most people liked to walk so slowly, to dawdle, to wander, so that from my point of view it was hardly exercise at all, and I was left with the choice of either walking by myself at a reasonable rate, or wandering along with everyone else.

We walked up the road to exercise, past the other houses and the hospital, and then round and round the yard at the top, with a large expanse of very green grass between us and the row of poplar trees which marked the fence, the public road outside, and freedom. Several houses would be on exercise at the same time, and it was possible to exchange news and gossip with people you knew who had been moved on to another house, or had been here the last time you were in. Again, I used to get the feeling of being a new girl at an old girls' reunion.

You learned a lot on exercise, because it was completely out of the officers' earshot. They just stood and watched us as we wandered round, and if we were cold, they must have been even colder. You learned about other inmates and their crimes, about the officers and their characteristics, about the other houses and other prisons. There was a lot of talk about how and why various people had been caught, and about various things that they had done and got away with. I learned how to evade a car following me down a motorway, how to break into various establishments, how to secrete drugs so that they 'would never be found' (by wrapping them in polythene and swallowing them), the best ways of setting fire to buildings, and committing murder. It was all very instructive.

Most of the conversation though was not about crime, but about people, people in the prison, and about families and friends outside. Most of these women had children, some of them had proper families with husbands and parents, and the talk was mostly about these children and these families. About how the children were reacting to what had happened to their mother, about the ways in which grandparents were caring for the children, about husbands who had gone off, about children who had been taken into care. I was left in no doubt that there is an extra penalty for women in prison when they are separated from their children, when they see them suffer and can only blame themselves. The talk always turned to children sooner or later, and when it did the women became at once serious and involved, unlike the normal 'carefree' faces they usually presented to the world.

There was little or no discussion of political, economic or international issues. Apart from a general feeling that 'Maggie' Thatcher was automatically to blame for everything that was wrong, these women were not interested in abstracts. They were interested in their own children and what was happening to them, and by extension, in other people's children too. My own daughters being grown up, I was rather out of these discussions, but they certainly made me feel extremely grateful that my children were grown up and that my parents were dead.

While we were going round the yard, I learned a lot about the other houses in Styal, and in particular 'Block 3'. In spite of the fact that its name suggested that it was some kind of punishment house, it was in fact the 'privilege house' and supposed to be the most desirable house in the prison. Block 3 was one of the houses that were being refurbished when I was there, and the girls belonging to it had been moved lock, stock and barrel to Wilson House while this was going on. I was given to understand by the other girls that they thought it very likely that I would end up on the privilege house, as I was the kind of trustworthy and quiet person who did. Glowing pictures were painted for me of the free and easy life the girls on that house lived, and I was eager to go there and join them. They did different and highly trusted work from the rest of the prison, such as cooking in the officers' mess, and cleaning their quarters. The orderly who helped in the gym was on that house, as was the reception orderly.

When I was moved from Davies on to Size, I was secretly bitterly disappointed that I had not been judged trusty enough to join the privileged girls on Wilson. Later, I was moved to Wilson, and there I did in fact spend the unhappiest time of my whole prison sentence. There were privileges, such as being allowed to go upstairs without asking, and the women were more intelligent and 'nicer' than most of them in the other houses, but perhaps because of this, they were harder to get along with, and there was an atmosphere of bitchiness which had been totally absent elsewhere in the prison. Who was it who said, 'Be careful what you want, because you may get it'? I wanted to be on Wilson, and when I was, I hated it.

But that was in the future. The present was the slow wander back down to Davies off exercise, and the afternoon's work. I think that the staff were often at their wits' end to know what to give us to do in the afternoons. Sometimes it was recleaning what had already been done in the morning. Sometimes we were taken out to other parts of the prison to clean, such as the administrative offices or the visitor's waiting room. I was deeply impressed on the day I had to clean the governor's office and I saw his rather fetching pale pink cloakroom. Sometimes we were sent to other houses to clean, notably Howard and Mellanby.

Howard was referred to by the girls as the Muppet House, and the women on it were known as Muppets. These were the inadequates, half of whom I suspect did not really know why they were in Styal in the first place. They would go up to the hospital when it was time for doses, walking even more slowly than the usual shambling Styal pace. There were two in particular who always went arm in arm; one was very tall, at least six foot, and very thin. The other was about five foot nothing, and as wide as she was short. Yet I never saw this incongruous couple other than arm in arm, and I am surprised it was allowed, for physical contact was forbidden to the rest of us. Howard was a lock-up house; that is, the inmates were locked up at night because they couldn't be trusted without constant supervision. Not many were locked up during the day. If you were that bad you would probably be on Brown, the second lock-up house. This was used as a kind of holding house for those who needed restraint, but were not bad enough to be sent to the punishment house. The numbers on Howard and Brown were in the region of ten each, as opposed to the twenty or more on an ordinary house. As the inadequates could not clean their own house properly, girls from Davies were frequently sent there to do the bulk of the work.

I was sent to Howard, but I was never sent to Mellanby, the other house regularly cleaned by Davies girls. Mellanby was the mother and baby unit, and mainly populated by tough Borstal girls, though there were some older women. If a woman was pregnant when she came in after sentence, she was likely to be sent to Styal because of the facilities there. Pregnant girls were sent to Fox House, which was next door to Mellanby, close to the hospital, and with a room in which a sister could sleep. When they went into labour, they were taken out of Styal to have their babies in one of the Manchester hospitals, so that the baby did not have to be born in prison. As soon as possible, often the same day, the girl was moved back into Styal. If she was keeping the baby, she and the baby went on to Mellanby House together. If she was not keeping the baby, she was moved as soon as possible to one of the other houses as far from Mellanby as possible.

It was not possible to avoid the babies completely, though. One would see them in their prams on the way to the hospital, or in their mothers' arms waiting to see the doctor. The prams were sometimes pushed round the grounds for the sake of the mothers' exercise, and whenever we went to canteen which was opposite Mellanby, there was a row of prams outside in the fresh air, and often the sound of a baby's cry as you went past. Babies stayed with their mothers for some nine months, and then the baby had to go outside, either into the care of relatives, or into the care of the local authority. It would not have been possible to have small children in prison, but it must have been terrible for a mother to be parted from her baby in this way. Presumably (but I never met any), a mother with more time to serve after her baby had been sent outside would be moved to an ordinary house. There were probably not many mothers in that position, most having served their sentence before the baby was sent outside. A sentence of a year would cover a full pregnancy and the first few months of the baby's life, even if the whole twelve months were served.

But it did sometimes happen that a woman faced a sentence which meant that she would have to be parted from her baby. While I was there, a twenty-two-year-old came in pregnant, with a four-year sentence for drugs. Clearly, she would have to say goodbye to her baby with a considerable length of time still to serve. Her child could well be three years old before the mother was released. On the other hand, there were girls on Fox House, the house for the pregnant women, who had a release date long before the date their baby was due. There were others, however, with whom it was touch and go whether their baby would be born the day before or the day after their release. The position was complicated by the fact that most of them seemed to have little idea of when their baby was due. It must have been a bit nerve-racking, wondering whether you would be released just in time or not. Fortunately, as these were mostly first pregnancies, the babies tended to arrive late rather than early, which meant the mothers were often free before the baby was born.

On my first or second afternoon on Davies, I and another woman were taken to clean the place where the officers received their training if they were interested in promotion. It made me feel at home, as it was well equipped with audiovisual aids of one sort and another. There was also a revealing poster on the wall, giving the spelling of various words: 'Governor', 'parole', 'offence', 'restriction', and so on. Knowing nothing whatever about the educational qualifications required in the prison service, I deduced from that poster that the level was not high.

Of more interest was another display, giving the history of Styal. I had been told (and was to be told again many times) that it had been a prisoner of war camp in the war, presumably the Second World

War. I had thought that two buildings on the campus looked remarkably like schools from the Victorian era, and so in fact they must have been, for I gleaned from the display that the place had been built towards the end of the last century as the latest and most up-to-date orphanage. The children lived in small groups in the houses, and there was one school for the little ones and one for the older children. The stable block was now Bleak House. Clearly the orphanage had been built by enlightened men, trying to get away from the Dickensian image of a nineteenth-century poorhouse, trying to make it as pleasant a place as possible. Indeed, if it were not for the eternal odour of depression which hangs over the place, Styal can look attractive in the late autumn sun, and with the snows of winter on its roofs it looks like a Christmas card.

We used to speculate sometimes about the lives that the children must have led here, about how they spent their days, whether they, like ourselves, were banned from walking on the grass. Were they allowed to play round the bushes? And what happened to them when they left? It occurred to me that some of the Manchester women here could very likely be the descendants of those children. It must have been a grim place to spend a childhood in spite of the efforts made to make it attractive by the standards of those days. It continued to be in use as an orphanage and then under the euphemistic name of a 'home' until after the First World War into the 1920s. It was then left to decay without a use being found for it until 1958, when the government took it over, not of course for prisoners of war, but for refugees from the ill-fated Hungarian uprising, just as more recently army camps were reopened to house the Vietnamese boat people. In the early sixties the place was refurbished and taken over by the Home Office for use as a women's prison, which it has been ever since. In the popular mind, the Hungarian uprising has become submerged and mingled with the Second World War, and the refugees transformed into prisoners.

So Styal has known, through its whole hundred years of existence, various types of extreme human misery. Being an orphan in the nineteenth century, a refugee and exile from your native land in the twentieth, or a combination of both those sorrows, a prisoner shut away from family and home – these are the people who for a hundred years have exhaled their various miseries until the air is full of sorrow. The place has absorbed suffering and cannot now be anything other than depressing. Sometimes when it was felt that we were in need of a little excitement, someone would pretend to see the ghost of a weeping child. Most houses were supposed to be haunted by these apparitions, and they could be heard as well as seen, crying hopelessly for the pity of a life blighted through no fault of their own. The women identified passionately with the sorrows of a child which seemed to be theirs as well. I never saw the ghosts, but I am prepared to believe that a place which has known nothing but human misery for a long period of time does take on an atmosphere of its own, and that this atmosphere can interact in some way with the minds of people in an emotional and receptive state.

10 Size, Fox and Wilson

I had been moved to Styal on Wednesday, 27 October. It was on my fourteenth day there, Tuesday, 9 November, that I was told during the morning that I would be moving, after lunch. But was not told where. They were always very secretive on Davies House. I had been hoping for a long while that I would be moving, and as I have said, I secretly expected to be sent to Block 3 with the other privileged girls.

So after dinner I went up and stripped my bed, putting all my bedclothes and all the possessions I had into one blanket, and tying it as best I could into a decent bundle. This was how prisoners moved round Styal, with their belongings in a blanket like so many refugees. I lugged this bundle downstairs, and stood in the hall outside the office, alongside the bundles of the two or three people who were also on the move. Then the system seemed to break down, for nothing happened for a long while, and I was left to lounge around in the common room for over an hour.

I was quite sorry when this life of luxury was interrupted by the voice from the office yelling my name. I was told to put the bundle on the office floor, and then it was checked item by item against my card, in the presence of the officer from Davies who was checking me out and the officer checking me in to . . . Size House. My heart sank when I heard that, and it seemed to me that I would now lose all my remission for sure, as they were known to be a lot of tearaways on Size, and only a few days ago the whole house had been taken 'down the road' to Bleak House for an investigation into some tomfoolery with the fire extinguishers which had happened at night.

However, mine not to argue or complain, mine to pick up my doubly checked bundle and go with the officer to Size. The atmosphere was completely different from the moment we entered the front door. First, the place was not super clean. In fact it was a bit like going from the sublime to the ridiculous, for parts of Size, notably the utility room, were decidedly dirty. Secondly, there was a much less neurotic and easier-going attitude on the house. Thirdly, of course, this was a working house, and most people were out working in the workroom or elsewhere, and the house felt empty.

Looking back, I am sure that I was put on Size because they thought I might give it a bit of stability. After the fire extinguisher episode, a lot of the worst mischief makers had been transferred elsewhere, and several new people were put on to Size, to give it a different atmosphere.

I was taken up to Dorm 1, shown my bed and my locker and left to unpack. I didn't like the look of Dorm 1 at all. On Davies I had had my little two-person dorm, but here there were four bunks, each with one up and one down, making eight people in all. Mine was an upper bunk in the corner. I unpacked, and then went down, but nobody seemed very interested in giving me anything to do, so I went into the common room and found Jeffrey Archer's *Kane and Abel* which I had long been meaning to read, and I settled down with that for the rest of the afternoon. At five o'clock or just before, all the others came in from work, and the place assumed the guise of bedlam. After some mistakes, I found a vacant place for my meal at one of the tables in the dining hall. Most houses had tables seating four, unlike Davies which had two refectory-style tables for everybody.

In the evening several girls went out to classes while the rest of us watched TV. I had had the usual interview with the education people before I left Davies, but there wasn't much they could do for me. I was not staying long enough for Open University, and the other classes in which I might have been interested, such as art, were fully booked. The head of education, knowing my background, had suggested that I might like to run a class, but I could see the disaster inherent in that situation, and anyway, as I told her, I was not up to it.

Dorm 1 when I finally got to it at 9.00 (late bedtime!) was even worse than I could have imagined. Eight noisy, foul-mouthed women, all shouting at once, and Radio 1 at full volume on someone's radio. Lights out and radios off were at 10.00, and then the fun really began. The radio was turned on, everyone was running in and out of bed and in and out of the dorm, there were violent arguments, and in the bunk below me, lesbian activities of an extensive kind were taking place.

I lay there and thought very carefully about what I was going to do about the situation. I knew I could not stand this until 12 January. Whatever else had been wrong with Davies, at least it was quiet at night. Yet I knew full well that if I complained, or if anything I said could be construed as grassing, I would be in for very serious trouble indeed. The noise went on and on, and it was not until the early hours that they quietened down and I got some uneasy sleep.

The next morning I was still debating the problem of what to do, when it was almost solved for me by the girl who sat next to me at breakfast. She was another obvious misfit in this place, spoke with a better accent than I did, and had come from an excellent background. Drugs had been her downfall; she had been caught couriering cannabis into the country in immense quantities. She was now the assistant cook on the house. She asked me if I was all right, as I wasn't looking well, and I told her quietly that I hadn't had much sleep. On finding out that I was on Dorm 1, she at once understood, and advised me to ask for a transfer to her dorm where there were only four people, all of them quiet.

It was fortunate for me that the officer on duty that afternoon when I made my request, was one of the nicest people I have ever met. How on earth she ever got into the prison service I cannot imagine, but I was jolly glad she had. At first she said she had no authority to move me, but then she must have done a bit of checking up because she came back and told me I could move. Nobody ever got her bed and belongings out of one room and into another quicker than I did. Later on, the principal officer for the house came round, and on being told that I had requested a dorm change wanted to know why. Looking her straight in the eye, I said I suffered from vertigo, and I couldn't sleep on the top bunk, and none of the others would change with me. The room into which I had moved had real beds, not bunks at all.

The officer didn't believe me, nor did the girls when they came back and found I had moved. But honour was satisfied, I hadn't told on them. I couldn't help my vertigo. I soon saw why dorm changes were discouraged, as several people were fed up that I had moved, and there was a rash of dorm-change requests. Yet that bed in my new

Dorm 4 had been vacant for several days, so if anyone had really wanted to move they could have requested a move even before I got on the house. There wasn't much ill feeling, and I was such a nonentity anyway as far as being 'one of the girls' was concerned, that soon nobody noticed me, whichever dorm I was on.

Dorm 4 was certainly quiet. Besides me, there was another older woman who also valued her sleep, and Jill, the assistant cook. The fourth bed was filled by three different people while I was there, but they were all quiet, and went off to sleep at 10.00 or soon after. We could hear the terrible noise from the other end of the corridor as people ransacked and rioted in Dorm 1, but nobody ever came to disturb us. We were the misfits.

For the rest of that week I was 'on the house' during the day, which meant that I stayed behind and did the cleaning with another girl. But how relaxed it was after Davies! We were told what to clean, and left to get on with it. When we had finished, our time was our own. Only once was I checked up on, and told that I had not cleaned behind the beds in my own dorm. Quite right, I hadn't. I did that every other day, not every day. In the afternoons I used to hide and read, and nobody ever came looking for me. I finished *Kane and Abel* that way.

Visits to the library happened on Thursdays in the evening, at irregular intervals, but often enough for me never to run out of reading material. I found it unbelievably strange not only to be allowed but encouraged to go out after dark. The library was with the canteen, right round the other side of the prison, so it was quite a walk to get there. An officer came with us, but she was hardly in control of the proceedings, as we were straggled out in a long line, with those in front out of sight. At one point we were only a few yards from the perimeter fence, but nobody seemed to bother. I felt so free that I wondered what on earth an open prison must be like if a closed one was so relaxed. What a contrast to Pucklechurch, and that line of officers guarding us across the few yards in broad daylight to the chapel.

This walk in the winter dark to the library was really pleasant, with the tang of cold in the air and, later, snow under our feet. It was always magic for me. And the library when I first visited it was a pleasant surprise. I had imagined a diet of Mills and Boon, but it was a proper

201

library, with more books in it which I wanted to read than I ever had time for. For slowly but surely my concentration was coming back, and I used to go to bed at 8.30 or 8.45 and read for an hour or so for the rest of my time at Styal.

On the Friday of my first week on Size, I was told that on the Monday I would start my real work, as assistant cook on Davies House. I was terrified, as that meant I would be working with that master cook, Petra, but it turned out to be a very happy time for me. Meanwhile, there was the weekend to get through, and weekends were unpleasant. All the girls were on the house, and it felt overcrowded. Everyone was trying to get their washing and ironing done at once, there was no peace and quiet in the common room, and of course we were not allowed upstairs. In the afternoons we watched TV, but I found that the weekend dragged terribly, and I was very glad on future weekends that, as a cook, I still had to go to work. It was a seven-day-a-week job, for which I was paid the high wage of £1.20. This was ample for me to buy all the letters I needed, things like handcream and shampoo, and a weekly feast. I had moved from Mars bars to plain Bounty bars, and every week I bought three and ate them all at once. I was also able to save money each week, which at Styal we were allowed to do, and it was added to the money in my property when I went out.

I began work in the Davies kitchen early in the morning on 15 November, which was a personal anniversary for me. Cooks were woken early by the night officer, and of course with Jill and I both being cooks that meant half of Dorm 4 was awake. We had to dress and stack our beds by the light in the corridor, though the others in the dorm usually got up early too: you could get to the basins in comfort then. One thing I did not like about Size was that there were no curtains round the basins as there had been in Davies. Apparently they had got pulled down at some point and the authorities were refusing to replace them, which was tough on those of us who had nothing to do with the episode. I could never bring myself to strip and wash at the basin with no privacy at all, but as a cook I was entitled to a daily bath anyway, so I did not really have to.

So it was a quick face and hands for me, into my clothes, and downstairs at about ten to seven to ask the officer to unlock the house door so that I could walk round to Davies, which was the next door house. It was still dark at that time, and nobody about at all, and I had a terrific sense of freedom in that short walk. I had to time it so that I arrived at the Davies front door before the officer went upstairs to wake up her people. Petra lived on Barker, which was the next house to Davies on the other side, and often we would arrive together.

That first morning I was in a great panic as to what I would be expected to do, but in fact it was all very easy, and I soon fell into the routine. My job was to do the toast, two slices each for however many women were on the house, to put out the little margarine pats, strictly one per woman, and weren't there some rows if I got it wrong! Meanwhile, Petra would be making the porridge and grilling the sausages, or whatever, as soon as I had finished the toast. Then I was supposed to wash up everything we had used before breakfast, but as the porridge or scrambled egg saucepan was invariably burned, I soon learned to hide them, leaving them to soak so that I could do them more easily later in the day.

Breakfast was at 7.30 and woe betide us if we were not ready on time. When the officer had given out the breakfasts, we would tidy the kitchen quickly, and then go with our plates to the spaces reserved for us. At ten to eight, when breakfast was over, we were free to go back to our own houses, to make our beds and wait for 8.30, at which time the whole prison went to work. Floods of girls went to the workroom, cooks to the kitchens, gardeners and maintenance women to wherever they were working.

There was not usually much time to spare in the mornings. I had the vegetables to do, and that was another aggravation. All the knives had to be handed in with the keys to the larder and the fridge, and if the officer was feeling bolshy, she would refuse to give me the knives, which meant waiting until Petra came before I could start work. If she had been to see the doctor or something, that could mean a long delay. Sometimes I might have to go to the stores for some supplies, and this meant quite a long walk round the bottom of the campus to the stores.

The stores were run by two catering officers who worked out the menus on a weekly basis. Each house had the same menu, but the food was what the cooks made of it. Most things were brought round to the houses by the stores orderlies, again on a weekly basis. A set quantity of sugar, butter and jam was delivered, and you had to make it last. Bread could be ordered by individual houses in more or less unlimited quantities, and things like flour and rice were available in the stores and could be had on request. We took large tins to bring home the booty in, but as we were usually short of something, voyaging to the stores was an almost daily occurrence when the weather was nice. I had to get permission before I went off the house, but this was easy: I would just appear in the office doorway with my coat on and the tins in my arms, and the officer would either just nod or give me an inquisition, depending on her mood.

Commodities such as sugar and fruit were not kept in the kitchen, but in the office. So was the dried fruit. It was an unusual pair of cooks, however, who did not have a little store of illegal goodies in the larder somewhere, and while the catering officer was liable to descend unexpectedly and check that we were not embezzling the rations, she rarely in fact found anything. Nor were we supposed to cook anything other than what was on the menu for that day. Poor Jill on Size was caught cooking biscuits one day and lost remission for it. 'Misuse of rations' was a serious offence, and rightly so, but in every kitchen I had anything to do with there were extra goodies for the cooks and their friends. When making biscuits it was always difficult to make the right number, quite genuinely so; as with the rock cakes and shortbread we often had for supper. Extras were always eaten, either by the cooks or by the officers. Some officers would always refuse everything, whether because of high principles or their diets I was never sure, but others would accept a cake or biscuit from time to time.

At first I did not like hiding in the larder and eating scones with mounds of jam. It seemed unfair, and also I was terrified of losing remission, but I got corrupted very quickly, and used to eat the extras with only a tiny qualm. I recall one day just before my release when I was cooking at Wilson, and the cook had just made an illegal baked jam roll for us. She had eaten her half, but I was washing up, so my half was hidden in a bowl on the draining board. I had just taken my first bite, when in walked the house principal officer, the person I most dreaded, who knew perfectly well that I was rarely up to any good. She used to come and take all the saucepans out of my cupboards looking for illegalities and improper washing up. On that particular occasion there was only one thing to be done. I plunged the beautiful jam roll in its bowl deep into the washing up water, making sure it couldn't float up again, and continued my washing up, keeping my jaws still until she turned her back for a second when I was able to swallow my mouthful.

I think that everyone in the prison, including the officers, knew that the cooks used to help themselves to perks of this sort, and although if they did catch anyone the officers would jump on them hard, by and large it was something they turned a blind eye to. The most indiscreet kitchen I knew was on Wilson, where I served under three cooks, one of whom was Chinese. She used to make herself Chinese food, and the kitchen often smelled like a Chinese takeaway, but the officers never seemed to notice. Under a later cook on Wilson, there was a special tin where the extra goodies were kept, and people on the house would wander in and help themselves. It was of course not allowed for anyone other than the cooks to be in the kitchen, but on Wilson this didn't seem to matter much.

I learned a lot from watching Petra, though I must say that since leaving Styal I have reverted to my former slapdash methods of cooking, but one or two things which we made at Styal, mostly for the vegetarians, have become absorbed into my repertoire. The Styal food was edible, but they were very mean with meat and, as I said about Pucklechurch, I can't see why they didn't give up meat, which was mostly fat and gristle, and use soya more often.

As assistant cook, my main function was to peel vegetables and wash up, but bearing in mind that we were cooking for about twenty, this was a full-time job. The vegetables would take most of the morning, and then there would be a mound of washing up to do. But Petra was very good, and often let me get my hands in the pastry bowl instead of keeping all the nice jobs for herself. We often had to get a lot of cooking done in the mornings, as Petra might have a visit, or be going to keep fit; but the normal thing was to cook the dinner in the mornings, and then do tea and supper together in the afternoons. Petra never seemed to have a disaster, never appeared flushed or rushed, and her food, as I have said before, was superb.

I had thought that this way of life would go on for the rest of my three months, and apart from the panic I used to get into in the afternoons trying to get all the washing up done before tea was served at five o'clock, I was quite happy with the routine. We ate breakfast and dinner on the same house we cooked for, and then returned to our own house, but we did go back to our own house for tea. This meant that if I did not get that dreadful washing up done I was late for tea, and mine would be shrivelled up on the cooker waiting for me. It was bad enough having to leave Davies House and the delicious tea Petra had cooked in order to go back to Size and eat what was invariably a second-rate version of what Petra had made. The washing up was a problem, because I could not wash the saucepans and tins until the food was dished out. We did not serve the food to the table in dishes, but put it straight out on to plates in the kitchen from the pans. We tried dishing up earlier, but the house then complained of cold food, so I took to hiding the worst saucepans overnight as well as after breakfast. Whilst I am sure the officers knew, they let me get away with it, as the alternative was to be washing up at half past five.

Certainly time went very quickly in the kitchen. There was rarely a moment to sit down, and we were on the go all day, seven days a week. From that point of view it was a very tiring job, and I don't think I could have done it for years. I would have had to ask for a work change at some point. But there were perks other than the extra food: the bath I could have every night after I had had tea, and the fact that I did not have to do any of the chores shared by the rest of the house, such as 'sweep up', 'wash up', or 'duty cook'. The duty cook had to peel a bucket of potatoes to help in the morning, and although we cooked the supper, she also had to get it out and warm it up if necessary, or make some toast. Whilst all that was going on, I could lie in my bath, and then sit in front of the television rubbing handcream into my sore raw hands which had been in washing up water for the greater part of the day. I used to go to bed almost immediately after supper and read myself to sleep in the blessed quietness of Dorm 4.

The routine was interrupted on a Wednesday by a kit check. It was not necessary to clean the locker as thoroughly as on Davies, but all kit had to be displayed on the bed, and we might have to wait an hour while the officer was checking the other dorms. It was a 'wind up', a very annoying waste of time. Many officers checked kit quickly, but some took ages, and it was cold in those dorms in December having just got out of the bath.

How quickly one gets into a routine. I felt as if I was living on Size and working on Davies with Petra for several months, but in fact it was only a little more than three weeks. On 2 December I was told by the officer on Size when I returned to the house after dinner that I would be moving to Fox House that afternoon. I did not want to go, as I had got myself nicely set up on Size, and I certainly did not want to join all those dreadful pregnant Borstal girls. I begged the officer to do what she could, but there was nothing she could do. It had been decided to move some of the stable older women to Fox to counter the atmosphere created by some particularly volatile Borstal girls; I was a stable older woman, and I had to go. So it was explained to me by the officer.

I was sent for during the afternoon and told to go back to Size and pack up my bundle. I moaned all the time about it, but I could not disobey. I felt safe enough now at Styal to moan. I really did not want to go, and threatened to request a house change the minute I got there. So it was the moving routine once more: bundle everything up, take it down to the office, have it checked, and then off with the officer to Fox House. We were usually allowed to move about the prison without an escort, but when moving around with a bundle, we were always escorted. Check again on Fox House and up to my dorm.

I hated life on Fox. The dorm was quiet enough because I was there with only two other people, and I made it clear that as I had to get up in the morning, I expected to be allowed to go to sleep at night. But the atmosphere on the house was horrible. There was a group of older women like myself, who had been similarly uprooted from other houses, on which they were happy, and made to go to Fox. The Borstal girls were every bit as awful as I had imagined, screaming and shouting the whole time. Mealtimes were like a bear garden. There did not seem to be any proper house officers, and a different officer was on duty every time I entered the house. Without officers who ared about the house, things soon deteriorated. A great deal of the atmosphere of a house depended on the officers. They could make it hell as it was on Davies, relaxed but controlled as on Size, or bad as on Fox.

What really upset me on Fox was that because there were no regular officers, I was often not called in the morning in time to get to work. Often I would be woken at 7.00 with the others, when I was supposed to have been on Davies by that time. The officers just did not seem to care, but the Davies officers certainly did, and I was always in trouble for being late. I began not to sleep properly because I was worried about being late in the morning. Had I been allowed an alarm clock, I would have been perfectly capable of getting myself to work on time but I had to depend on the officers.

In fact the whole thing was a complete waste of time, as although it seems to me that I was on that awful house for months, I was only there for eight nights before I was moved again. So they might just as well have left me on Size for all the good I did on Fox. I certainly tried to get off Fox by talking to the most sympathetic of the Davies officers, explaining the problems I was having with not being woken up in the morning, and asking her if there was anything she could do. She arranged to phone the Fox officer to remind her to wake me, but I think she also saw to it that I was moved again.

But it was not only my place of residence that was changing. There were great upheavals on Davies House itself. Petra had heard the result of her appeal, and her sentence had been reduced from four years to eighteen months, which meant that she had only a couple more weeks to do and would be home for Christmas. What a super surprise that was for her! It meant, however, that she was no longer a long-stay prisoner, and so she had to move from Barker House, where the women were all doing sentences of over three years. The prison authorities had a theory that putting short- and long-stay prisoners together upset the ones with really long sentences, so where possible people with long sentences were put on the same houses. They did not therefore live in an atmosphere of people constantly going home, but in one of settled time-serving. For the same reason, the lifers were kept on their own house, Patterson, where they had special privileges, such as being allowed to have personal possessions in their dorms, and living no more than two to a dorm, or in single rooms. During my time there were so many lifers that Patterson was full, and the others had to be put on ordinary long-stay houses.

So Petra was moved from Barker to Wilson. She was also taken out of the kitchen, as the job of cook was one for a long-term prisoner. So I had a new boss, a younger woman who was serving a long sentence, again for drugs offences. Dita was a Turkish Cypriot who had been studying at the London School of Economics when she had been caught couriering large amounts of hard drugs into the country. She was a very striking looking girl, but she suffered agonies of embarrassment with her facial hair, which she normally kept under control with electrolysis. But of course there were no such facilities in Styal, so poor Dita had to grow her beard. She was temperamental by nature, and not nearly such a good cook as Petra, though she did her best, and the longer she cooked the better she got.

I suffered at her hands because she was forever turning the cooker up too high and burning the food well and truly on to the bottom of the pans. She was also very disorganized and was in a perpetual flap which I found very wearying after Petra's calm and confident approach. We got on quite well, but I was not helped by the fact that I arrived so late in the mornings just as Dita was trying to settle in as a cook. She would sometimes flare up at me as a way of relieving her own panic, and I found it hard to take. I think we would have got on better had I stayed, but I was moved shortly after Dita came.

Yet another upheaval happened to Davies House. It was decided in the middle of December to do away with the Assessment House, and make it a house for prisoners serving between two and three years, a kind of medium-stay house. People who fell into this category from all over the prison were suddenly moved on to Davies, and the atmosphere was appalling for some time. Everybody hated Davies, and it was a terrific blow for the women to be moved back there from a house where they had probably been happy. I waited with interest to see what would happen. The Davies officers continued at first to be as bloody-minded as they had always been: I even saw Dita, who was one of those moved, called out of the kitchen five minutes before breakfast-time because she had not stacked her bed properly! The women could cope with Davies for a fortnight when they first came in, but three years of that kind of petty-mindedness was not tolerable. After a short while, however, there was a big meeting of Davies House women and officers with the assistant governor, as a result of which things improved for the women and new officers began to come on to Davies, including one whom I liked very much, who was a very good officer, firm, fair and not petty minded. The old Davies officers began to appear less often, and were given other jobs to do around the prison.

At the time of this changeover, there were three women on Davies who were very short-stay prisoners indeed: three of the first women from Greenham Common to be sentenced to prison. They had been held at Drake Hall Open Prison, but had become an embarrassment to the authorities because there was a large camp of other Greenham women and local CND members at the gates. The situation was felt to be a security risk, so the women were moved to Styal, their camping supporters following them. I think they came in on the Thursday, and were due for release on the Monday morning. They certainly brightened up the place, both because of their obvious inappropriateness in Styal, and because their supporters sent in several million flowers. Davies was full to bursting with the most lovely flowers, and the hardier pots and bunches were put outside on the grass for the whole prison to enjoy. Some flowers may have been sent to other houses; I know the officers took some home, and I just hope they asked first.

I used to talk to these Greenham women whenever I could, and was impressed by their intelligence and sincerity. They were given a lot of support by most of the women on Davies, and they were shocked by their experience of prison. I know that they had been convicted of offences such as obstruction, but in a very real sense I felt that they were the first political prisoners in this country. They were not really in prison because of obstruction or refusal to pay a fine, but because of their political beliefs. I didn't like it at all. Also, they were treated worse than the rest of us: we were left free at night, but they were put together in a dorm at night with plastic pots, and locked up. I never understood why that should be.

People going out had to have a special early breakfast in order to get through reception by 8.00, so the Greenham women had breakfast at 7.00 on that Monday morning, and I was able to wish them well. They went out to a rapturous reception from their supporters, and from the press, and we saw it on television that night. I was amazed at the large numbers who had been keeping vigil outside Styal while the women were inside.

I was just settling into my new routine of living on Fox and cooking with Dita on Davies when I was told that I was on the move again, away from Fox and Davies. I was to move across to Wilson, and be assistant cook there. So at last I was to go to the privilege house. The officer who told me seemed to think that I should be overwhelmed with gratitude, but I was a bit choked off at having to move yet again. I was only in the prison for a few weeks and already I had been shunted round more than most people were in months or years. And because the officer thought I should be grateful, as if some great favour were being bestowed on me, I moaned more than I might have done in order to be difficult.

It was 10 December, my daughter's birthday, when I did up my beastly bundle yet again, and trailed it from Fox to Wilson, right from one side of the prison to the other. Trailed is the right word, as I discovered when I got to Wilson that one of my blankets had been dragging in the mud all the way. And so I entered Wilson, the privilege house, where I had wanted to be, and where I was actually allowed to stay for the last month of my sentence.

Wilson was a funny house. The officers were mostly pleasant, though there was one I disliked and the feeling was mutual. The house principal officer was a dragon. I had had nothing to do with principal officers before, but this one was always on the house looking for trouble, of which there was quite a lot while I was there. The women were a mixed bunch and, as I have already said, I think that because they were 'nicer' than the average prisoner, they were also bitchier. The privileges mostly consisted of being allowed upstairs without permission, and having the pick of the jobs going at Styal: being allowed outside the prison to clean the officers' quarters or work in the mess, or having other trusty jobs such as reception orderly or gym orderly. Wilson was also a more amenable place to live than some of the other houses, as it was better kept, less shabby, and better decorated. It also had curtains round its washbasins.

I had more problems on Wilson with the other women than I had had before. Again, as at Size, I had to ask for a dorm change. This was not because of any unsavoury goings on such as the nightly happenings in Size's Dorm 1, but because two women of my own age would not stop talking to each other until the early hours of the morning. The others in the dorm were very annoyed with me when I asked the two natterers to shut up so that I could sleep. I had got used to sleeping at ten or half past, but it seemed that nobody on Wilson needed to sleep except me. Unlike the women on Size, the whole house took it personally when I got a transfer to another dorm, and I did not make things better for myself by saying truthfully in answer to their question that I did not prefer life on Wilson, and had been much happier on Size. How I missed my lovely quiet dorm!

My attitude was also somewhat coloured by the onset of 'gate fever'. When I had been on Wilson for a week, I only had a little more than three weeks more to do, and I was becoming less and less prepared to try to fit in. I just wanted to be left alone, allowed to sleep and work, and get past Christmas into the New Year. I did not want any hassle from the other women, and as I would be leaving so soon I could not be bothered, with one exception, to form relationships. Life in the house largely went on without me, and I suspect that I was probably the least popular member of Wilson for the time I was on it.

The one exception was Doris, a sweet quiet woman who had only another couple of months of a long sentence to do. She was a real worrier and, like me, not really part of the house. Her job was orderly for the big administrative block outside the prison, and she used to worry all the time that her work might not be up to standard. When I changed dorms, she had the bunk below me, and we used to have quiet chats in the dorm in the evening while the others were watching TV. Nobody else had much time for Doris, she was too quiet, and she came to regard me as her best friend, and she cried when I was released, though we had only known each other a short time. In order to get her cleaning done, Doris had leave for work early: she always got up with me at 6.30, or rather she got up at 6.15, and made sure that I was up at 6.30, and then I would get her breakfast and she would be off to work before the others were woken at 7.00.

By changing dorms I had got away from the natterers, but I had made myself very unpopular with another girl in my new dorm, who was probably the most disturbed person I met during the whole of my eight months. Her name was Lee, and she was in for 'Paki bashing'. She was a really violent type, and was only on Wilson because with other violent prisoners on another house she was nothing but trouble. At least the Wilson girls were not violent, and the authorities must have felt that she could be contained in the non-violent atmosphere. From the first day I appeared on the house, Lee had it in for me. She had to have someone to hate, and I was that person.

Lee accused me quite falsely of being a grass. This interested me as an example of how gossip goes round a prison. When I had been moved from Size to Fox, it happened to coincide with the discovery of lesbian activities on Size, and some of the girls concerned had been punished. Because I had been moved at that time, the rumour had started that I had grassed on the lesbians, and had been moved from Size for my own protection. I had dealt with this on Fox, but on my first night on Wilson, Lee made me aware that the rumour had followed me there. She said she was going to get me for it, as she herself was a lesbian. I think she was one of the few genuine lesbians in Styal, as – like at Pucklechurch – most of them were playing with it for the sake of the drama and excitement it provided.

The thought of being 'got' by Lee was a sobering one, as I had no doubt that she would half kill me if the opportunity arose. I remember seeing her on the first kit check night I was in her dorm laying out a pair of white trousers, legs covered in rusty stains. She was angry about those trousers. They were ruined she said, ruined. The stains just would not come out. It was blood: those were the trousers she had been wearing when she was arrested, having kicked a Pakistani almost to death. It disgusted me that she could continue to wash and wear those trousers and complain about their condition. Lee was utterly callous, and totally devoid of any feeling whatsoever for anyone else . She was totally self-centred, and every evening the dorm would have to listen to her long stories about herself and her girlfriend. There were two bunks and a single bed in the dorm, and Lee used the occupant of the single bed as a kind of mother figure, talking to her endlessly about her life and problems. Listening in return was something Lee never did. It was self, self, self all the time. I was horrified to see the extent of the damage which had somehow been done to that woman. For she was a woman in her mid-twenties, though in attitude and behaviour she might have been twelve or fifteen.

I felt very sorry for Lee, but overwhelmingly I felt afraid of her. She used to refer to me as 'That'. 'I really hate That up there', she used to say, jerking her fist at me as I sat in bed in my bunk pretending to read. 'One day I'm going to kill That, I really am.' I believe, too, that if we had had to live together for very long, she might have done. Lee saw to it that I got as little sleep as possible but, luckily for me, she herself seemed to need a lot of sleep, and would often fall asleep quite early. I never felt safe sleeping until she did; once she was sleeping nothing wakened her. Many times as I dressed in the early morning to the accompaniment of Lee's snores, I felt that I would like to wake her up to pay her back for keeping me awake, but I never did, partly because I did not wish to be so petty, and partly because I was afraid.

In those days around Christmas, a strange atmosphere descended upon the house. One woman was actually taken off Wilson and put on a lock-up house because she was found wandering around downstairs in the middle of the night. She said she was sleepwalking, but I didn't believe it. A whole group of other girls got into serious trouble for making a ouija board out of a plate and some Scrabble letters, and getting caught sitting in the corridors frightening themselves to death with it. The atmosphere became as brittle as ice; we lived in the constant expectation that something awful was going to happen.

To cope with this, people became very silly, and there was a lot of St Trinian's behaviour. People's beds were pulled to pieces, mattresses hidden in other rooms, pillowcases put into cisterns, apple pie beds made. The staff got more and more fed up with what was going on, and the whole house was lectured by its officers and by the principal officer. We were warned that we were not behaving like people on a privilege house should behave. On a couple of occasions we had babysitters in – the night patrol made its headquarters on Wilson House because we could not be trusted to behave ourselves. This was a tremendous scandal in the rest of the prison. Even one of the house officers got into trouble, because she had covered up for the ouija board girls.

The authorities tried a bit of moving about. Jenny, the policeman's daughter who had been with me on Davies House, was brought in, but she only ended up in trouble for taking rations from the kitchen to put down someone's bed. It was only a carrot and bit of flour, but of course technically it was 'misuse of rations' and a serious offence. Poor Jenny got 'busted' for it, lost her privileged job outside and was demoted to being a house cleaner. Jenny used to sit at my table for meals, and there was a permanent atmosphere of near-hysterical humour. Lee hated all this laughing and the fact that she was not the centre of attention, and used to stage great dramas in the dining room. These were usually centred round the fact that she could not eat the awful food, which was no doubt a dig at me.

It is actually very hard to eat on the house you cook for, especially on Wilson, where so many of the girls were cooks, either on other houses or on the officers' mess. They all thought their own cooking was superb, and ours appalling, and it could get very unpleasant if the cook had had a disaster, as was bound to happen from time to time. The girls on the officers' mess never seemed to eat anything, and I was sure they used to get better rations illegally where they worked.

And so Christmas came, dreaded by us all. There were carol services, to which I did not go, not trusting my self-control. I had requested that no cards be sent in. I wanted to ignore Christmas if I could. We were not allowed to have our cards out on our lockers anyway, though we were allowed to decorate the common room. A list appeared on the noticeboard detailing the Christmas arrangements, and they did try to lay on two or three days of festivities for us. There were sporting events and a couple of films, one of which was 'Porridge', which we thought was an odd choice. I went to see that film, but let everything else pass me by.

For one thing, Christmas was a very busy time for cooks. There were not many extra rations, but they all had to be collected from stores and put in the larder. There were mincepies to make, the cake to ice, and even more vegetables to prepare. We had Brussels sprouts for Christmas Day, and as they were about the size of marbles, and I had to do enough for twenty women, that took a long time. So I was well able to hide from Christmas in the kitchen, which I did. Also, I was getting really tired by this time.

On Christmas Day itself, breakfast was late and dinner was early, so we had a mad panic in the kitchen. The officers were trying very hard indeed to lift our spirits and create a good atmosphere, and I respect them for the way they behaved: it couldn't have been much fun for them either. But most of the women had children at home, and despite all attempts to lighten the atmosphere, a sense of deep gloom pervaded the whole prison, and I came across more people having little weeps in corners on that day than at all other times combined. On Christmas afternoon, I retired to the kitchen and spent the whole time washing up entirely alone. The cook had gone back to her own house at my suggestion, and I declined all offers of help. I wanted to make the jobs last, so that I could keep well away from the television and the sentimental atmosphere it engenders on Christmas Day, which I find quite hard to take at home, never mind in prison.

By the end of Boxing Day, there was a lot of ill-feeling on the house, resulting entirely from the extra stress of coping with Christmas. I avoided the common room completely. Everyone was very glad indeed when work began again, either on the day after Boxing Day, or the day after that for some. Life got back to normal, and we forgot Christmas as quickly as we could. I think that those in prison at Christmas time suffer an extra punishment. We had one girl who went out just before Christmas, and one girl who went out just after. One was overjoyed; the other very depressed.

Then came the new year, which is a happier time in prison, as it marks another huge step forward in one's sentence. Now you could say, I get out this year or next year, or in only another two years. The people who can't look at it that way are the lifers, and particularly those there on Her Majesty's Pleasure, who do not know how long they may have to serve. The cook I was working under at that time was one of these, a young girl in her early twenties, who was in for an IRA offence. I do not know how she coped with the uncertainty of not knowing how long she was to remain in prison. Every two years she was allowed to request a release date. So far she had not been given one. It had been a horrific IRA bomb, but she had been seventeen or eighteen at the time, not at all political, not even Irish. She had just got carried too far on her rollercoaster, as I had on mine, and she was a different person now.

So with January came a new attitude for me. My release date was the 12th, a Wednesday, and I became even more solitary and cut off from the life of the prison. I used to go over to the hospital twice a day for my medicine, answering the call of the officer who more often than not would simply shout 'Doses!', and leave us all to make our own way there and back. I used to walk slowly, and on each journey I would pass at a distance from the main gate, and it became a ritual to look at it and whisper ten, nine, eight, or however many days I had left. This was partly in eagerness, but mostly in apprehension. I had only been in eight months, but I was afraid of going out. All those problems were waiting for me outside the gates, and I didn't much fancy having to go out there and get to grips with them. I became quite depressed and withdrawn.

I applied for a clothing grant, as I had been in long enough to qualify for one, and one afternoon I was sent for to go and choose my clothes. I was allowed a skirt, a jersey, a coat, three pairs of the monstrosities known as 'grant knickers', two pairs of long socks and a pair of shoes. All were cheaply made and quite hideous, but at least they were new clothes, and therefore quite exciting. I wore them proudly to my last visit, when my daughter and I arranged that she should meet me at the gate on the day of my release. I was beginning to feel unreal again, as I had done in the early days.

I decided that I quite liked Styal. I liked the houses, especially with snow on their roofs. We had quite a fall in January, which led to speculation about what would happen to someone on her release date if it was a bad winter like 1976 and everything had ground to a standstill. The authorities would have to let you go, but suppose you could not make it into Manchester? I liked walking across to the hospital, it was all very peaceful, very safe, very secure.

But I did not like that principal officer, who had now found another way to make my life a misery. She insisted that I should thoroughly clean the cooker every day at one o'clock. That was fine, except that the house officers expected me to go out on exercise at just after one. For a while I got out of exercise (it had got too cold for me to enjoy walking round and round now), but then they decided that I must go to exercise with the others, and then clean the cooker before the cook started using it again. I used to come in from exercise, pull the whole cooker to pieces, and get a bowl of soapy water beside me on the floor, knowing that in five minutes the cook would come rushing in and have a fit at the sight of the cooker in pieces and tell me to put it back together again or tea would never be ready.

Another job, which I only did once, was cleaning out the grease trap on the drain. This was a hellish invention, which collected not only grease but everything else other than water which went down the sink. Told to clean it out every week by the PO, I stumbled on the fact that nobody knew what I was supposed to do with all the gunge I had extracted. 'What do I do with this?' I demanded of my officer. It could not go in the swill bin, it could not go in the dustbin. Holding her nose, she suggested I buried it in a flower bed, but the ground was like iron. So I simply dumped it on the flower bed, and there it remained, stinking to heaven until I left Styal. I enquired what other houses did, and the answer was that nobody ever cleaned out the grease trap.

Those last days went very quickly. I had hoped to be allowed to remain in the kitchen until at least the Monday before the Wednesday of my discharge, but I was taken off kitchen work a week before my release. This meant that my last days were spent as my first, as a house cleaner. I used to take my time about everything, pottering round with brooms and dusters, sometimes working efficiently, more often getting the sags and staring out of windows at the Styal campus, wondering what on earth was to become of me.

I was given absolutely no preparation whatsoever for discharge. 'The Welfare' saw me, and having ascertained that I would be met by my daughter and could go to her house, that was that. Nobody knew or cared what my circumstances were, what problems I would face, what could be done to stop me repeating the offence and returning. Only my own probation officer, who came to see me during her Christmas holiday which she had spent at Leeds with her family, seemed in any way concerned about what was to happen to me, and whether I could cope with life outside. I count myself fortunate that I had somewhere to go and someone to care for me. Nobody in Styal would have cared otherwise. Of course I had heard about the appallingness of prison aftercare, but to hear about it is one thing, experience it another.

The Monday before I was to be set free, Lee got a letter. It was from her girlfriend, and I suppose it was the lesbian equivalent of a 'Dear John'. Lee's girl had finished with her, she said, and not for another woman either. She had met a man and was going to settle into heterosexuality. Lee went berserk. She refused to go to work, she behaved in a very dangerous and threatening way towards everybody, even the staff. I dreaded that night, as I thought that surely there would be trouble. And there was. The officer said goodnight to us, and I noticed that she remained in the doorway with the door open behind her. No way was she coming into the dorm, but I had to spend the night there. I wondered what would be left of me by the morning, and whether I would lose remission and not get out on Wednesday after all.

When the officer had gone, Lee began crying and wailing to her motherly figure. Several people came into the dorm from other dorms on the house to try to console Lee, but she would not be consoled, and was slowly working herself up into a state. I lay with my face hidden in the sheets, but kept one eye on Lee in case her fury came in my direction. Fortunately, Lee had forgotten me. When she had goaded herself into losing control, she leapt out of bed and began to smash up the furniture. Those lockers were quite substantial, but she had amazing strength, and she had the doors off and the sides splintered with a very few blows. She was only using her hands. In the bunk below me I could hear Doris quietly praying. I did not dare to do even that, but tried to prepare myself for when Lee hit me with a piece of smashed locker.

There was utter chaos. Lee rushed out of the dorm, the others in tow, and began to create mayhem in the washrooms. It didn't last for long. The night patrol must have been aware of the possibility of trouble, for they arrived in full strength. They found almost all the girls on the house out of bed (an offence) and in the wrong dorms (a serious offence). Taps were on in the washroom, and the floor was flooded. Lee, with amazing presence of mind considering the state she was supposed to be in, had leapt back into bed. When the night patrol came to our dorm, all five of us were in bed, and nobody knew anything about the smashed furniture. They looked to Doris and I to tell them what had happened, but neither Doris nor I were that stupid. The officers stood in the middle of the wrecked room and had no alternative but to accept that none of us had heard anything, none of us had seen anything, none of us could understand how the locker came to be in that state, or how the clothes and bedclothes had come to be everywhere.

The night patrol settled down on the house, for which I was very thankful, as it meant I could sleep in comparative safety. They warned us before they left that there would be serious trouble in the morning. Lee went to sleep almost straightaway, and I lay awake for a while wondering whether I would lose remission as a result of all these goings on, and if that happened whether I would be glad or sorry. On the whole, faced with the possibility of another week or fortnight on this house, I thought I would be very sorry indeed, and it was a healthy sign that I was beginning to prefer freedom with all its uncertainties to further imprisonment.

In the morning, the promised trouble materialized in the shape of the principal officer and the senior officer for the house, and a full-scale investigation, not only into the previous night's troubles but also into the episodes of recent weeks on Wilson. Put all together, these episodes were making the staff wonder what on earth had happened to their privilege house. Many of the girls were not allowed to go to work at all. Some went to work and were recalled for questioning. Lee was told to go to work, but managed to spend most of her time hanging around the house, from time to time bursting in and demanding to see an officer.

Throughout the time I was on Wilson, I was interested to observe the reactions of the rest of the house to Lee's behaviour, and the lenient way in which she was treated by the officers. Lee was allowed to get away with behaviour which would simply not have been tolerated from any of us. She was very much a special case, and the other women accepted this, taking it for granted that Lee was not like the rest of us, and that her very disturbed personality merited special treatment. As a teacher, I had often had this kind of situation to deal with, and I had always wondered how I would feel if I were in the position of a child seeing another child get away with types of behaviour disallowed to me. Now I knew: you understand the difference, tolerate it, and accept that this person is treated differently, and that this is fair.

Half way through the morning, the assistant governor herself arrived on the house, and the investigation was hotted up. There was a horrible atmosphere on the house, with women sitting about in small hostile groups, each wondering what the other women had said, and what they would say when it was their turn. The cleaners were still supposed to be cleaning, but as it was evident that no officer was going to check anything, we merely left a few brooms lying about, and did nothing.

I was given a fair deal of attention on the last day of my imprisonment. I was sent for and interviewed no fewer than four times. The line that they took was, firstly, that I was going out the next day, and so could afford to reveal all I knew about what was happening on Wilson – sexual, psychic, violent or just plain illegal. Secondly, I was surprised and interested to note, they appealed to me on the grounds of being one of them. They reminded me who I was, or rather, what I had been, and assumed that therefore I must be on their side. Come on, ex-deputy head, you'll help us, won't you? As for every single other day of my time inside, they had studiously avoided treating me in any way differently from any other woman, I was a bit taken aback by this sudden reversal.

This was a fascinating situation for me to be in, and I found, somewhat to my consternation, that I tended on the whole to be on the side of the women rather than the officers. Having only been in prison for eight months, I would not have expected the beliefs and attitudes of a lifetime to have become eroded; yet so it was. I had had plenty of experience myself in being the authority figure conducting the investigation, and had used the very techniques with my recalcitrant schoolgirls which I observed the principal officer and assistant governor to be using on me. I felt compromised by my desire to be the reasonable and law-abiding person which I really was, and to tell the authorities everything I knew (which was quite a lot, in common with every other woman on the house), and the devil which prompted me to give them no help at all because they were 'them' and somehow on the opposite side. I knew from my own experience on the other side of the desk that if I held out and refused to say anything, there was absolutely nothing that the officers could do. I recognized the techniques and resisted them, and again felt a deep satisfaction at defying the system – which ought to have been totally foreign to my nature.

There was also the practical consideration that if I told them how the furniture got smashed, Lee would certainly smash me that night. I had no compunction in letting the officers know that I was not talking because I was afraid, and although I did not name Lee, they knew who I meant. Lee was a bully, who terrorized not only me and Doris, but others as well. Eventually I was told by the assistant governor that Lee was going to be transferred off the house with immediate effect, and I am sure that Wilson was the better for her going. I still felt unable to tell what I knew, and they ended up very diappointed in me. Another girl did actually reveal who had smashed the furniture, but I wonder to this day if as soon as my back was turned she did not put it about that it was me and not her who had told, as no one likes to acquire the reputation for grassing.

In addition to the excitement of this investigation, I had other calls on my time that last day. I had to see the doctor, who glanced at me to ascertain that I was still alive, and then surprisingly said that he hoped I would get the psychiatric treatment outside which the judge had recommended I should have inside. I had to see the governor, who never so much as glanced at me, merely told me in a bored tone how much money I had due to me, signed something, and then snapped 'All right, go' when I stood there waiting for some further sign of life from him. I thought perhaps he might wish me well, or tell me not to do it again, or something at least, but there was nothing, nothing at all. I had to bundle up all my belongings and take them over to reception, to be united with the rest of my property, checked and searched and put ready for me to claim the next day.

As in a dream, it was teatime, and my last bathtime, and suppertime, and bed. Bed in a strangely quiet dorm without Lee ranting on. I felt in some way guilty about her, as though I should have done more to help her, but she was so disturbed and she hated me so much, that I do not really see what I could have done. Anyway, she was gone , and I was to go tomorrow. Doris, who had only another month to do herself, asked me how I felt, for now without Lee the rest of us could talk to each other. Doris was trying to imagine what it must feel like to be going out tomorrow. I felt excited, of course I did, but also weighed down with worry about whether and how I would be able to survive outside. Could I make a living? Could I go back to my house in that little village? Could I meet people again? I was not expecting to be able to sleep, but I did sleep, dreamlessly and well. My last night in captivity.

Doris woke me early the next morning. It was still dark, but it looked as if it would be another cold, dull day. Doris was very emotional, and kept hugging me and crying. I knew she would miss me, because I was one of the few people who bothered to talk to nervous, introverted Doris. How she came to be in prison I cannot imagine: yet another complete misfit. I was supposed to have my breakfast with her before she set off as usual for her cleaning work on the admin. block; but I was too strung up to eat anything. I was also supposed to go across to reception before the others all got up at seven, but on that morning, of all mornings, everything went wrong.

The front doors of the houses were locked every night, and opened again in the morning by the duty officer, who then had the job of rousing the cooks, unlocking the kitchen, and then waking the rest of the house at seven. But this morning there was no officer. The front door remained locked, as did the kitchen, so it was just as well I wasn't hungry. Doris was hungry, though, but there was nothing we could do except hang around outside the office by the front door and wait for the officer to come. The cook lived on another house, but the assistant cook was there with us, yawning and irritable. I knew how she felt. It is a rush to get breakfast for twenty women: it must be ready at 7.30, as they have to get to work, and if you can't get in the kitchen by about ten to seven, you are going to have problems. Often I had fumed at officers making my life more difficult by not coming on time and then taking their time to unlock the kitchen, out of spite sometimes I'm sure.

So there we stood, Doris wanting her breakfast, the assistant cook wanting to get into the kitchen, and me with my bundle of blankets and my last few possessions wanting to be released. But the officer did not come and did not come. It got to be seven o'clock, ten past, a quarter past. We took counsel with the women who had got up of their own accord, and decided to go and wake up the other women ourselves. It wasn't just our house. All over the prison houses were in darkness where there should have been lights; kitchens were empty where they should have been occupied. I stood there with my bundle, feeling disorientated, but wondering what we would do if no officer ever came again. Suppose it was a revolution, or war, and we just stood there dumbly waiting to be unlocked, as the animals in the zoos will wait when it does happen, and there is nobody left to unlock them or feed them ever again?

It was nearly 7.20 when the officer did arrive, refusing to answer any questions as to what had happened, though rumour soon spread that it was something to do with the IRA girls. When the prison was disrupted it usually was something to do with them, and we heartily wished they were back in Durham (on one occasion we missed a whole half hour of visiting time because of an IRA rescue threat). I had to wait while the officer sorted out the cook and dealt with the routine things she had to do in the morning. Then she phoned over to reception for an escort, because, of course, as I had a bundle I was not allowed to walk alone along the path I had walked alone hundreds of times.

So I left Wilson House for the last time, and glad I was to see the back of it too. A short walk in the dawn light to the old building which housed reception, where I was pleased to note that I was the only prisoner due for release that day. The usual routine: undress, leave clothes in the room, strip search, clothes searched, dress again, property searched and united with the rest of it, sign for it – although I hadn't checked it and didn't know whether or not it was all there, but at that stage, who cared? The officer on duty was the one very humane woman I had got to know on Davies, and I was glad that the last officer I would see was one who seemed to think that the function of the prison service was to help prisoners make sense of themselves and their lives rather than one of the officers who could not care less about individual prisoners.

Then I had to wait for the chief officer. While I waited, breakfast was brought to me, and I was surprised to find that I could actually eat quite a lot, which I did, because the officer had been kind enough to have it sent over for me since she knew I had had none on the house. I waited in a state of limbo until another officer appeared to escort me to the chief, that same chief whom I had known at Pucklechurch, now promoted to Styal. Seeing her again rounded out the whole experience, and for once I did stand to attention and recite my name and number, J74937, as I was supposed to do. Again she quietly made the atmosphere informal with her 'Hello Audrey'. Her concern that I had somewhere to go and that I should not come back was rather different from the governor, I thought.

The chief gave me the money I was due, and I signed for it. She asked if all my possessions were in order, and I naturally said they were. She gave me forms to take to the DHSS, and another form which I had to read and then sign in duplicate, binding myself not to possess a gun for a period of five years. This is apparently standard practice for the release of people who have committed a violent offence, but it came as a shock to me. What good they think it would do in the case of a real criminal I cannot imagine. I have never had a gun, and certainly have no intention of having one, but there it is.

The chief wished me well, and I went back into my little room to wait for the magic hour of 8.00, for although it seemed to me that I had been in reception for several hours, it could not have been longer than twenty minutes. At last the nice officer came in and said, 'Right Audrey, it's nearly 8.00. We might as well go.' So I went and picked up my bags from where they had been put after being searched, and we strolled up the path towards the gate. Styal has two gates, one in the perimeter fence, which is locked and manned, and one higher up at the top of the drive, which is open all the time. We went through the gate in the fence, the officer handing whatever documentation was necessary to the male officers on guard. Then we strolled up towards the top gate.

I was in no hurry. I had the rest of my life, after all. Though, being an emotional person, a lump did rise in my throat as I went through that locked gate, opened now to return to me my freedom. The end of an experience which will live with me for the rest of my life. The officer was concerned enough to talk to me as we walked, saying that she was sure that prison had not done me any good, and it was up to me to see that it hadn't done me any harm either, and that I never

225

came back. She also reminded me to be careful, as I was still under a suspended sentence.

Wishing to try to be helpful in some way, and perhaps to atone for my lack of cooperation the day before, I asked her whether she knew that the search carried out on prisoners was useless without a medical examination, as the vagina, being an organ designed to stretch enough to accommodate a baby on its way into the world, had been found to be a useful repository for a large number of things which were also on their way into the outside world, through prison gates. I hadn't told her anything she didn't already know. She said that they had to do something, and the strip searching was the only thing possible unless there was a change in the law to permit medical examination. This was not actually my point, I did not wish to suggest that the searches should be intensified, but rather abandoned.

And so we arrived at the top of the drive, by the open main gates, where staff cars were driving in. The officer escorted me right outside the gates, and looking down the road we could see my younger daughter coming towards us as fast as she could. She would have been waiting outside, but we had fooled her by coming a little early. The officer said goodbye and good luck, I said goodbye and thank you, and then ran down the road towards my daughter. We met and embraced, and there didn't really seem to be anything to say at all.

We walked down the road towards the station, and a long road it was. I thought of my daughter coming all that way in bad weather to visit me. On some days she must have got soaked. I tried to take notice of what I was feeling, but I cannot honestly say that I felt anything very much. I was glad it was behind me, but I wasn't overcome with joy, or with the sense of freedom, or any such thing. I just plodded down the road, and it seemed such a long road. And I knew only too well that just being outside the gates instead of inside them did not really make a difference to anything at all which mattered to me. Just as eight months previously being inside instead of outside had not made the slightest difference to anything.

We went to Styal station and got tickets to Manchester, or rather my daughter got the tickets. I was content to let her look after me; it seemed quite natural somehow. The idea was that I would return with my daughter to her flat, spend some days there, and then my elder daughter would drive up to Manchester to collect me, and I would spend some time back at home with her to see if I thought I could live there again. If I could not, then I could return to Manchester and stay with my younger daughter until I had got myself sorted out. I was not particularly keen to go home; it seemed that while I was in Manchester I was still away from the real hard concrete problems which I would have to face as soon as I returned home.

11 Release and After

Life after release from prison is strange. Everything has changed, yet strangely everything is the same. As I sat with my daughter in the little train from Styal to Manchester, I felt two totally contradictory feelings at once. First, I felt absolutely normal. I was in a train, going to my daughter's house. People got on and off, commuters on their way to work, reading newspapers, saying nothing; an entirely normal and familiar scene. I felt that I had every right to be sitting on this train among them, and it was hard to believe that half an hour before I had been a prisoner. Perhaps eight months is simply not long enough for the hand of institutionalism to settle over one. I was not afraid to be free, I was not elated, it all seemed entirely natural as if I had had a nightmare and was now awake.

Yet at the same time, I felt set apart, branded. I was sure that everyone must realize that I had been in Styal, that I was an ex-convict, that although I sat quietly and normally among them, I had things in my head which they would have condemned me for had they spoken to me. I had been arrested, on trial, imprisoned; and these things set me apart from those who had not, irrevocably, like a woman who has had a child is never quite the same person as she was before, and between her and her childless sister there is a gulf fixed which, while it is impossible to explain properly, everyone can sense. This feeling I have has persisted, and will not be shaken off.

I was deeply afraid of meeting people I knew. I was afraid to go home, in case they shouted at me in the streets. I was afraid of what they said to each other, of what they might say to me, of what they might think and not say to me. If I felt branded among strangers on a train, what would I feel back in my little village? It was very good for me not to have to go straight home, but to be able to stay for a while in Manchester, where I was unknown.

In the afternoon of the day of my release, we decided to go into the city centre and look around the shops. Here I got my first surprise. I had been expecting, and so had my daughter, that I would have problems coping with the crowds, as I don't like masses of people at the best of times. In fact, that was no worse for me than usual. Indeed, the noise and bustle were quite a treat. What I did find was a terrible physical tiredness, which I was ashamed to admit to. At last I had to tell my daughter that I could not go any further, and we went home. I suppose it should have been obvious that after eight months without walking, I would not be able to walk for an extended period, but I have always taken the perfect functioning of my body for granted, and suddenly to find that I could not walk round the shops for a couple of hours without becoming totally exhausted was a great shock to me.

Having been thus alerted to the poor physical condition I was in, I made other experiments, and found that I got tired and out of breath ridiculously easily. I felt very annoyed about this: my life for years past had been one long rush, my idea of relaxation a walking holiday in the Welsh mountains, and now I could hardly do anything. It was more as if I had come out of a hospital than a prison. I also felt cheated – all of those exercises I had done in my cell at Pucklechurch had evidently had no effect whatsoever. All my muscles seemed to have turned to fat, or rather to have shrunk and been replaced by fat. Later, at home, I began a ruthless campaign to get fit again. I cycled furiously for miles, timing myself round a series of circuits, pushing myself until what had taken an hour took only half an hour; until I could stay on the bike up hills where at first I had had to get off and walk.

After four months of this, I undertook my first long walk. To make sure I couldn't cry off, I abandoned my car, took the train to Cheltenham, and arranged for my husband to pick me up at Winchcombe, about ten miles away the way I wanted to go. I did it, though I was far more tired at the end of it than I should have been. I shall keep at it though. I cannot bear to think that my days of walking in the Rhinogs and climbing Cader from Corris, returning via Llanfihangel and Tal y Llyn, are over. And as anyone who knows the Rhinogs will realize, you have to be fit to spend all day among them. I will not let prison take that from me. I could not do it at the moment, but when

I next stand on the summit of Cader or Arran Fawr, then I will have conquered this particular legacy of my prison experience.

I do not disguise from myself that it may be a lot easier to free myself of the physical side-effects of prison, than the mental ones. I still feel quite surprised that if I want to get in my car and go to Manchester, for example, I can do so. I am haunted by the feeling that I ought to tell somebody what I am doing. I can't quite believe in my freedom. The first couple of times I went to London, I was convinced that the police were following me, that they would not leave me alone in London. I kept looking over my shoulder. When I come out of a shop, I often have a tingly feeling in my back, expecting a hand on my shoulder. I am not and never have been a shoplifter, but I am now irrationally afraid that I will inadvertently take something and end up back in prison. My suspended sentence does indeed hang over my head. From time to time I get sudden cravings for sweets, and I am still grateful that I can go into a shop and buy what I like. All those months of having to wait until the day for canteen have clearly left their mark.

The first time I felt my irrational fear of shoplifting was on my second day of freedom. My daughter had a lecture, and I had said that I would be perfectly happy just looking at the shops again for an hour. I wanted to buy some wool, and one or two other things. I was indeed quite happy, until spotting some tights in a January sale. I picked up one pair and took them to another counter to compare them with a second pair. It was all totally innocent, but a fear suddenly burst upon me that I might be accused of shoplifting and rapidly end up back in the prison from which I had only been released the day before. I felt ill with fear, hastily replaced both pairs of tights and went to the ladies room to recover. I had to wait quite some time until I felt able to go back into the shop. From that time until the present, I have been afraid in public places that I am suddenly going to be arrested again for something. I know it is irrational, but it is also real. I feel all the time as though people are looking at me, ready to mock, ready to pounce, and I am still sure that the telephone is tapped.

I do not feel any differently about myself as a result of my imprisonment. Whatever else it has done, it has not altered my own self-image. It comes as a shock to me therefore to find that some other people regard me as being a different person because of what has happened to me. That is a very hurtful experience, and some of the people I would have most expected to rely on are the ones who have turned away from me as if I had leprosy. How valuable that makes the love and loyalty of those who have not turned away. How true is the old cliché that trouble shows us who our friends really are.

One way in which other people's attitudes were brought home to me with some force was what happened as a result of my article in the *Guardian*. Several people responded to my appeal for help to reform the remand system. I wrote back, suggesting one or two ways in which they could help, and saying that as I thought publicity was the most important factor, I would be delighted to address small groups on the subject, perhaps in people's homes. It should have occurred to me, but it didn't. I felt just the same. But back came the letters, asking exactly what crime I had committed, and explaining that they could not really ask me into their homes to meet their friends until they had checked up on what sort of criminal I was.

I read these letters with shock. I still don't see myself as any kind of criminal, but of course the rest of the world does. Having been reminded of this, I could quite see their point of view. I had hoped that my private life could remain private, because the point at issue was the state of our remand centres, not the reason I had been in one. That would have been valid had I been a murderer or an IRA terrorist, but I could see that if I was inviting myself to people's houses they did have a right to ask what I had done. That left me with an agonizing problem, because while I wanted to do everything in my power to help the victims of the remand system, I was not at all sure that I could bring myself to tell over and over again the very long and complex story of what happened to me. In fact, I could not, and wrote back giving all the details of my life of high respectability before prison, and saying that I felt emotionally unable to discuss my crime.

I think it would be easier now for me to cope with that kind of situation if only I had actually been charged with what I did intend, which heaven knows is bad enough. I find it almost impossible to face up to the fact that I have been convicted of incitement to murder, am therefore legally guilty of it, and will carry that for the rest of my life. I find it totally impossible to discuss, except as a very formal and anonymous concept. I can talk to my typewriter about it, but I cannot write it in a letter to a friend. If only I could have been charged with what I did, and convicted of what I did, I am sure I would have the courage to grit my teeth and admit to it. But imagine having to tell people that you have been convicted of incitement to murder, when you are innocent of that? Of course, more than one innocent person has been hanged for murder, so I suppose I have nothing to complain about compared with them.

Needless to say, my ultimate employers, the DES, also had to have their say. While I was still in Styal, I had had a letter saying that in view of my conviction, the Secretary of State was considering whether or not I was a fit person to remain as a qualified teacher. Of course, they could not exactly take away my qualifications, but they could certainly put me on what teachers know as the 'black list'. This is a list of people, who in the opinion of the DES are no longer fit to teach because of something they have done, which is circulated to local authorities. Most of the people on the list are those whose sexual predilections make them unfit to be in charge of children. Some are chronic alcoholics, one or two are drug abusers. And, of course, any teacher who gets into trouble with the law and ends up in prison is an obvious candidate for the black list.

So I had not been surprised, though I was very upset, when just after Christmas, and while I was still in Styal, I received that recorded delivery letter from the DES. It said that in view of what had happened to me, the Secretary of State had to consider my suitability to continue as a teacher, and invited me to submit whatever documents I wished in order to help him come to a fair decision. Although I was upset, I fully realized that the DES had every right to take such action, and also I was grateful that at least someone in authority was prepared to listen to and to consider my point of view, my version of the story. I had been very shocked by the way my headmaster and the local authority for whom I had worked had not made the slightest attempt to ask me what had happened before my trial, and had presumably been satisfied with the inaccurate newspaper reports after it. At no time did the chief education officer or any of his officers contact me in any way, and the letters I had from my headmaster were of a personal nature. It was as though I had died, as far as they were concerned. I still wonder at that attitude. I still wonder how they could just write me off like that, because I was arrested. No presumption of innocence until proved guilty in the world of education!

I wrote back to the DES saying that I would submit my documents at the end of February. I then collected together anything which I thought might help: my psychiatrist's report, the list I drew up for my solicitor of the stresses I had been under before my arrest, my last job application form and my c.v. which give background details of my career, and copies of testimonials. I then sat down and wrote out for the first time what had happened to me, and why I had done what I did. I sent the whole lot off, the DES mulled over it for about six weeks, and then I had another letter inviting me to attend for interview to put my case in person.

Elizabeth House, York Road, London, the headquarters of Education, was depressingly like a prison when I visited it on a warm May afternoon. Every door was guarded, and nobody could get in or out without a pass. Visitors had to be given a piece of paper authorizing their presence, and were not allowed to walk about unescorted. I was taken to the lift from the reception desk, met at the relevant floor, and escorted into the office of someone who I imagine was a very senior civil servant. The man who had escorted me remained, and took copious notes in longhand of everything I said. My appointment had been for two o'clock, and it was to be a quarter to five before I emerged, shattered.

The senior civil servant was very courteous, but very shrewd. He appeared neither friendly nor unfriendly, and it was impossible to know how he was taking what I said. Had I been trying to act a part, I would have found it very difficult indeed, but as all I had to do was to tell the truth, it was easier. We went all through my life, all through my career, and then again through the story of the events leading up to my breakdown and my arrest. I had been expecting the interview to last for half an hour, or an hour at most, but for two and three-quarter hours I was answering his questions. He was evaluating me all the time, deciding what sort of a person I was, how much of what I said he could believe, giving me time to trip myself up if I was lying. He asked one or two questions which nobody else had ever thought to ask. He was very good at his job. At the end of the interview, I had not the remotest idea what he thought about me or about what I had said.

It was a gruelling experience for me, but I managed to get through without emotion, except at the end when we were discussing the implications of my being put on the black list. When I left, I had no idea what the outcome was going to be, but the man who had been taking notes escorted me back to the lift and took my hand in parting and wished me luck, with sympathy and sincerity in his eyes. So I knew that he at least believed my story. I was again grateful that I had been given the chance to put across my point of view, and such a generous allocation of time in which to do it. The contrast between the way the DES treated me and the way my local education authority had treated me was doubly highlighted.

I then had to wait a long time, because my case was to go to the Secretary of State himself, and the Prime Minister chose that time of all times to call a general election. My case could not be considered until the election had been held and the Secretary of State was back at work again. It was the end of June before the recorded delivery letter came, and I did cry as I read the words: 'The Secretary of State has decided that he will not, on this occasion, determine you to be a person unsuitable for employment as a teacher'. I felt really vindicated that this was the result of being able to tell my own story in my own way. The DES had given me a fair chance, and had not condemned me. Had the letter said otherwise, I would have been really upset, because to keep my status as a teacher had become very important to me: a kind of touchstone against which to test the rest of my life. To lose that status would have been a worse punishment than going to prison.

I did not think that because I had this magic letter, I could now go out and get a job. The whole point of my status is purely an academic one, because I knew, and know full well, that I shall never actually teach again. In teaching, as in everything else, there are too many people looking for too few jobs for any employer to consider someone who has been in trouble, regardless of the rights and wrongs of the case. I myself have gone through many huge piles of application forms, looking for any reason to put one more on the reject pile, to reduce the number to be considered. A spell in prison, for whatever reason, would see any application that I might make going straight on to the reject pile.

Neither could I get a job without a suitable reference from my headmaster, and I knew that he would not give me one, because he had made up his mind that I was not suitable to teach. Made up his mind on God knows what evidence, as he has never bothered to talk to me about what happened. He wrote me off, unheard, long before my trial. When I received the DES decision, I wrote to him asking if, whatever his personal feelings might be, he would bear in mind when writing a reference for me that the DES had fully considered my case and felt I was still a suitable person to be a teacher. I received a noncommittal letter in return, and such a vitriolic one from his wife that I did not write again.

My barrister said in court before I was sentenced that I would be punished in many ways, and I suppose this was the kind of thing he had in mind. A professional person is in so many ways dependent on what other people think of him or her: and if those other people refuse to consider that there may be another side to the story, then the case is hopeless. I am well aware that I am far from being in a unique position. Many, many professional people are in a similar situation, because having a breakdown, or getting into trouble unless you are a member of the 'criminal classes', is unforgivable in the eyes of other professional people. I wonder why? What is it about doctors, lawyers, teachers which makes them condemn so deeply one of their number who falls, in this case so deeply that they will not even ask what happened?

I have thought a lot about it, and it seems to me to spring from a terrible arrogance, or perhaps a terrible unacknowledged fear that they, too, may not be as perfect as they would like to think they are. Of course I did wrong. Of course I deserved to suffer for it. And part of the suffering which will never go away is the knowledge that by what I did I harmed the school and my colleagues there. But I do not see why that automatically disqualifies me from further contact with my profession. I may well be a better teacher because of what has happened to me, and certainly there is no way in the world in which I am a danger to the young. I should certainly be a better teacher now than I was during the time of my breakdown. My real crime, as is always the case, was being discovered. Teachers are only as human as the rest of us, and have dubious morals of many kinds, yet they can go on teaching so long as they are not found out. I was found out.

I hope that this does not read as if I am making out a case for my return to teaching, because that is not my intention. I am sufficiently realistic to know that whatever the academic arguments may be, the facts are that I shall never teach again. My good character is blemished, and for me, this may as well be Victorian Britain, and I a girl who made one mistake. I am only asking why we consider it necessary for our professional people to appear to be perfect. Would it not be a lot more honest to admit that none of us is perfect? Given that the individual case has been examined, as mine was by the DES, should there not be forgiveness and reinstatement? For me there will be neither, and that is also part of the punishment, but perhaps in the future such things will not happen. One of the terrible things about an arrest is that it almost always carries with it loss of employment, utterly regardless of guilt or innocence, or of the circumstances of guilt. I think this is wrong.

So one of the things which ex-prisoners have to face up to in the months immediately following their release is the fact that, whatever they may think of themselves, however deeply they may know that they are still the same person that they always were, the mere fact of imprisonment will have changed the attitudes of other people towards them. There will be a certain amount of unpleasantness, and some real vindictiveness. I count myself among the fortunate in that I have had very little of the latter, and I have had a great deal of support. In particular, many of my neighbours have gone out of their way to show me kindness and make me feel that I need not be an outcast.

When I first came home, I felt that it would be impossible to live in such a small village, and so we made a real attempt to sell the house. But our house is a rambling old Victorian vicarage, and it has proved impossible to sell it. So I have had to live here, and very good for me it has been. Gradually, as the weeks have become months, and it is now well over a year since I was released, I have gradually got my confidence back. At first I would not go into the shops in case I was recognized, and used to go out of my way to other towns to shop. Now all that remains is that I am unable to walk through the village. Fortunately, the house is right at one edge of the village, so that I can walk or drive along the lanes where I hardly ever meet anyone. But only last week I left my car in the garage after a service until my husband could collect it because (was I afraid, or ashamed?) I had to walk through the village to the garage to get it myself. I wonder whether this is a weakness, or a proper sense of my own disgrace. As yet, I cannot answer that.

In April, while I was still trying to find my feet, I had a bad shock. My solicitor phoned, and told me that the police wanted to see me again. I am very grateful to the Bristol police for the way they handled this episode. They could have just appeared on my doorstep to question me, and that would have frightened me to death. Instead, they approached me through my solicitor, and arranged to interview me in his office. The questioning was nothing really to do with me in fact. They were trying to establish a case against a private detective in Bristol, who apparently had actually taken money to go and murder a local solicitor's wife. He was not the same detective as I had consulted, but they wanted to know from me, yet again, why I went to a Bristol detective, and whether I had heard that a detective in Bristol would do this sort of thing. But I could tell them no more than they already knew from me, and the whole thing was largely a waste of everyone's time. It was also tremendously upsetting for me, as it brought back to me the whole horror of my arrest, and the vile-tasting atmosphere of those days, at a time when all I wanted to do was to forget.

I was worried after that that the police would always be after me for one thing or another, but in fact they have not been. Yet still when a policeman appears on the doorstep I am afraid, which is quite silly as never at any time have I regarded the police as my enemies. They did what they had to do it seems to me, and I bear them no grudge. It just is a bit alarming to open the door to a policeman, even if all he wants is to see my husband about a traffic accident, or to bring the sad news that his father has died. I think my shock must have shown on these occasions, because the police have always said, 'Don't worry, it's all right, but could we just see . . .'

And to satisfy my need to help and serve the community, I have

237

my campaign against the remand system, of which this book is a major part. The whole concept of the penal system is not one which meets with instant sympathy on the part of the general public, yet reform is needed here more urgently than anywhere else in our society.

I have found it difficult, as an ex-teacher, to know what to do with my instincts to care for the young. Forbidden any longer to care for children, I have found a way out by caring for animals, and am an active member of a local animal charity concerned with rescuing and re-homing unwanted or neglected animals. We call ourselves Animal Concern, and I act as a foster home for cats and kittens until new homes can be found. At present I have two adult cats and seven kittens waiting for a home. It seems to me that anyone who has a genuine concern for human beings must also be aware of the rights and needs of other forms of life, and I feel that in caring for these abandoned animals I am doing something of real value not only for them, but also for all life, including the human children I can hear playing in the school playground along the road. If we were to turn our backs on the need of any living thing, every living thing would be the poorer.

So this is how I have found a way of life for myself, a crusade in life and a purpose in life. I still do not feel very different from the way I felt before; I still seem to have the same needs and the same energies. All that has changed is the channel through which I express them.

12 Conclusion

I have written this book about the eight months I spent as a prisoner in England in 1982 because I cannot rest until I have added my voice to that small but growing number of voices which are telling us as a society that all is not well with our system of justice, with our penal system. It is so easy, I know, for ordinary citizens to be reluctant to concern themselves with the penal system on the grounds that the system is for criminals and will never touch them.

I wish to state that English prisons, and even more so the remand centres, are full of innocent people. If you trust the police never to arrest an innocent person, then you are not being realistic. The police are fallible, they are human, they make mistakes. Please don't get the idea that it could never happen to you; it could, easily. I know many people to whom it has happened. I know of many more. You could be arrested and held on remand for month after month. If this did happen, think what you would lose. What would happen to your family? Your job? Your house?

I would like to concentrate in this conclusion upon the evils of the remand system. It seems to me that quite a lot has been said recently about the state of our prisons, but that the remand centres, which in my opinion, having experienced both, are considerably worse, are never mentioned. Efforts are being made in our prisons to provide reasonable conditions and a reasonable way of life for prisoners, but the prisoners on remand are forgotten about, which is ridiculous, since there must be more innocent people in the remand centres than in the prisons.

There are three main things wrong with our remand system: too many people are held in custody; they are held for too long; and they are held under shocking conditions.

In 1982, the number of people held for some period of time in custody because bail had been refused was 62,871. Think of that figure for a minute: 62,870 people and me. In the same year, the population of Aldershot was 33,750, of Chelmsford 58,320, of Lincoln 76,760. Or you could have rounded up the whole population of Guildford (58,470) and still not have as many people as were held on remand in 1982. Very considerable numbers of people are held on remand in any period of time you care to consider. Of these 62,871 people held in 1982, on 30 June 3598 were women.

I cannot understand why so many people are remanded in custody. Of the people with whom I spent my five months on remand, it seemed to me that very few represented any kind of threat to society. Most were either ill, or inadequate, or had made one mistake. I am not arguing for the abolition of remand centres. I understand that there are some criminals who do represent a threat and should be kept in custody. What I am saying is that the population of our remand centres could be reduced today by between 50 and 75 per cent, without anyone being adversely affected.

The situation is made worse by the fact that when these prisoners come to trial, many of them are either found not guilty, or given a non-custodial sentence. In 1982, of the 52,606 prisoners whose sentences were known when the Home Office compiled its statistics, 40 per cent were either found not guilty, or given a non-custodial sentence. This means that 19,464 people had been held in custody for some length of time, but when they came to trial they were not in fact considered by the courts to merit being held in custody. And 1578 were acquitted and should not have been held at all. These are the figures for one year. I am justified in saying that there is in this country a vast and growing number of people who have been quite wrongly held in custody. Roger Cook of the BBC 'Checkpoint' programme interviewed some of them in 1983, and very bitter they were too.

The reasons why police oppose bail in so many cases, and why magistrates listen to them, would make a fascinating study, but it is beyond the scope of this present book. I can see that from the police point of view, after apprehending someone, they do not want to run the risk of them escaping and having to be traced and arrested all over again. Yet, throwing thousands of people into custody every year should not be acceptable to society, and I cannot understand why there is not more of an outcry about it.

It seems to me that there are solutions to the problems of what to do with people who have, to a greater or lesser extent, to be controlled while awaiting trial. In 1982, it cost £263 per week to keep a woman in custody. It must be more now. This money would be better spent on providing facilities other than remand centres. Money could be saved by allowing more people, especially first offenders, to be remanded on bail, perhaps on conditions such as the surrender of passports or daily reporting to the police. This already happens, of course, but it should be extended.

Greater use should be made of proper psychiatric facilities. In my case, for example, a bed was waiting for me in a proper psychiatric hospital, but I was not allowed to take it. I had to go to the remand centre. I have mentioned the diagnosed schizophrenic whose weeks on remand with no proper care certainly made her worse. I have mentioned Caroline and Corinne, who were sent at their trial to psychiatric hospitals where they should have been all the time. I would like to see every magistrates' court having the facility to send people to psychiatric hospitals to await trial. The length of time they stay there should rest with the doctor in charge of the case rather than with the police and the courts. I would not wish to see special units for this purpose: they would no doubt end up being as bad as the hospital wings of prison and remand centres. Offenders should be sent to a local hospital, where they can mix with the rest of the community, and can continue their treatment after their trial, if necessary, in the same way as everyone else.

There should also be a tremendous increase in the number of places available in bail hostels. In its report 'Too Many Prisoners' (1980), the Parliamentary All Party Penal Affairs Group came out in strong support of the use of bail hostels to provide controlled accommodation for those who at present await trial in custody because of their homelessness and rootlessness, rather than because they are a threat to society. So many people on remand are there because they are inadequate or retarded, or otherwise unable to cope. A spell on remand does them no good at all: a spell in a properly run bail hostel, where they could be given support and help, would perhaps do them some good in the long term. There is a need for more places such as this where the inadequate can be sent after trial instead of to prison, but to my knowledge this scheme is only theoretical and these bail hostels do not as yet exist in sufficient numbers. They should.

An absolute end should be put to the practice of remanding people in custody for reports. I have seen many people come in for reports, sit about for two and a half weeks, and see the doctor and the probation officer for half an hour just before they go back to court for sentence. I have more than a suspicion that in these cases the courts are using the remand centres to administer a 'short, sharp shock'. If this is the case, they should be stopped from doing so at once. People can have their whole lives ruined because they have been on remand in custody for three weeks. That is long enough to lose a job, be evicted from a home, and become the cause of gossip to the neighbours so that life after release is intolerable. Magistrates should think about these things before packing people off to remand centres in the way they do at present.

In fact, I do not think anyone should be remanded in custody, unless they are hopeless recidivists or they are being accused of very serious offences. For many of these groups, and for everyone else, arrangements other than remand in custody would be more suitable, more humane, cheaper, and better in the long run for the whole of our society.

Accepting that there must be some people for whom the remand centre is the only place where they can await trial, there is still no excuse whatever for the length of time which at present elapses between someone's arrest and their sentence. In 1982, the national average waiting time between committal and trial was 14.6 weeks, while in London it was 23.6 weeks. Imagine yourself held in custody for all these weeks in the conditions I have described. And then remember that those figures refer to the time between committal and trial. You may well have already been on remand before being committed for trial for an additional eight, twelve or sixteen weeks. I was arrested on 13 May. My trial began on 6 October. Whether a person is held in custody, or remanded on bail, to make them wait for such lengths of time is inhumane, and ought not to be allowed in a civilized society. Cases are supposed to be heard within eight weeks of committal, but in 1982 only 57 per cent of the cases of those in custody were heard within this limit, and only 34 per cent of those allowed bail. (In London the figures were 30 per cent and 6 per cent respectively.)

For this delay I blame the courts and the legal profession. Courts must sit longer and more frequently while there is such a backlog of cases to hear. How can they go on holiday throughout August and again for three weeks at Christmas knowing that the remand centres are'full of people waiting for trial? It simply cannot take months and months to prepare a case, except where a case is really complicated. I imagine that most solicitors would be pleased to have a more rapid and immediate turnover of cases. At present when the case comes to trial, everyone is talking about events which happened months, if not years ago. Better, surely, to bring a case to trial within the shortest possible time, and if this might jeopardize a defendant's case then his solicitor could be allowed to request an adjournment. Let the norm be that trials take place as soon as possible and the long-delayed trial be an exception, instead of the other way round as it is at present.

In May 1980 Leon Brittan himself, when he was Minister of State at the Home Office, made a speech in Scarborough in which he said:

> . . . it is important not to lose sight of the damage that is done to the fabric of the criminal justice system by any sort of unnecessary delay, whatever the type of case. Even relatively trivial charges can cause great distress to the defendant. And it is axiomatic that the staler the evidence that is given, the lower the quality of the criminal process must be.

The factors affecting waiting times for trials include such things as the number of judges, court accommodation and staff, the hours during which courts sit, as well as more technical matters about the conduct of cases, their scheduling, and the number of charges a prisoner may face. Reform in all these areas is long overdue. Scottish law provides that a maximum of 110 days may elapse between committal and trial, and if a defendant is not brought to trial within this period, he or she must be released. Very few people have to my knowledge been released under this law, so if the Scots can get on with the job within a time limit, why cannot the English?

I am, however, alarmed that Mr Brittan now proposes to bring the 110-day rule to England as a solution to the problem of delay. This is still over three months, and this period begins at committal. Given a wait of two months (it can be much longer) from arrest to committal, a person could still be held before trial for nearly six months. If we are to introduce time limits, I would rather see committal followed by trial within two weeks, given that by the committal stage the prosecution has prepared its case, and had it accepted by the Director of Public Prosecutions as being a case to answer. The defence case should by that time be largely known, and I suspect that most barristers only turn their minds to a case shortly before it is to be heard anyway. A fortnight's work should be enough. I met my barrister for the first time on 4 August, but I decline to believe that he was occupied with my case to the exclusion of all else for two months. I suspect he largely forgot about me until he had dealt with his other cases in September, and then turned his attention to mine. I would also like to see a definite and reasonable time by which the police must have sent their papers to the DPP, and a limit of no more than one week for the DPP to consider the case. In the vast majority of cases these limits would be sufficient; in those few where it would not be possible, a defence solicitor could again request a delay. But the aim should be for as little delay as possible.

I am aware that there would be an outcry from the legal profession if these proposals were seriously put forward. Yet in no way would speeding up trials affect the amount of work solicitors or barristers did and the amount of money they could make. It would merely mean that someone arrested, as I was, in May might have a chance of being tried in June or at the latest July. That interval is horrific enough. I cannot describe what it is like having to wait week after week after week for trial. I cannot imagine how my friend Gillian, who had to wait a year before her trial, coped. I only know that I saw her going steadily downhill with the strain. I used to visit her in Pucklechurch after I had been released from Styal, and I saw what waiting for a year for trial had done to her.

In America they have the Speedy Trial Act, which requires that a defendant be indicted within thirty days of arrest, and where there is a plea of not guilty, the trial should take place within seventy days of indictment. In the name of humanity, why can we not do the same in this country, whose legal system was once the envy of the world, but is now almost medieval in its approach? I appeal to whoever reads this book to put themselves in the place of a prisoner, who is possibly innocent, certainly innocent in the eyes of the law, held in custody for these unbelievable lengths of time. Only, it seems, when there is a sufficient groundswell of outrage against a wrong will the politicians act. Only when people are aware of the facts can they be outraged by them. That is the sole reason for this book.

I hope that the relevant chapters of this book will have made my readers aware of what it is like to be held on remand in England in the 1980s. The conditions are not justifiable even for convicted criminals, but I repeat once more, people in remand centres are not convicted criminals. Most of them are innocent. Innocent because they never committed the offence with which they are charged. Innocent because they are retarded, inadequate or mentally ill, and did not understand what they were doing. Innocent, all of them, because they have not been proved guilty. I persist with this fundamental assumption of English law. If we are going to assume that everyone who has been arrested must be guilty, then God help human rights in England.

So why, why do we treat people on remand as though they were guilty? Why do we lock them up with plastic pots, strip search them, humiliate and degrade them? Why do we deny them access to their families, open their mail, herd them through the long boring day with little to do and no outlet at all for any creativity? Why do we deny them medical care, psychiatric help, common human dignity?

Why cannot our remand centres be places where people can be helped with dignity, with humanity, to come to terms with whatever defect in their characters has put them into the centre in the first place? Why, for instance, could a remand centre not be part of a local complex containing a health centre and a day centre? In very few cases are remand prisoners dangerous to themselves or other people. The few who are must of course be separately contained, but I do not believe that in England in 1982 there were 62,870 dangerous lunatics on remand, and me.

Finally, there is the fact that nobody is entitled to compensation as a result of being wrongfully arrested and held in custody. They may be held for a year, and then acquitted at their trial. They may well be perfectly innocent. They may have lost their job, their house, their family. Their life will have been ruined. Yet they cannot get any compensation whatsoever, unless they can prove that the police acted with overt malice or the courts displayed an extraordinary degree of eccentricity by remanding them in custody; and it would be next to impossible to prove this. Probably the police quite genuinely made the arrest thinking that they had the right person, and the courts, as in my case, sent them off to the remand centre because they believed it to be the right place for them, whatever the actual facts. Compensation is sometimes awarded to people who have been found guilty but are later proved to have been innocent all the time, particularly if the case has been taken up by the press; but the thousands of people every year wrongly held in our remand centres get no compensation whatever, despite what they may have lost. And all compensation is a matter of grace, not of right. Surely the law should be altered here?

This therefore is my testimony against the remand system as it operates in the England of the 1980s. I call upon all men and women to think about and to feel within themselves the evil of this system within our society, and to stand with me and say: This wrong we will no longer tolerate, this evil we will no longer condone, this inhumanity we will no longer support. These are our fellow creatures, more in need of our compassion than most, and more in need of the protection of the law than of its punishment. And until they are found guilty by the due process of law, let them no longer be treated worse than the convicted criminals in our prisons.

Index

Index

Index

Index

Fontana Paperbacks: Non-fiction

Fontana is a leading paperback publisher of non-fiction, both popular and academic. Below are some recent titles.

You can buy Fontana paperbacks at your local bookshop or newsagent. Or you can order them from Fontana Paperbacks, Cash Sales Department, Box 29, Douglas, Isle of Man. Please send a cheque, postal or money order (not currency) worth the purchase price plus 15p per book for postage (maximum postage required is £3).

NAME (Block letters) _____

ADDRESS _____ _____

_____